Gregg
Shorthand Manual
Simplified

JOHN ROBERT GREGG

LOUIS A. LESLIE

CHARLES E. ZOUBEK

shorthand written by **CHARLES RADER**

Gregg Publishing Division

McGraw-Hill Book Company, Inc.

NEW YORK CHICAGO CORTE MADERA, CALIF.

DALLAS TORONTO LONDON

GREGG

Shorthand Manual

Simplified

SECOND EDITION

GREGG SHORTHAND MANUAL SIMPLIFIED, SECOND EDITION

Library of Congress Catalog No. 54-12669

June 1961-RRD-9

PUBLISHED BY GREGG PUBLISHING DIVISION
McGraw-Hill Book Company, Inc.
Printed in the United States of America

Acknowledgments

The publishers acknowledge with deep appreciation the suggestions received from scores of teachers for improving the teaching of Gregg Shorthand. Wherever feasible, these suggestions have been followed directly or indirectly in the preparation of *Gregg Shorthand Manual Simplified,* Second Edition. The publishers wish to make special acknowledgment of the contribution of Mrs. Madeline S. Strony, who, as a member of the staff, works closely year after year with literally hundreds of shorthand teachers throughout the nation on the improvement of shorthand instruction.

Finally, the publishers wish to recognize the contribution made by Mr. Charles Rader, who not only wrote the beautiful and artistic shorthand in this book, but also assumed a large share of the responsibility for the technical accuracy of the material.

PREFACE

Most Widely Used System. Since the publication of Gregg Shorthand in 1888, the system has been learned and used by millions of writers. The flexibility of the system, which enables the writer to use it with equal effectiveness for personal, stenographic, and reporting purposes, has made Gregg Shorthand the most widely used system in the world. The successful use of Gregg Shorthand not only in English but also in the many foreign languages to which it has been adapted is striking evidence of the genius of the inventor, John Robert Gregg, in devising the most efficient shorthand alphabet in more than 2,000 years of shorthand history.

Gregg Shorthand Manual Simplified. In 1949, the *Gregg Shorthand Manual Simplified* was issued. The simplification of the system that the new text presented and the many helpful teaching and learning advantages that it offered immediately appealed to the shorthand teaching profession. The simple and logical principles governing the construction of outlines and the substantial reduction of special forms and exceptions made the student's task of speed development an easy and pleasant one. The marginal reminders, which help to improve the student's ability to spell and punctuate concurrently with the development of his shorthand skill, have made a real contribution to the ultimate goal of the shorthand course – *accurate and rapid transcription.*

Simplified Outlines Retained in Second Edition. Teachers who have enjoyed using *Gregg Shorthand Manual Simplified* will find teaching from the Second Edition an even greater pleasure. In the Second Edition all the helpful teaching and learning features of the initial edition have been retained. The principles and the outlines have not been disturbed – *there are no changes in outlines.* Nor are there any changes in the organization of the book. Like the initial edition, the Second Edition is organized into 10 chapters, which are divided into 70 lessons. The theory is completed with Lesson 53, with each sixth lesson a "breather" in which no new theory is presented. Lessons 54 through 70 are supplementary and contain systematic reviews.

New Teaching and Learning Features. During the years that *Gregg Shorthand Manual Simplified* has been on the market teachers have shared with us many valuable and practical suggestions designed to make the teaching and learning of Gregg Shorthand even more effective. These suggestions have led to the incorporation into the Second Edition of new features that should do much to create and maintain the student's interest and to prepare him even more thoroughly for dictation and transcription. These features include:

I. Greater Transcription Emphasis. The initial edition of *Gregg Shorthand Manual Simplified* was unique in its attention to pretranscription training. That edition was the first to teach spelling and punctuation concurrently with shorthand. In the Second Edition the emphasis and attention to pretranscription training are considerably increased.

1. Applied Vocabulary Studies. Beginning with Chapter 2 each Reading and Writing Practice opens with an applied vocabulary study consisting of several expressions for which the meanings are provided. The expressions are selected from the Reading and Writing Practice. These applied vocabulary studies will help to overcome a major transcription handicap – a limited vocabulary.

2. Extension of Marginal Reminders. The marginal reminders in the Second Edition are introduced in Chapter 6. The explanations of the marginal reminders appear with the lessons in which they are introduced. In addition, the student is given step-by-step instructions on how to treat the marginal reminders in his homework. To impress the correct punctuation and spelling on the mind of the student, the punctuation marks and spelling words appear in red.

3. Pretranscription Quiz. Beginning with Chapter 8 the last letter in the Reading and Writing Practice appears without marginal reminders. A number of words have also been omitted from the shorthand. As a pretranscription training device, the student is called on to supply the proper punctuation and the missing words.

II. Assistance with Homework and Class Participation. Gregg Shorthand Manual Simplified, Second Edition, takes special cognizance of the problem of getting homework done. Many of its new features are devoted to the accomplishment of this function in learning and developing skill in shorthand.

1. Talks with the Student. Each of the ten chapters is introduced by a talk with the student on some phase of his shorthand study. These talks are accompanied by stimulating and meaningful photographs. In addition, they give the student step-by-step suggestions on how to practice.

2. Shorthand Reading Material in Lessons 1 and 2. To give the student the feeling of accomplishment from the very beginning, reading exercises are now provided in Lessons 1 and 2. In these exercises the few words for which the shorthand outlines have not been learned are given in longhand.

3. Reading and Writing Prac-

tice Previews. In Chapters 1 through 5 the transcript of words and phrases in the Reading and Writing Practice that might cause the student difficulty in reading are given in the margin of the shorthand. These previews help speed up the student's reading in the early stages and prevent discouragement.

4. *Check Lists.* To keep the student constantly reminded of the importance of good practice procedures, an occasional check list is provided. These check lists deal with writing shorthand, reading shorthand, homework, proportion, etc.

5. *Reading Scoreboards.* At various points in the Second Edition, the student is given an opportunity to determine his reading speed through a scoreboard that enables him to calculate the number of words a minute he is reading. By comparing his reading from scoreboard to scoreboard, he receives some indication of his shorthand growth.

III. Theory Presentation Helps

1. *Theory Presented in Small Segments.* The theory in each lesson is presented in small learning units, thus making for easier teaching. This arrangement also makes for easier learning for the student who must study without the constant guidance of the teacher. Full explanations of the theory are given; and, wherever necessary, the student's attention is directed to specific points that will make the theory easy for him to understand.

2. *Recall Charts.* In the last lesson of each chapter a unique recall chart is provided. This chart contains illustrations of all the theory taught in the chapter. It also contains illustrations of all the theory the student has studied up to that lesson.

IV. Practice Material Improvements

Approximately 50 per cent of the material in the Reading and Writing Practice exercises is new. The new letters and articles were chosen not only for the richness of their shorthand content but also for their interest and informational values. The material that has been retained from the initial edition has been revised to bring it up to date and to make it read more smoothly by shortening and simplifying sentences.

Even though the vocabulary is restricted by grading considerations, the material is smooth and natural from the earliest lessons.

Gregg Shorthand Manual Simplified, Second Edition, is offered to the teaching profession with gratifying satisfaction in the wide-scale and successful use of the initial edition and with full confidence in the modern, progressive teaching and learning features of the new edition.

The Publishers

CHAPTER 1

Shorthand Is Easy

Gregg Shorthand is written by millions of people the world over. It is a system that is easy to learn, easy to write, and easy to read.

When you have learned Gregg Shorthand, you will have acquired a tool that will help you obtain an interesting and profitable position in business. In addition, Gregg Shorthand will be of great personal value to you.

If you can write longhand with any degree of fluency, you will have no difficulty writing Gregg Shorthand. The strokes you will use in writing Gregg Shorthand are the same ones that you have been accustomed to writing in longhand. In many ways, Gregg Shorthand is easier to learn than longhand. Skeptical? Well, just this one illustration should convince you. In longhand, for example, there are many different ways to express the letter r, all of which you had to learn. Here are a few of them:

In Gregg Shorthand there is only one way to write r, as you will discover in the first lesson.

When you have completed Chapter 1, you will be delighted and amazed at the amount of material you have covered and the

Shorthand opens the door to profitable positions in many interesting lines of work.

progress you have made. In Chapter 1 you will cover more than half the alphabetic strokes of Gregg Shorthand. Those strokes will be presented to you in such a way that you will have no difficulty learning them and recognizing them in the words in which they are used. In addition, you will become acquainted with two shorthand devices that will enable you to write shorthand more easily and rapidly—brief forms and phrases.

When you have completed Chapter 1, you will be equipped to construct outlines for literally hundreds of words in the English language. Your shorthand vocabulary will, in fact, grow so rapidly that by Lesson 4 you will be able to read actual business letters, just like those that the stenographer in the business office takes from dictation.

The skill that you eventually attain in shorthand will, of course, depend on how well and how regularly you practice. If you practice regularly, you will be able to watch your skill develop; and with each lesson your study of Gregg Shorthand will become more and more fascinating.

Good luck to you with your study of Gregg Shorthand.

GENERAL
FREIGHT
AGENT

CBS

Courtesy Columbia Broadcasting System

LESSON 1

Group A

1. Silent Letters Omitted. In the English language, many words contain letters that are not pronounced. In Gregg Shorthand we omit all silent letters and write only those sounds that we hear in a word. For example, for the word *say* we write *s-a*, omitting the *y*, which is not pronounced; for the word *knee* we write *n-e*, as the *k* and the final e are not pronounced; for the word *cat* we write *k-a-t*, as the *c* is pronounced *k*.

2. S-Z, A. The first shorthand stroke you will learn is the letter *s*. It is approximately the size and shape of the longhand comma and is written downward. The same stroke represents the sound of *z*, as in the words *saves* and *seize*.

The second shorthand stroke you will learn is the letter *a*, which is a large circle. It is simply the longhand *a* with the final connecting stroke omitted.

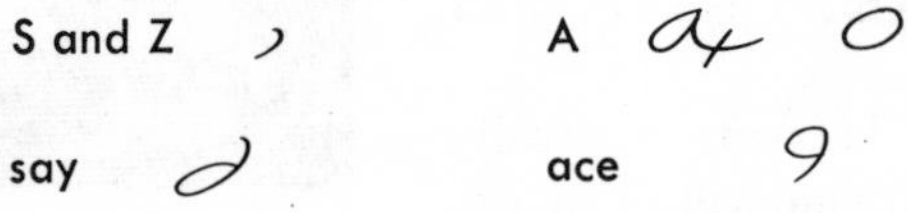
S and Z
A
say
ace

Did you notice that the *c* in *ace* has the *s* sound?

3. F, V. The shorthand stroke for *f* is the same shape as the stroke for *s*, except that it is larger – about half the height of the space between the lines in your shorthand notebook. The shorthand stroke for *v* is also the same shape as the stroke for *s*, except that it is much larger – the full height of the space between the lines in your shorthand notebook. Both *f* and *v* are written downward.

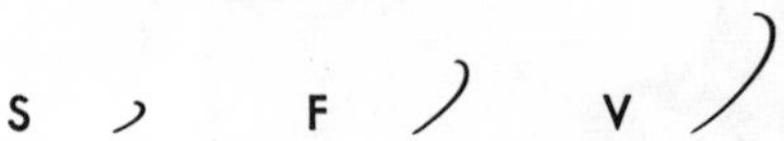
S
F
V

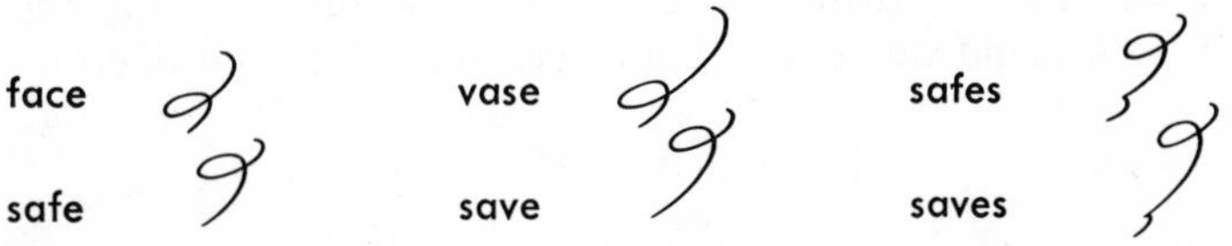
face
vase
safes
safe
save
saves

Did you notice that the final s in *saves* has the z sound?

4. E. The shorthand stroke for e is a tiny circle. It is simply the longhand e with the two connecting strokes omitted.

E

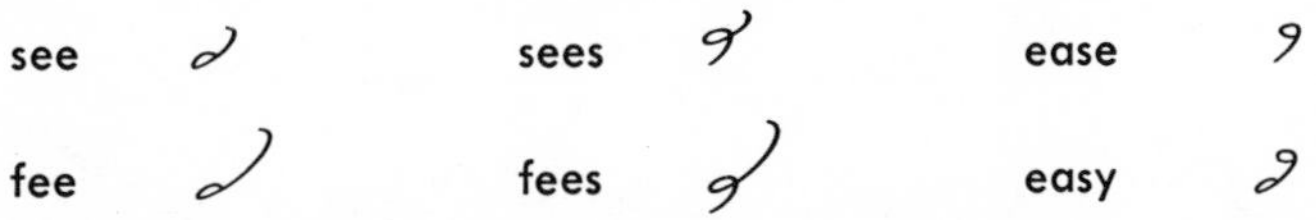
see
sees
ease
fee
fees
easy

Did you notice that the y in *easy* is pronounced e and is therefore represented by the e circle?

Group B

5. N, M. The shorthand stroke for *n* is a very short straight line; the shorthand stroke for *m* is a longer straight line. Both *n* and *m* are written forward.

N
M

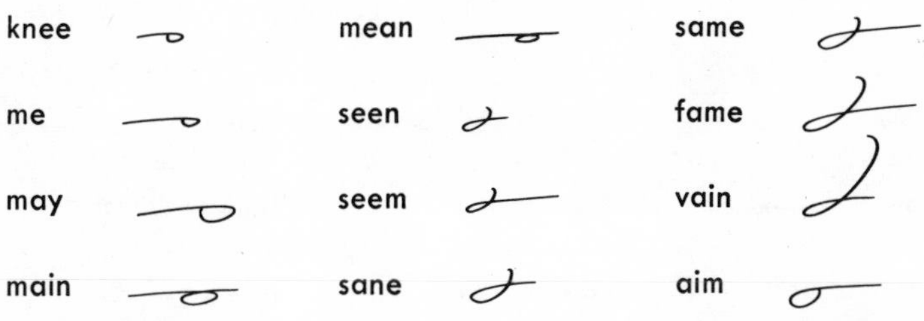
knee
mean
same
me
seen
fame
may
seem
vain
main
sane
aim

Did you notice that the *k* is not written in *knee* because it is not pronounced?

6. T, D. The shorthand stroke for *t* is a very short upward straight line; the shorthand stroke for *d* is a longer upward straight line.

T  **D** 

T

tea		**team**		**seat**	
eat		**neat**		**stay**	

D

day		**need**		**feed**	
aid		**made**		**deed**	

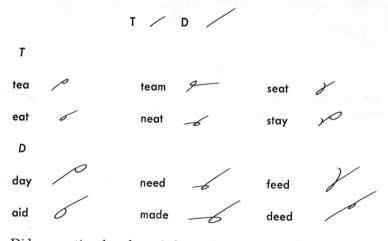

Did you notice that the *a* circles are large, the *e* circles tiny?

Group C

7. O, R, L. The shorthand stroke for *o* is a small, deep hook. The shorthand stroke for *r* is a short forward curve. The shorthand stroke for *l* is a longer forward curve.

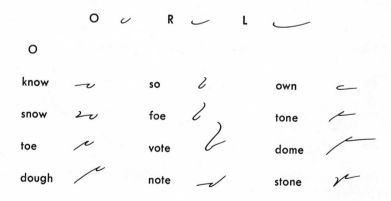

O  **R**  **L** 

O

know		**so**		**own**	
snow		**foe**		**tone**	
toe		**vote**		**dome**	
dough		**note**		**stone**	

R

ray		ear		fare	
rate		dear		free	
raid		mere		tore	
trade		near		store	

L

lay		ail		fail	
late		nail		flame	
laid		mail		stole	
lead		reel		roll	

Did you notice the slight change in the slant of the *o* when it comes before *n, m, r, l?*

8. H. The shorthand character for *h* is a dot written above the following vowel.

heat	 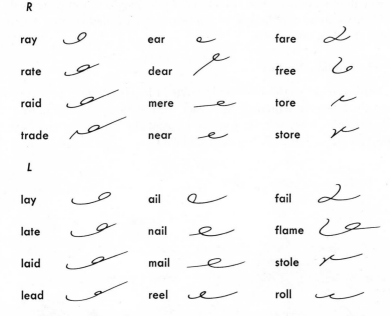	hate		whole	

9. Omission of Minor Vowels. Sometimes a vowel in a word is slightly pronounced or slurred. Such a vowel may be omitted if it does not contribute to speed or legibility.

leader		hearer		even	

10. Punctuation and Capitalization

Period		Paragraph		Parenthesis	
Question Mark		Dash		Hyphen	

For all other punctuation marks, the regular longhand forms are used.

Capitalization is indicated by two short upward dashes underneath the word to be capitalized.

11. Reading Practice

With the aid of the few words given in longhand, you can already read the following sentences. Spell each word aloud as you read it, thus: *f-r-a-t, freight; r-a-t, rate.* If you cannot read the word after you have spelled it, refer to the key that is given below.

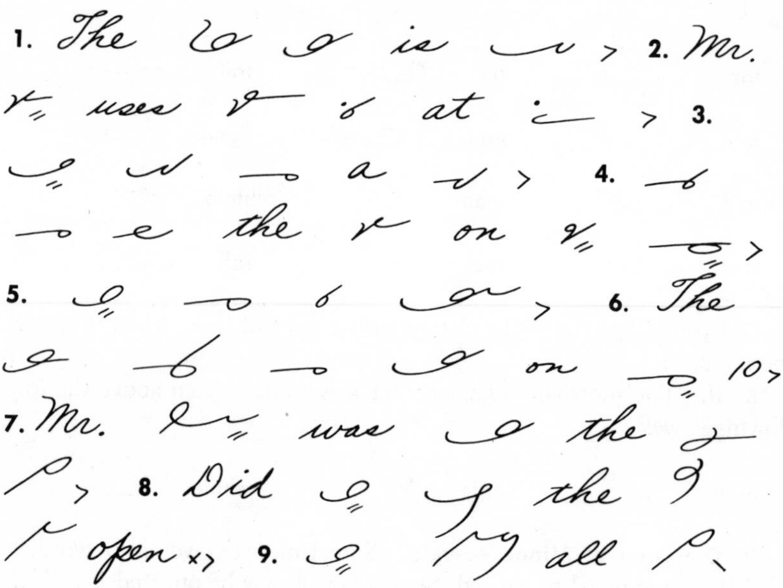

1. The freight rate is low.
2. Mr. Stone uses steam heat at home.
3. Lee wrote me a note.
4. Meet me near the store on East Main.
5. Ray may eat later.
6. The rain made me late on May 10.
7. Mr. Taylor was late the same day.
8. Did Ray leave the safe door open?
9. Ray drove all day.

LESSON 2

Group A

12. The Left S and Z. In Paragraph 2 you learned one stroke for s and z. Another stroke for s and z is also used in order to provide an easy joining in any combination of strokes – a backward comma, which is also written downward. For convenience, it is called the left s. At this point you need not try to decide which s stroke to use in any given word; this will become clear to you as your study of shorthand progresses.

S and Z 

eats		nears		roads	
toes		names		sales	

13. P, B. The shorthand stroke for *p* is the same shape as the stroke for s given in Paragraph 12, except that it is larger – approximately half the height of the space between the lines in your shorthand notebook. The shorthand stroke for *b* is also the same shape, except that it is much larger – approximately the full height of the space between the lines in your shorthand notebook. Both *p* and *b* are written downward.

S  P  B 

P

pay		praise		hope	
pays		people		open	
pair		plain		paid	
spares		paper		pain	

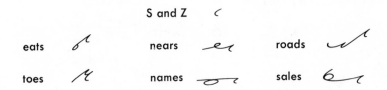

B

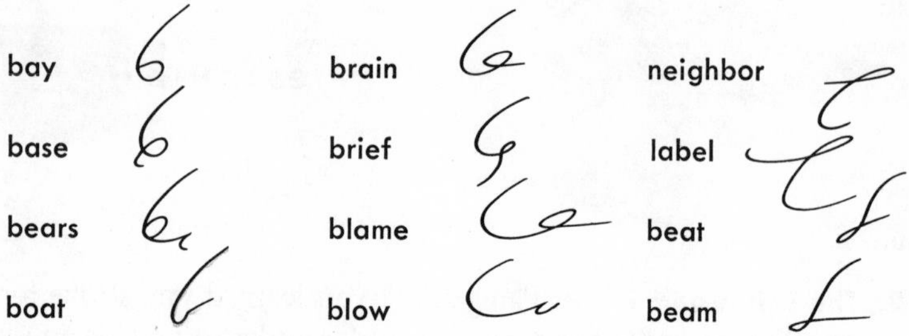
bay
brain
neighbor
base
brief
label
bears
blame
beat
boat
blow
beam

Did you notice that *pr, pl, br, bl* are written with one sweep of the pen, without a pause between the *p* or *b* and the *r* or *l*?

14. K, G. The shorthand stroke for *k* is a short forward curve. The shorthand stroke for the hard sound of g (as in *game*) is a much longer forward curve. It is called *gay*.

K
G

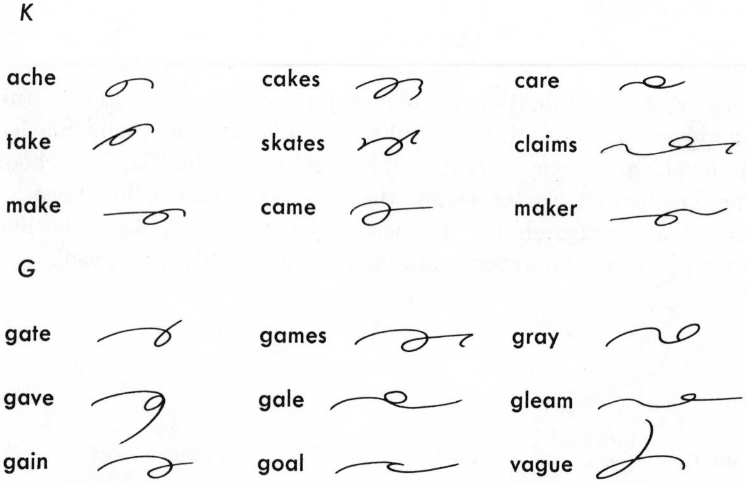
K
ache
cakes
care
take
skates
claims
make
came
maker
G
gate
games
gray
gave
gale
gleam
gain
goal
vague

Did you notice that *kr* and *gl* are written with one smooth, wavelike motion; that *kl* and *gr* are written with a hump between the *k* and *l*, *g* and *r*?

Group B

15. Sh, Ch, J. The shorthand stroke for *sh* (called *ish*) is a very short downward straight stroke. The shorthand stroke for *ch* (called *chay*) is a longer downward straight stroke approximately half the height of the space between the lines of your shorthand notebook. The shorthand stroke for *j* is a long downward straight stroke approximately the full height of the space between the lines of your shorthand notebook.

Sh  Ch  J 

Sh

she		shows		shade	
show		showed		shape	

Ch

each		reaches		chair	
teach		chains		cheap	

J

age		rage		changes	
cage		gauge		range	

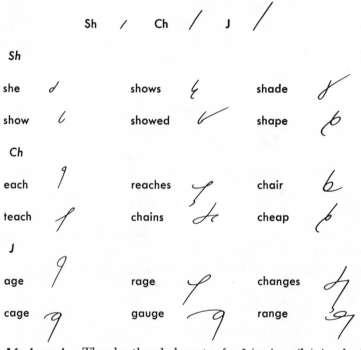

16. Long I. The shorthand character for *ī* (as in *mile*) is a broken large circle, thus: 

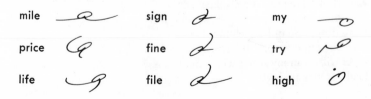

mile		sign		my	
price		fine		try	
life		file		high	

17. Reading Practice

With the aid of the few words given in longhand, you can now read the following sentences. Remember to spell each word aloud as you read it and to refer immediately to the key below when you cannot read a word.

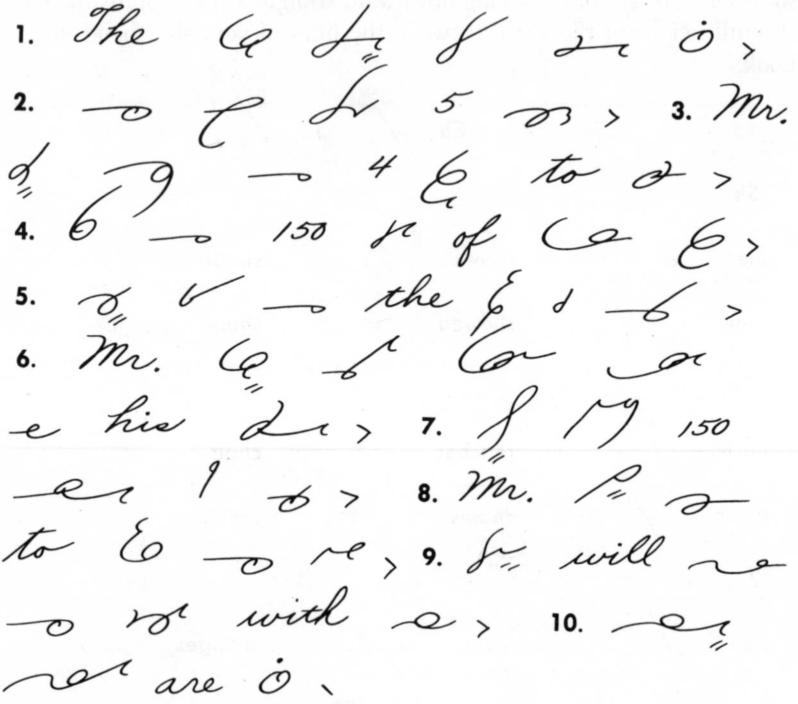
1. The
2. 5
3. Mr. 4 to
4. 150 of
5. the
6. Mr. his
7. 150
8. Mr. to
9. will with
10. are

1. The price James paid seems high.
2. My neighbor baked five cakes.
3. Mr. Chase gave me four papers to sign.
4. Buy me 150 sheets of plain paper.
5. Kate showed me the speech she made.
6. Mr. Price needs brighter lights near his files.
7. Dave drove 150 miles each night.
8. Mr. Day came to spray my trees.
9. Peter will clean my skates with care.
10. Gail's grades are high.

LESSON 3

Group A

18. Ă, Ä, -ing. In longhand, *a* represents the sound of ă (as in *has*) and ä (as in *mark*) in addition to the long sound of *a*. In shorthand, the large circle for *a* also represents the sounds of ă and ä.

At the end of words, *-ing* is represented by a dot.

Ă

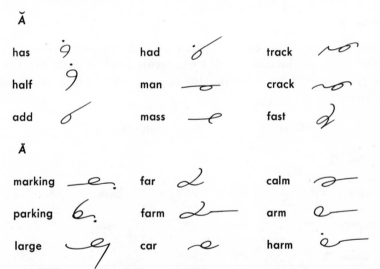

has		had		track	
half		man		crack	
add		mass		fast	

Ä

marking		far		calm	
parking		farm		arm	
large		car		harm	

19. Ĕ, Ĭ, Obscure Vowel. The tiny circle for *e* also represents the sound of ĕ (as in *help*), the sound of ĭ (as in *trim*), and the obscure vowel heard in *her, church*.

Ĕ

help		head		selling	
telling		check		settle	

Ĭ

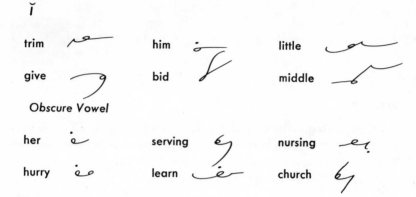

trim	him	little
give	bid	middle

Obscure Vowel

her	serving	nursing
hurry	learn	church

Group B

20. Th. Two tiny curves, written upward, are provided for the sounds of *th*. At this time do not try to decide which *th* stroke to use in any given word; this will become clear to you as your study of shorthand progresses.

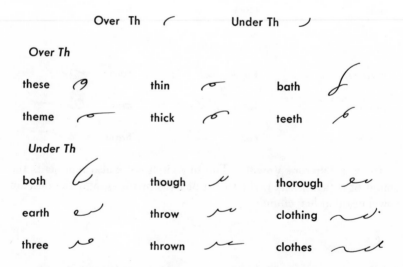

Over Th   Under Th

Over Th

these	thin	bath
theme	thick	teeth

Under Th

both	though	thorough
earth	throw	clothing
three	thrown	clothes

21. Brief Forms. The English language contains many common words that are used again and again. As an aid to rapid writing, brief forms are provided for many of these common words. For example, we write *k* for *can; th* for *the*. You are already familiar with this process of abbreviation in your longhand. You will recall that you write *Mr.* for *Mister, memo* for *memorandum, Ave.* for *Avenue*.

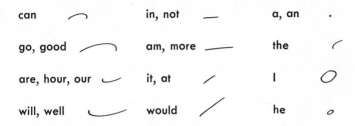

can		in, not		a, an	
go, good		am, more		the	
are, hour, our		it, at		I	
will, well		would		he	

Did you notice that some of the outlines represent more than one word? You will have no difficulty selecting the correct word in a sentence; the sense of the sentence will give you the answer.

22. Phrases. The joining of the outlines for many simple words is another aid to the development of speed. This joining of simple words is called "phrasing." Here are a number of useful phrases built with the brief forms you have just studied.

I can		he cannot		in the	
he can		I am		at the	

23. Reading Practice

If you have studied diligently the material presented in Lessons 1, 2, and 3, you will be able to read the following sentences without difficulty. As an aid to your reading, you will find in the margin the meaning of some of the outlines that might "stump" you. (For complete suggestions on how to read shorthand, see pages 32 and 33.)

at least

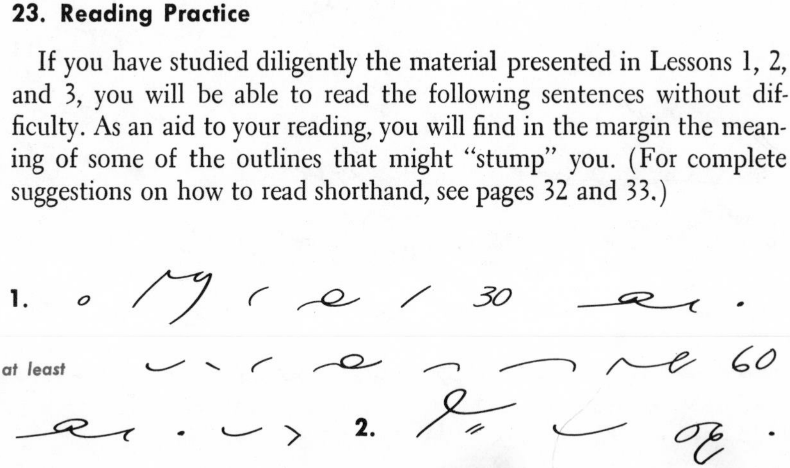

post
Italy

he may
course

I can
cancel

he gave

if it
snows

magazine

firm
secretary

jacket
fit

camera

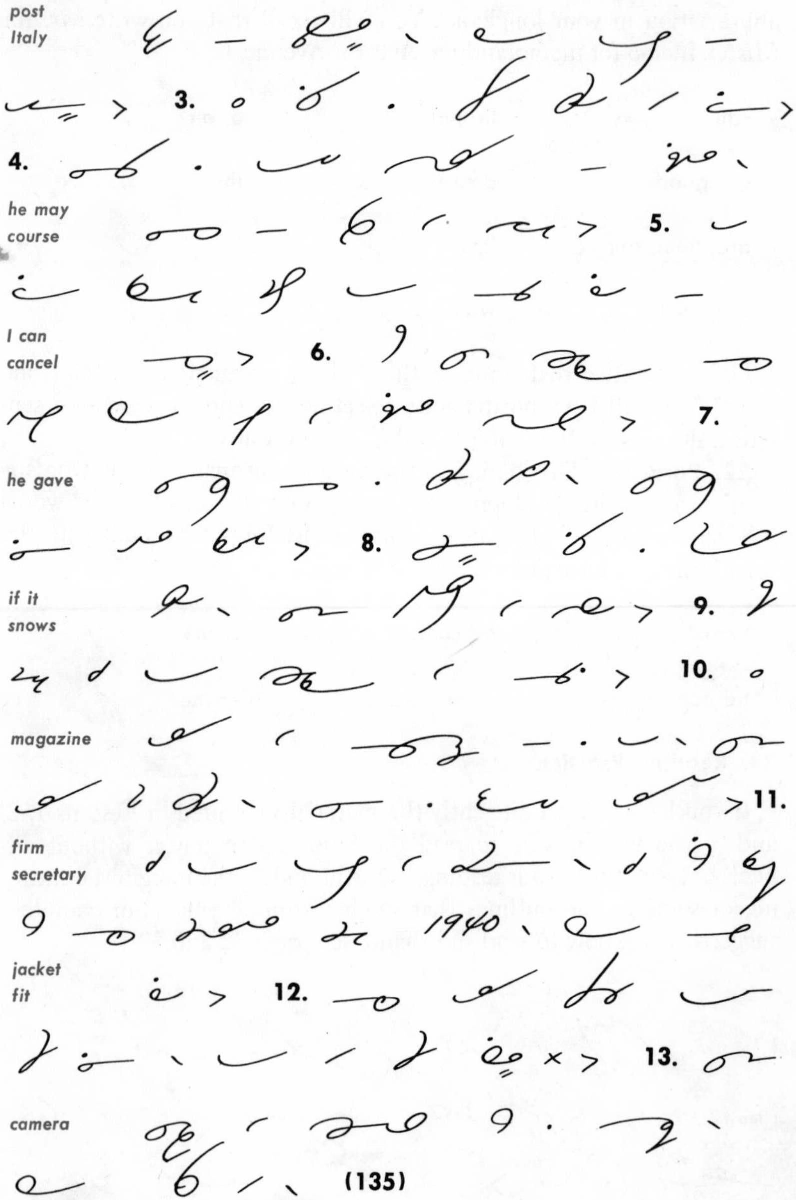
3.
4.
5.
6.
7.
8.
9.
10.
11.
1940
12.
13.

(135)

LESSON 4

24. Ŏ, Aw. The small, deep hook that represents *o* also represents the vowel heard in *top* and the vowel heard in *law.*

Ŏ

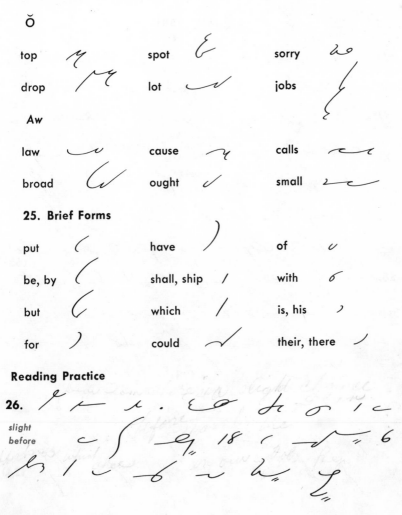

top	spot	sorry
drop	lot	jobs

Aw

law	cause	calls
broad	ought	small

25. Brief Forms

put	have	of
be, by	shall, ship	with
but	which	is, his
for	could	their, there

Reading Practice

26.

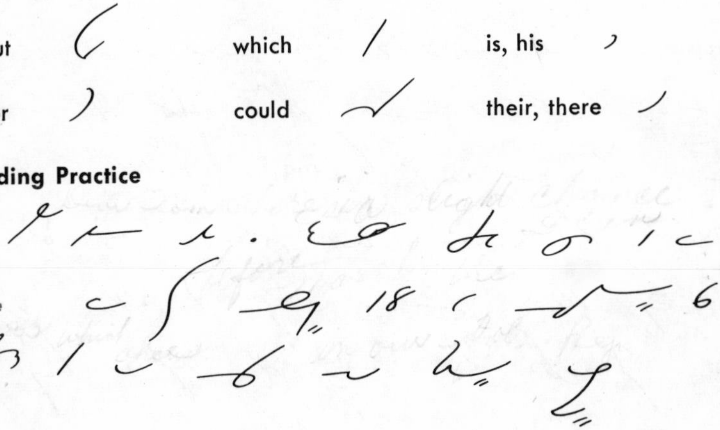

slight
before

I could have

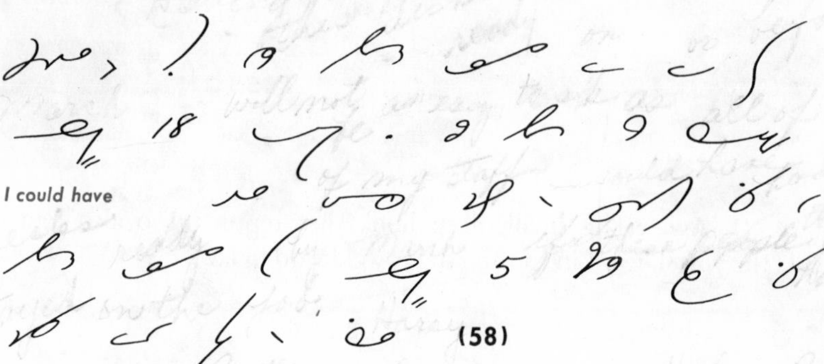

(58)

27.

retire
dean

(55)

28.

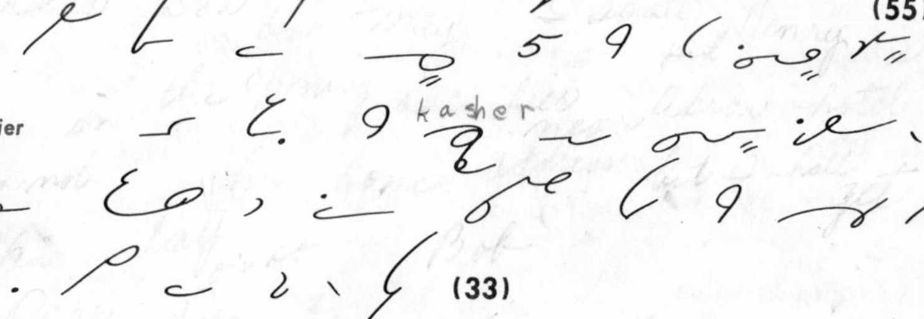

cashier

(33)

29.

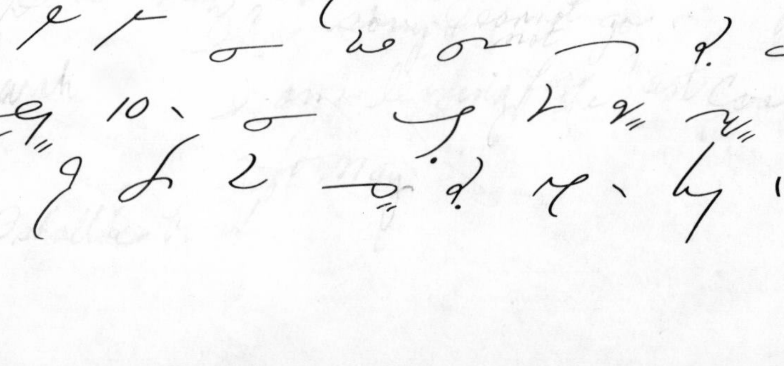

(24)

LESSON 5

30. Ses. The sound of *ses* is represented by joining the two forms of *s*.

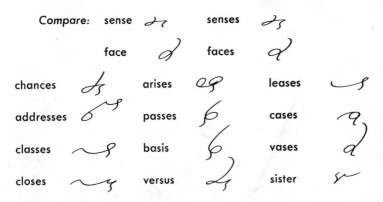

Compare:	sense		senses	
	face		faces	

chances		arises		leases	
addresses		passes		cases	
classes		basis		vases	
closes		versus		sister	

Did you notice that the ses stroke also expresses *sis* (as in *sister*) and *sus* (as in *versus*)?

31. T for *to* in Phrases. In phrases, *to* is represented by *t* before a downstroke.

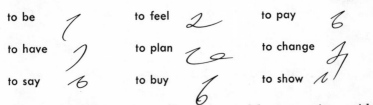

to be		to feel		to pay	
to have		to plan		to change	
to say		to buy		to show	

32. X. The letter x is usually represented by an *s* written with a slight backward slant.

Compare:	miss		mix	
	fees		fix	

box relax tax

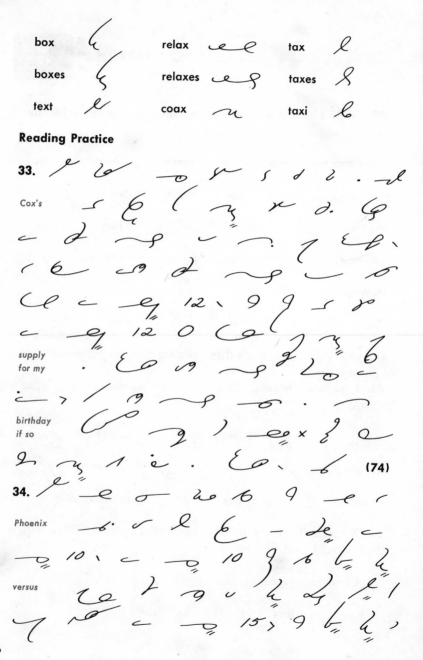

boxes relaxes taxes

text coax taxi

Reading Practice

33.

Cox's

supply
for my

birthday
if so

(74)

34.

Phoenix

versus

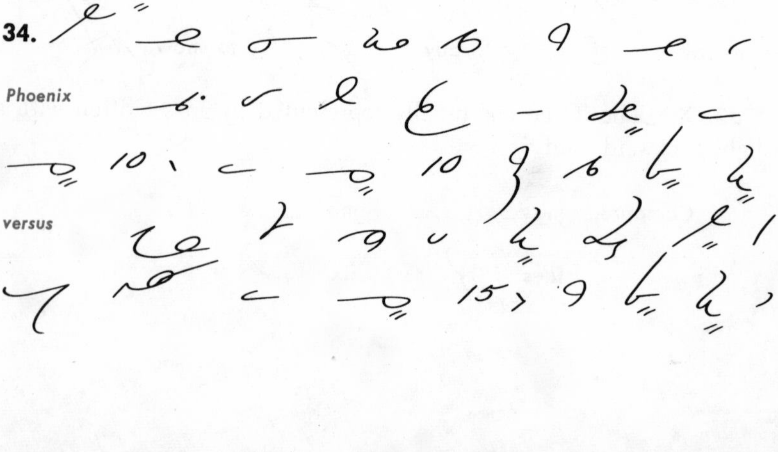

(76)

35.

listing attached

I need

(40)

36.

starting

(34)

37.

better salary

vacancy

(32)

LESSON 6 Recall

There is nothing new for you to learn in Lesson 6. In this lesson you will find a simple explanation of the principles that govern the joining of the strokes you have learned thus far, an interesting chart that will enable you to see how well you remember the things you studied in Chapter 1, and a series of short letters in shorthand.

Principles of Joining

As a matter of interest, you might like to know the principles under which the words you have already learned are written. The joinings of the shorthand characters are so easy and natural that it hardly seems necessary to give rules or explanations. However, notice the groups into which the joinings naturally fall.

38. Circles are written inside curves, outside angles.

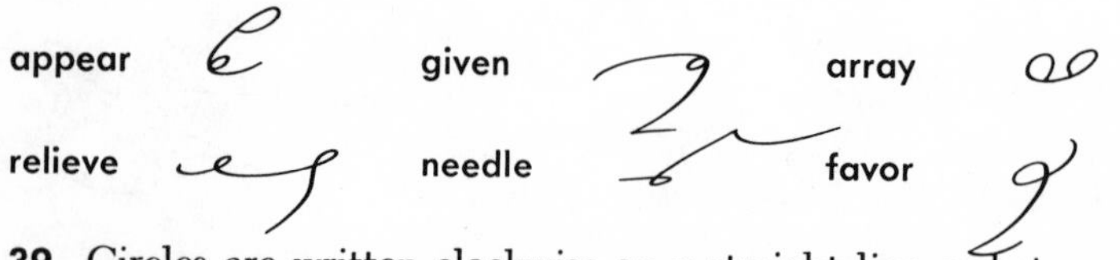
appear
given
array
relieve
needle
favor

39. Circles are written clockwise on a straight line or between two straight lines in the same direction.

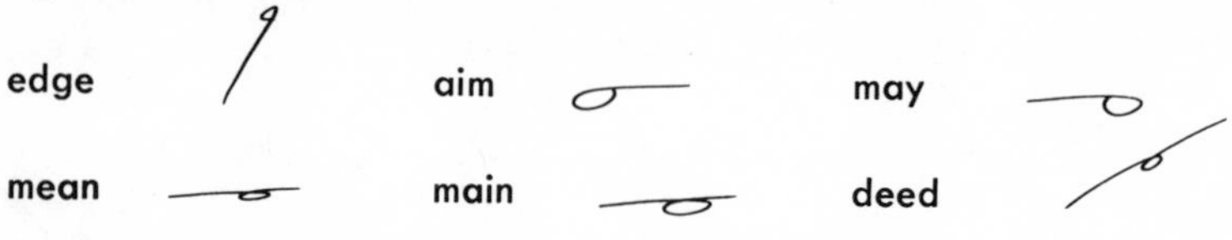
edge
aim
may
mean
main
deed

40. Between two curves in opposite directions, the circle is written on the back of the first curve.

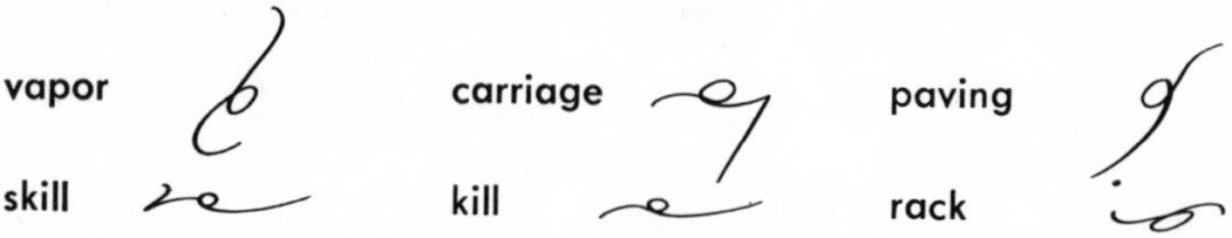
vapor
carriage
paving
skill
kill
rack

41. The *o* hook is written on its side before *n, m, r, l* unless a downward character comes before the hook.

own  home  knowledge 

bone  bowl  zone 

42. The over *th* is used in most joinings; but when *th* is joined to *o, r, l,* the under form is used.

these  both  thread 

43. The exact placement of a shorthand outline on the line of writing is of no importance. As a matter of convenience, however, the base of the first consonant of a word is placed on the line of writing. When *s* comes before a downstroke, however, the downstroke is placed on the line of writing.

dome  names  space 

44. Recall Chart. This chart is divided into three parts: (1) words that illustrate the principles, (2) brief forms, (3) phrases. As you read each word, spell it to yourself aloud, thus: *a-r-m, arm.* You need not spell the brief forms and phrases.

The chart contains 84 words and phrases. Can you read the entire chart in 9 minutes or less?

Words

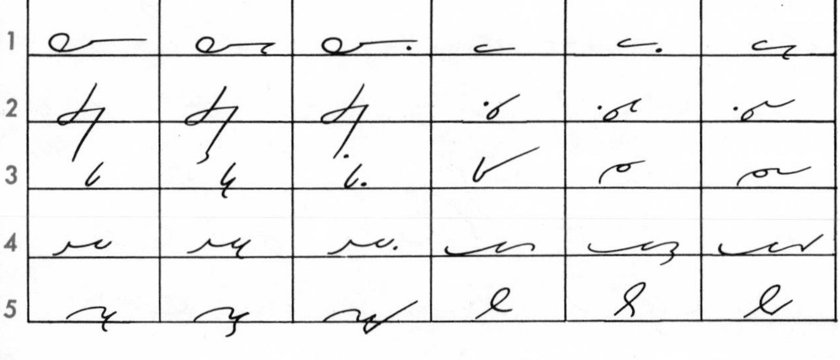

Brief Forms

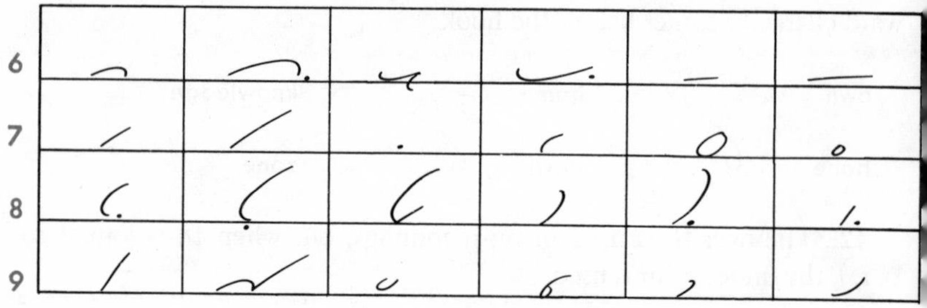
6
7
8
9

Phrases

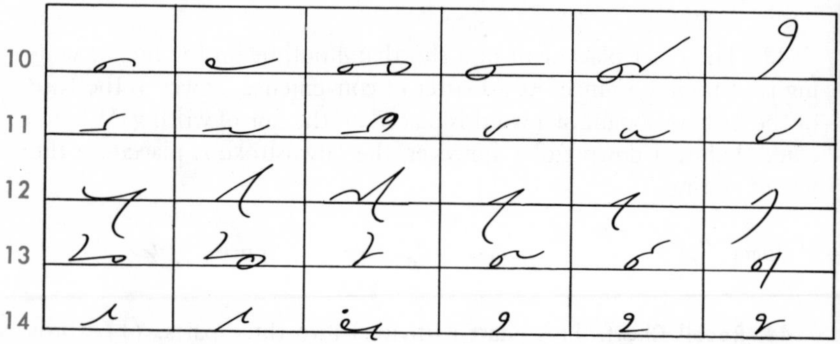
10
11
12
13
14

Reading Practice

45.

baseball
players

gym (57)

46.

private

sorry
sincere

(54)

47.

lease
premises

Akron 11:45 10

6

(49)

48. 15

Meade
Broad 16

(33)

CHAPTER 2

Your Practice Program—Reading

To make the most rapid progress in shorthand, you must practice efficiently. By practicing efficiently, you will achieve two important results: First, you will get the greatest benefit from the material on which you practice; second, and no doubt very important to you, you will be able to complete each lesson in the shortest possible time.

To begin with, choose a quiet place in which to practice—and resist that temptation to turn on the radio! Then follow these easy steps:

Word Lists

1. Place a card or slip of paper over the type.

2. Spell each shorthand word aloud if possible, thus: *m-e-s, mess; t-a-x, tax*. By reading aloud, you will be sure that you are concentrating on each word as you work with it.

3. If the spelling of a shorthand outline does not immediately give you the meaning, refer to the type key. Do not spend more than a few seconds trying to decipher an outline.

4. After you have read all the words in the paragraph, reread them in the same way. This second reading should be easier and you should not have to refer to the key so often.

5. In reading brief forms and phrases, it is not necessary to spell.

Letters and Articles

1. Before you start the Reading and Writing Practice, have a blank piece of paper or a card and a pencil handy.

2. Read the shorthand aloud.

3. When you come to a shorthand outline that you cannot read, spell it. If the spelling gives

The student studies the word lists by placing a card over the key and reading the shorthand words aloud. She then reads the Reading and Writing Practice, writing on the card any outlines that she cannot read after spelling them.

you the meaning, continue reading. If it does not, write the outline on your sheet of paper or card and continue reading. Do not spend more than a few seconds trying to decipher the outline.

4. After you have gone through the entire Reading and Writing Practice in this way, repeat this procedure if time permits. On this second reading you may be able to read some of the outlines that escaped you on your first time through. When that happens, cross that outline off your sheet or card.

5. Finally—and very important—at the earliest opportunity ask your teacher or your classmates the meaning of the outlines you could not read.

Note: Instructions for writing shorthand are given on pages 56 and 57.

Remember, during the early stages your shorthand reading may not be very rapid. That is only natural, as you are, in a sense, learning a new language. If you do each day's lesson faithfully, however, you will find your reading rate increasing almost from day to day.

What's Ahead?

In Chapter 2 you will meet only three new alphabetic characters. Most of your work will be concerned with the study of useful devices that will help you write more rapidly and easily.

In Chapter 2 you will find a new feature that will be extremely helpful to you as you work with each Reading and Writing Practice – an Applied Vocabulary Study, which gives brief definitions of expressions that may be unfamiliar to you.

Be sure that you read each Applied Vocabulary Study before you begin your work on the Reading and Writing Practice.

LESSON 7

49. Brief Forms

that  them  *you, your 

right, write  were, year  *to, too, two 

must  Mr., market  *Yours truly 

desire, Dear Sir 

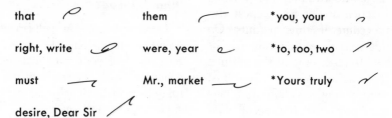

*The hook in this outline represents the sound of oo, which you will study later.

50. Word Beginning Ex-. The word beginning ex- is expressed by es.

express  extreme  expense 

explain  extra  exclaim 

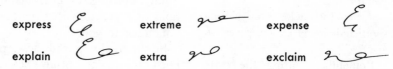

Reading and Writing Practice

51. Applied Vocabulary Study. To help you understand the meaning of the practice material, a number of expressions are defined briefly at the beginning of each Reading and Writing Practice. The meaning or explanation given applies to the use of the expression in the practice matter; it does not cover all the possible meanings or uses of the expression. Once you add these expressions to your vocabulary, you will find that you will be able to read the shorthand more easily.

Excessive, too much, too high. *Exhibit,* show. *Asset,* something of value.

52.

sheet
realize
hesitate
write me

(71)

53.

easy chairs
ago
I thought

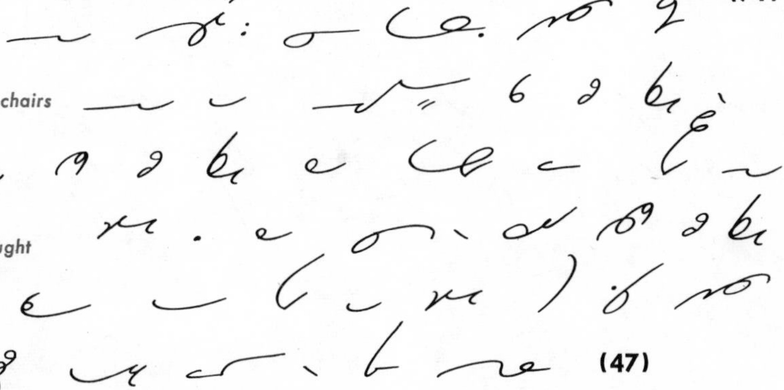

(47)

54.

you can have
Harris's

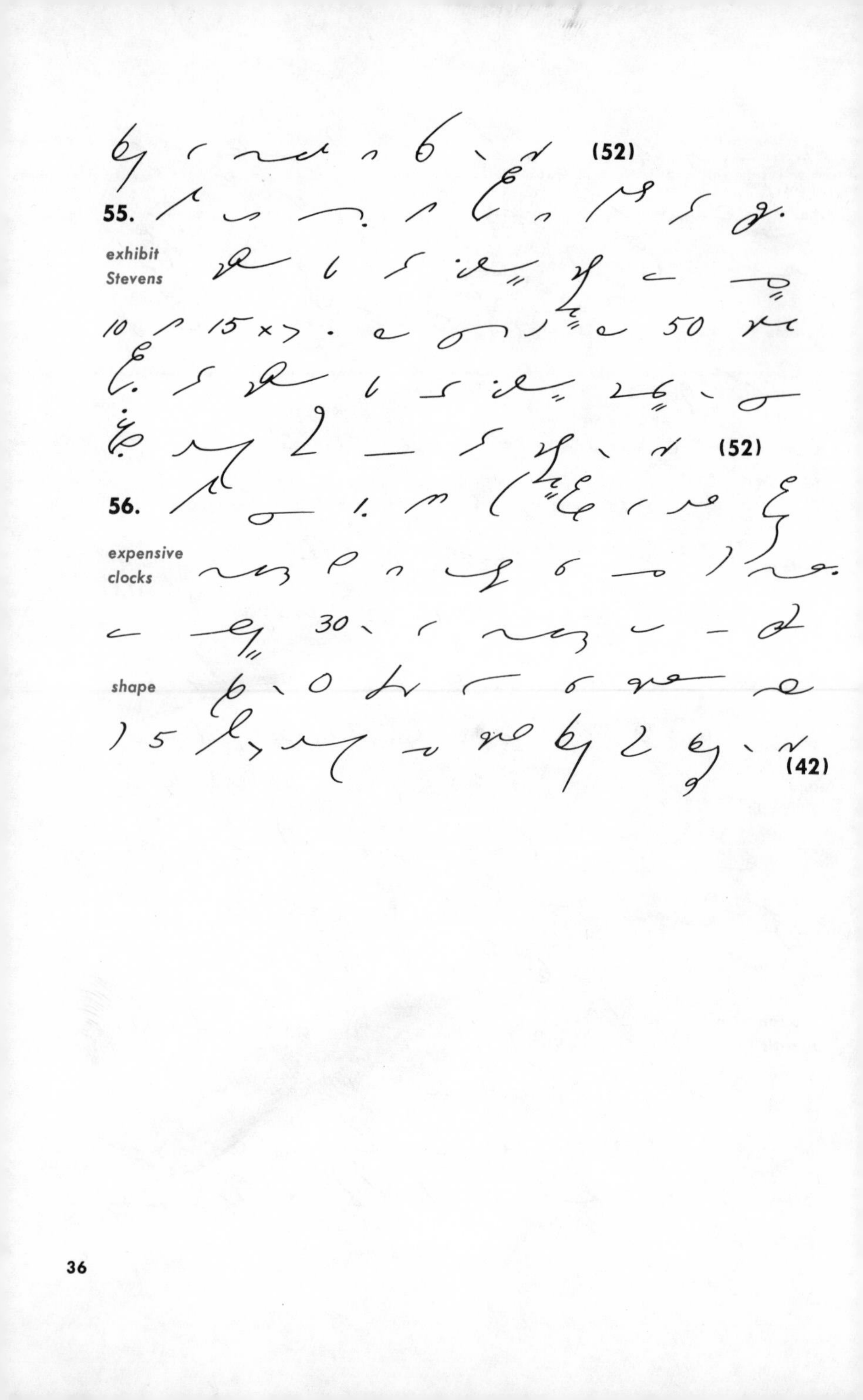

(52)

55.

exhibit
Stevens

10 15 50

(52)

56.

expensive
clocks

30

shape

1 5

(42)

LESSON 8

57. Word Ending -tion. The word ending *-tion* (or *-sion, -shion, -cian*) is represented by *sh*.

nation		section		fashions	
ration		occasion		physician	
action		operation		national	

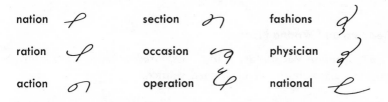

58. Word Endings -cient, -ciency. The word ending *-cient* (or *-tient*) is represented by *sht; -ciency,* by *shse*.

patient		efficient		efficiency	

59. Word Ending -tial. The word ending *-tial* (or *-cial*) is represented by *sh*.

social		initials		special	
partial		financial		essential	

60. Amounts and Quantities. You will find the method of expressing amounts and quantities shown here especially useful in business dictation.

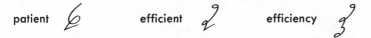

500		$5		5 o'clock	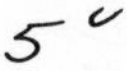
5,000		$5,000		$5.50	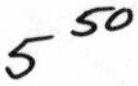
500,000		$500,000		5 cents	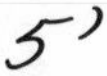

Did you notice that the *n* for *hundred* is placed *underneath* the figure?

61. Disjoined Past Tense, -er, -or. The shorthand character representing the last sound of some words is omitted. In such words, the past tense is represented by a disjoined *t*; derivatives in *-er, -or* are written with a disjoined *r*. The disjoining indicates the omission of one or more shorthand characters.

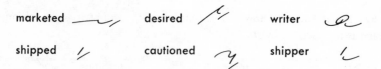

marketed	desired	writer
shipped	cautioned	shipper

Reading and Writing Practice

62. Applied Vocabulary Study. *Essential,* necessary. *Vexation,* annoyance. *Expiration,* end. *Cautioned,* warned.

63.

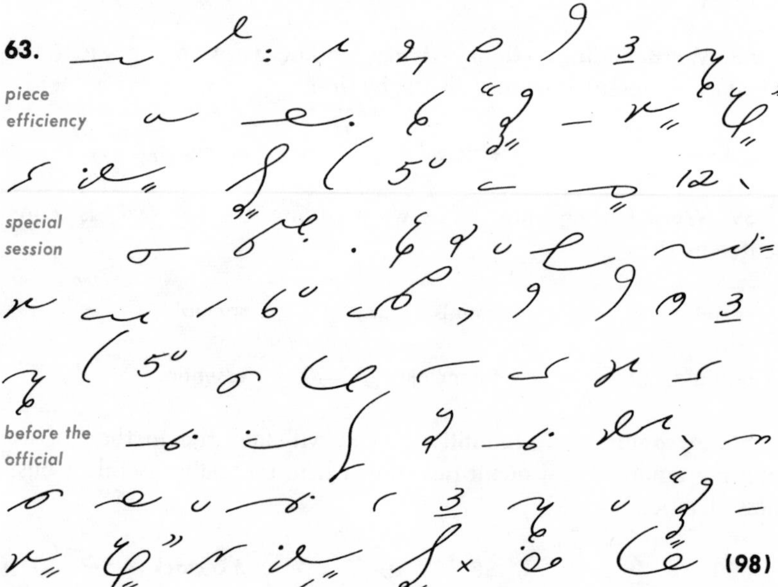
piece
efficiency
special
session
before the
official
(98)

64.

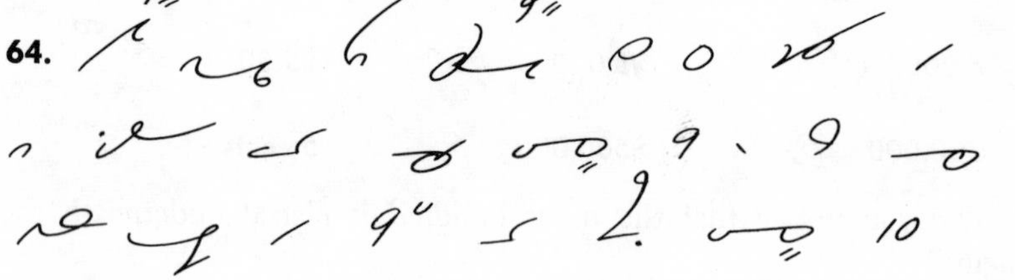

Murphy

he gave me

expiration

I would have

(133)

65.

cautioned

physician
exception

(60)

LESSON 9

66. Brief Forms

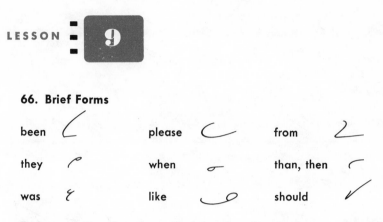

been	please	from
they	when	than, then
was	like	should

Did you notice that the outline for *than-then* is the over *th*, with *n* added without an angle?

67. Been in Phrases. The word *been* is represented by *b* in some phrases.

had been	you have been	it has been
have been	have not been	there has been
I have been	has been	should have been

68. *Able* in Phrases. The word *able* is represented by *a* in some phrases.

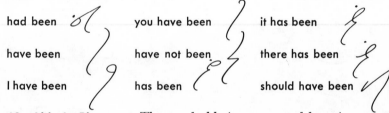

have been able	has been able
I have been able	should be able
I have not been able	to be able
had been able	you will be able

69. Word Ending -ly. The word ending *-ly* is represented by the small circle.

fairly | early | nearly
briefly | only | merely
sincerely | openly | daily

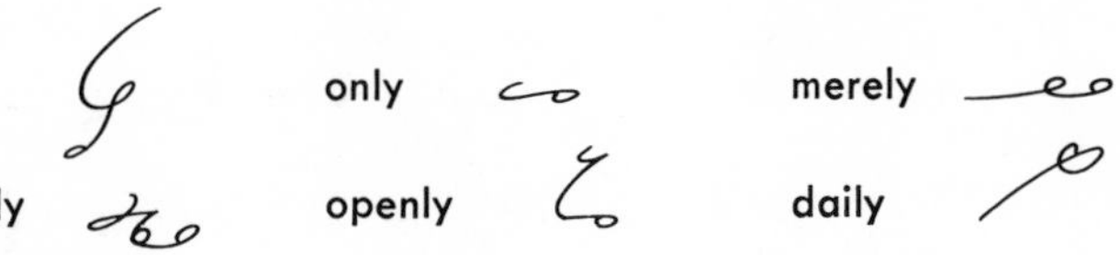

Did you notice how the circle for *ly* in *daily* is added to the other side of the *d* after the *a* has been written?

70. Word Endings -ily, -ally. The word endings *-ily, -ally* are represented by a loop.

readily | hastily | nationally
easily | heavily | totally
family | especially | occasionally

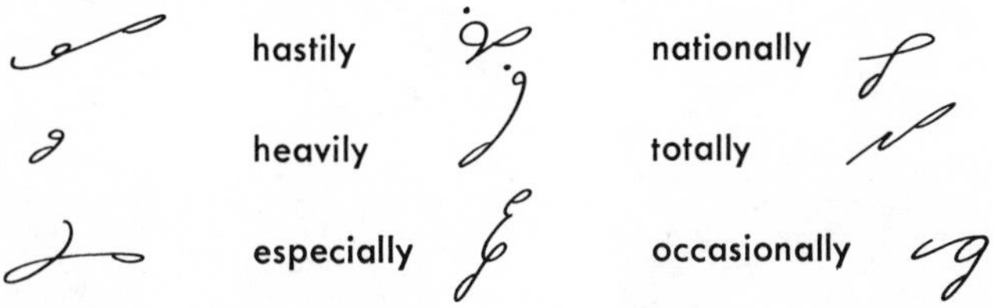

Did you notice that the loop is long and flat; that the same-sized loop represents both *-ily* and *-ally*?

Reading and Writing Practice

71. Applied Vocabulary Study. *On the road,* traveling as a salesman. *Vacancy,* job opening. *Range,* cooking stove. *Burner,* the part of a stove where the flame is produced.

72.

Fresno
family
hire
with him

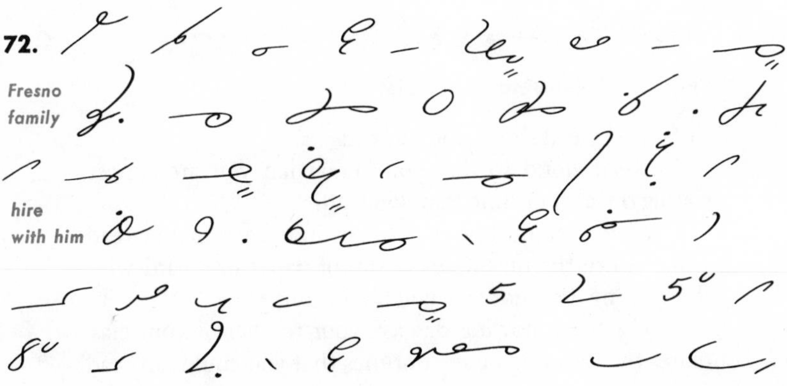

I liked
eagerness
vacancy

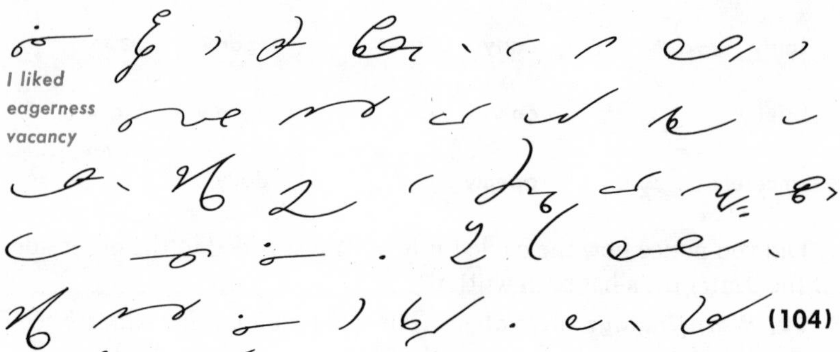

(104)

73.

highly
honor

course
recall

Shorthand Reading Check List

When you read shorthand, do you

1. Read aloud so that you know that you are concentrating on each outline that you read?
2. Spell each outline that you cannot immediately read?
3. Write the outline on a slip of paper or a card when the spelling does not give you the meaning?
4. On the following day ask your teacher or your classmates the meaning of any outlines that you could not read?

10

(93)

74.

kitchen burners

250

350

(60)

75.

drafty

thorough lower

(74)

LESSON 10

76. Oi. The sound of *oi* is represented by

toy	toil	noise
oil	soil	joining

77. Word Endings -ure, -ture. The word ending *-ure* is represented by *r*; *-ture*, by *tr*.

failure	figure	nature
secure	procure	picture

78. Word Endings -ual, -tual. The word ending *-ual* is represented by *l*; *-tual*, by *tl*.

annual	actual	actually
gradual	factual	annually

79. Word Beginning Re-. The word beginning *re-* is represented by *r*.

receive	reply	reception
reserve	receipt	reopen

80. Word Beginning Be-. The word beginning *be-* is represented by *b*.

began	became	below
begin	beneath	because

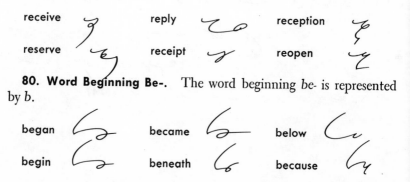

81. Word Beginning De-. The word beginning *de-* is represented by *d*.

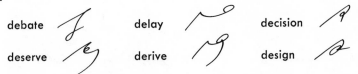

debate delay decision
deserve derive design

82. Word Beginnings Dis-, Des-. The word beginnings *dis-, des-* are represented by *ds*.

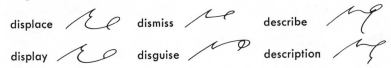

displace dismiss describe
display disguise description

83. Word Beginning Mis-. The word beginning *mis-* is represented by *ms*.

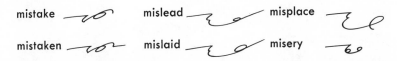

mistake mislead misplace
mistaken mislaid misery

Reading and Writing Practice

84. Applied Vocabulary Study. *Text*, short for *textbook*. *Operating schedule*, timetable. *Annual*, yearly. *Depot*, railroad station.

85.

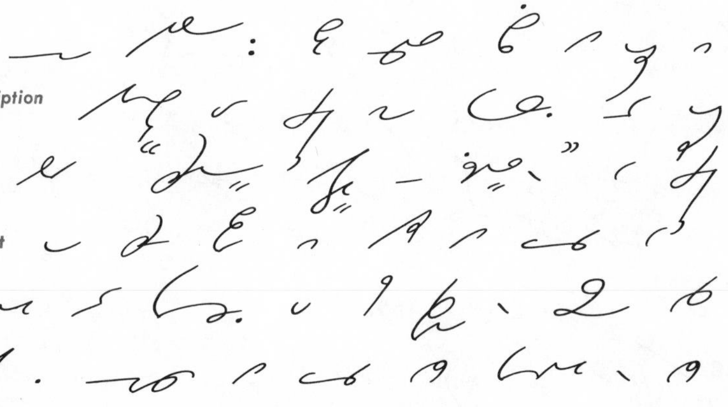

description
text
except

actually
feature
schedule
Joyce

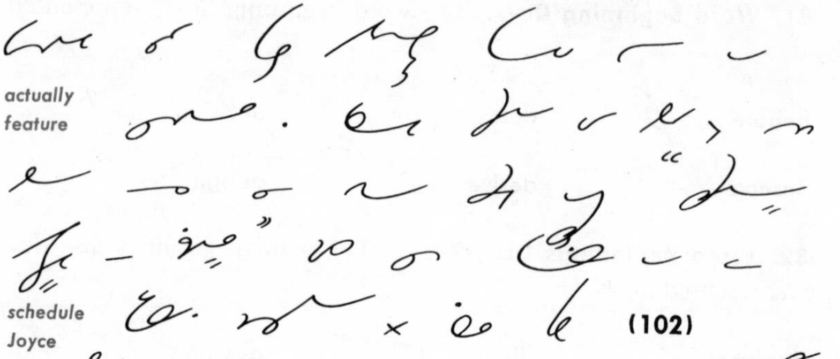

(102)

richly

86.

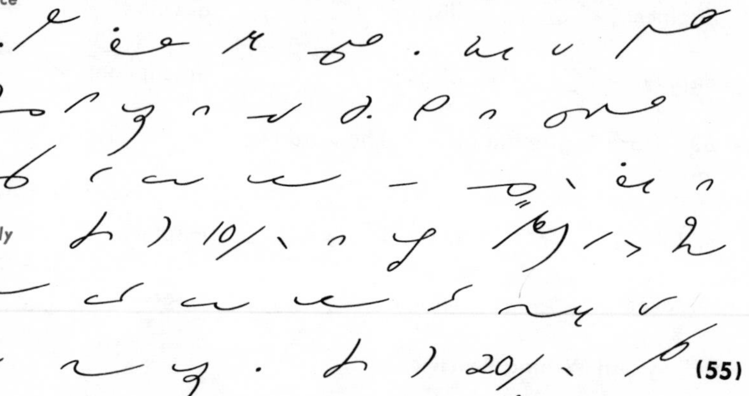

(55)

annual
annoyance

87.

(60)

88.

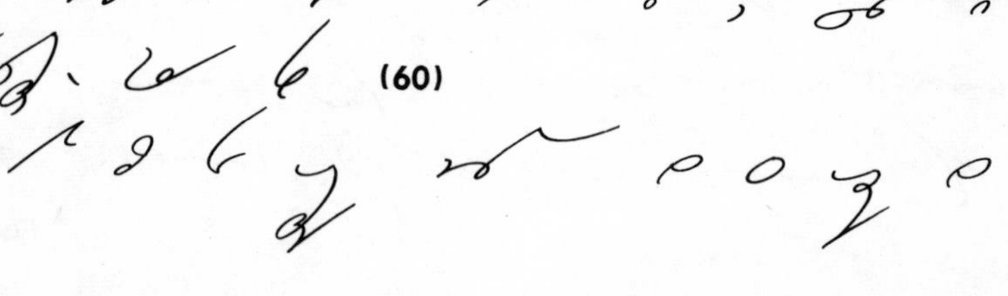

Akron
lecture

research

they have
essays

(117)

89.

taxpayer
simply

(53)

LESSON 11

90. Brief Forms

*and, end	bill	what
side	after	most
business	all	Mrs.

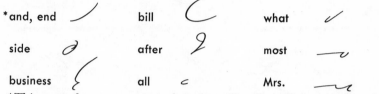

*This *upward* curve represents the *nd* combination, which you will study later.

91. Long I and a Following Vowel. Any vowel following long *i* is represented by a small circle within the large circle.

Compare: line   lion

science	trial	appliances
diet	diary	reliance

92. Ia, Ea. The sounds of *ia* (as in *piano*) and *ea* (as in *create*) are represented by a large circle with a dot placed within it.

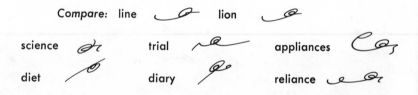

piano	appreciate	create
mania	initiate	area

93. Joining of Hooks and Vowels. Hook and circle vowels are joined in the order in which they occur.

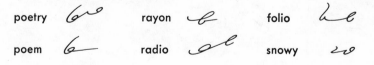

poetry	rayon	folio
poem	radio	snowy

Reading and Writing Practice

94. Applied Vocabulary Study. V*ia express,* by way of express. *Rayon,* a kind of cloth. *Replenish,* fill again. *Deviating,* departing.

95.

Lydia
Ryan

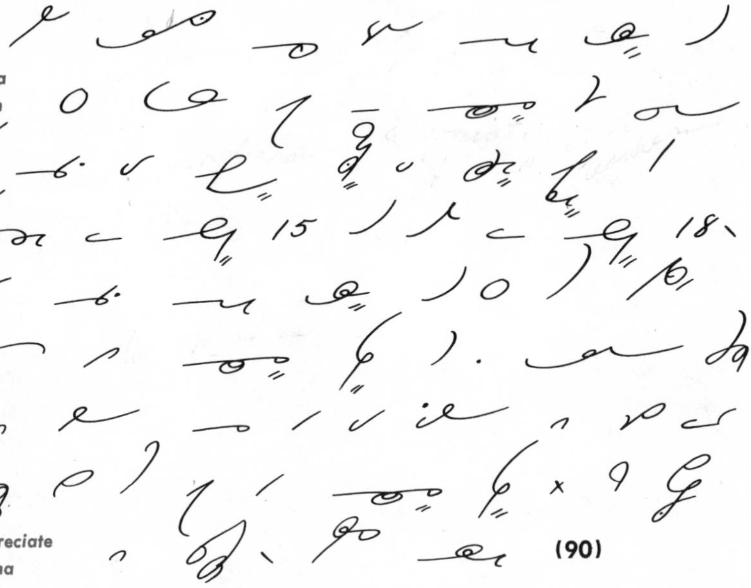

appreciate
Diana

(90)

96.

Roy
Norse

via
so far

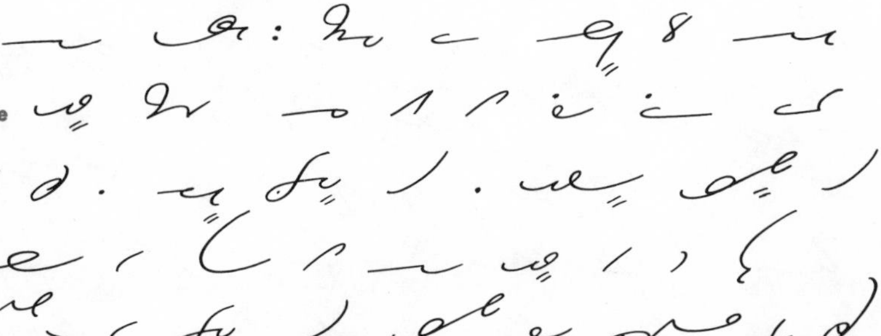

ill will
of all

(123)

97.

buyer
rayon

replenish

(74)

98.

deviating

Julian

(53)

LESSON 12 Recall

Lesson 12 is a "breather" for you; it has no new shorthand devices for you to learn. It contains a few more principles of joining, a helpful recall chart, and several short letters in shorthand that you should have no difficulty reading.

Principles of Joining

Here are the principles that govern the writing of the new words and phrases with which you have been working in Chapter 2.

99. The word *been* is represented by *b* after *have, has, had.*

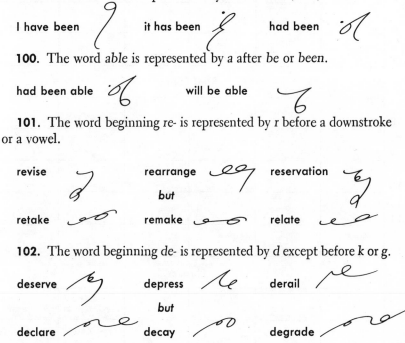

I have been  **it has been**  **had been** 

100. The word *able* is represented by *a* after *be* or *been.*

had been able  **will be able** 

101. The word beginning *re-* is represented by *r* before a downstroke or a vowel.

revise  **rearrange**  **reservation** 

but

retake  **remake**  **relate** 

102. The word beginning *de-* is represented by *d* except before *k* or *g.*

deserve  **depress**  **derail** 

but

declare  **decay**  **degrade** 

103. Recall Chart. This chart contains all the brief forms in Chapter 2 and one or more illustrations of all the shorthand devices you have studied in Chapters 1 and 2.

The chart contains 84 words and phrases. Can you read the entire chart in 9 minutes or less?

Words

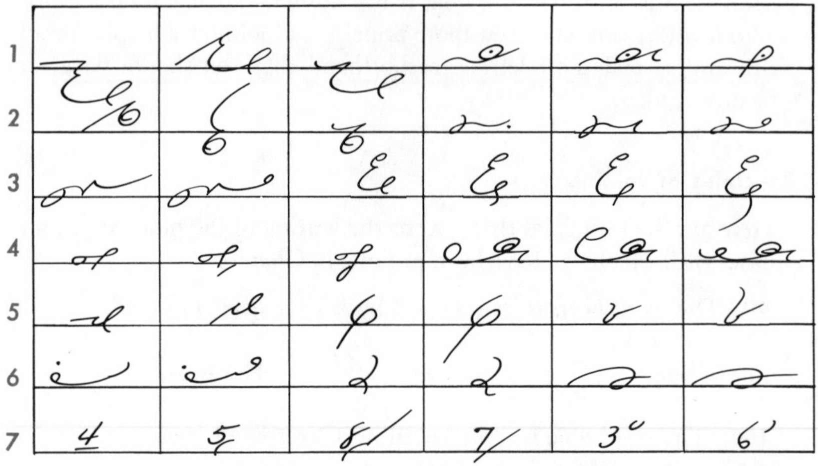

Brief Forms

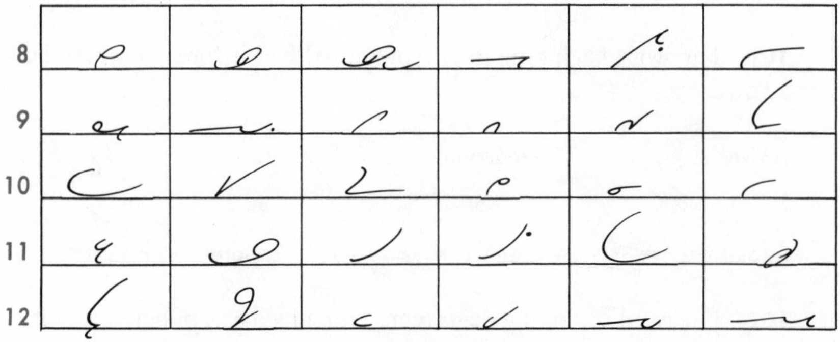

Phrases

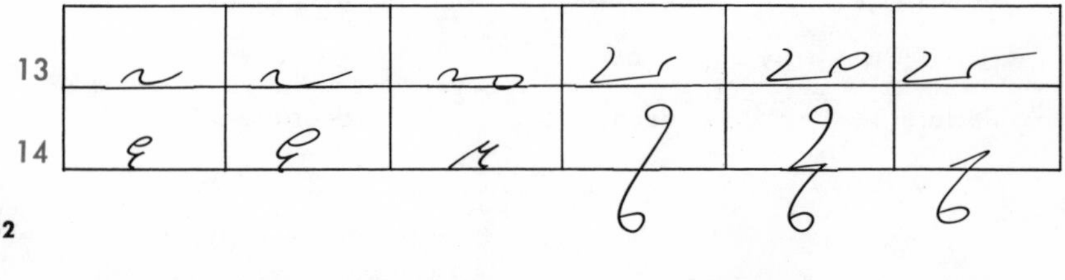

Reading and Writing Practice

104. Applied Vocabulary Study. *Branch,* a local office. *Associates,* fellow workers. *Dismal,* gloomy, dreadful. *Reaction,* response, one's feeling about something.

105.

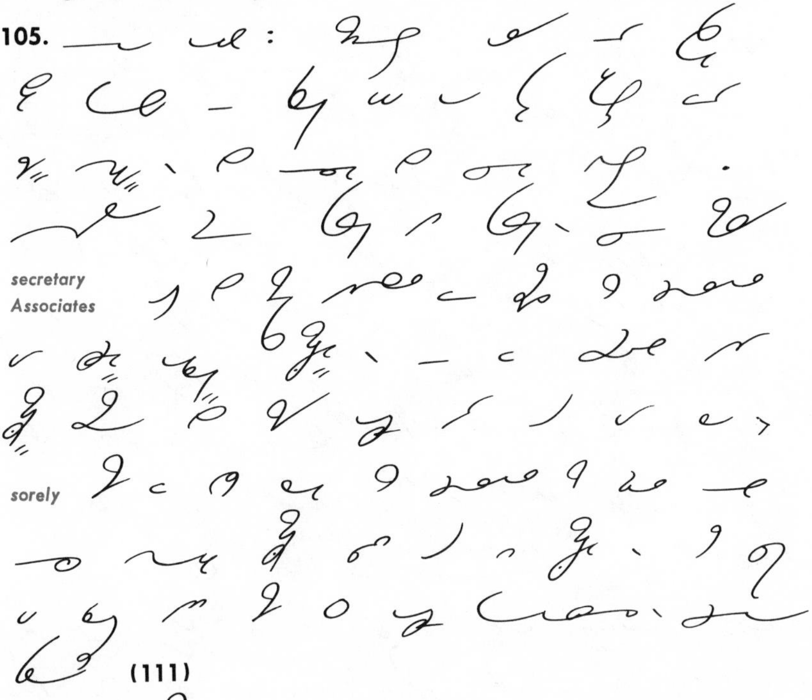

secretary

Associates

sorely

(111)

106.

dismal

(60)

107.

8 cents
of his

(82)

108.

appreciate
to show

better
realize

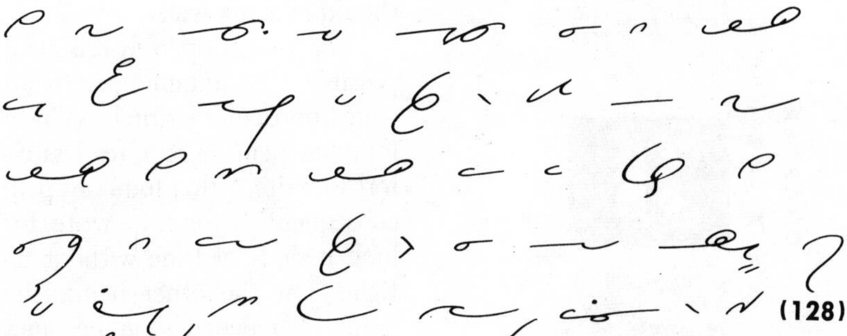

(128)

109.

Peoria

reaction

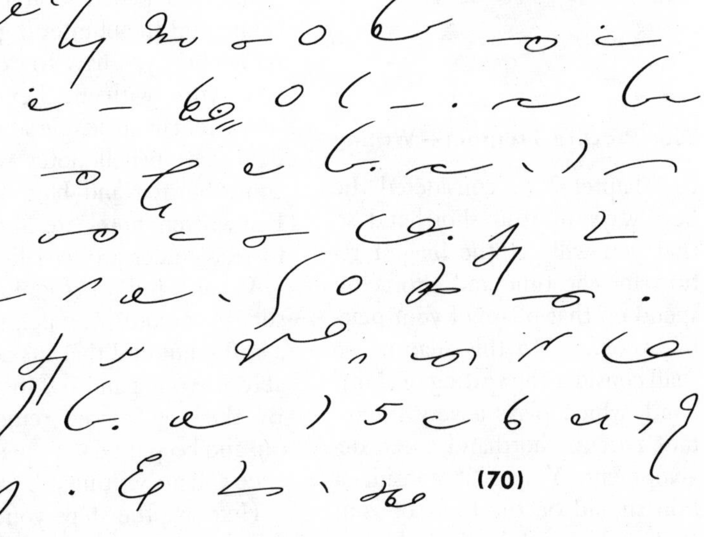

(70)

CHAPTER 3

Your Practice Program — Writing

In Chapter 2 we considered the best ways to read shorthand so that you will get the biggest return for the time and effort you spend on that phase of your practice program. In this chapter we shall consider the writing of shorthand, which plays a very important part in shorthand speed development. Your first consideration should be the tools of your trade—your notebook and your fountain pen.

Your notebook. The best notebook for shorthand writing is one that measures 6 by 9 inches and has a vertical rule down the middle of each sheet. If the notebook has a Spiral binding, so much the better, as the Spiral binding enables you to keep the pages flat at all times. The paper, of course, should take ink well.

Your fountain pen. If it is at all possible, use a fountain pen for all your shorthand writing. Why a fountain pen? It requires less effort to write with a fountain pen; consequently, you can write for long periods of time without fatigue. On the other hand, the point of a pencil soon becomes blunt; and the blunter it gets, the more effort you have to expend as you write with it. Pen-written notes remain readable almost indefinitely; pencil notes soon become blurred and hard to read. Pen-written notes are also easier to read under artificial light.

What kind of fountain pen should you use? Any pen that has a stiff point and that fits comfortably in your hand is satisfactory. By the way, always remove the cap and keep it off your pen all the time you are writing.

Here are the steps you should follow in copying each Reading and Writing Practice:

1. Read the material you are going to copy, following the suggestions given on pages 32 and 33. *Always* read everything before you copy it.

2. Read a convenient group of words from the printed shorthand; then write the group, reading

aloud as you write.

3. As you copy from the printed shorthand, you may decipher some of the outlines that you wrote on your slip or card when you read the material before copying it. When that occurs, cross the outlines off your list. Be sure to ask your teacher or your classmates the meaning of any outlines that remain on your list or card.

4. Remember that in the early stages your writing may not be very rapid, nor will your notes be so pretty as those in the book. With regular practice, however, you will soon become so proud of your shorthand notes that you won't want to write any more longhand!

What's Ahead?

In Chapter 3 you will cover nine more alphabetic strokes, after which you will have only ten of the easiest strokes to learn. The brief forms are moving along, too. When you learn those in Lesson 17, you will have covered almost half the brief forms of Gregg Shorthand.

You are in for a little surprise in Lesson 18, where you will find three amusing fables written in shorthand. Perhaps you did not realize that your shorthand vocabulary has grown to the point where you can read articles and stories in shorthand!

Official
GREGG
Shorthand Notebook

The efficient shorthand writer makes sure that his pen is filled, that his pencil is well sharpened, and that he has enough blank pages in his notebook on which to write.

LESSON 13

110. OO Hook. A tiny hook expresses the three vowel sounds heard in the words *who, up, foot*. You are already familiar with this stroke through the brief forms *you-your, to, Yours truly*. The hook is deep and narrow.

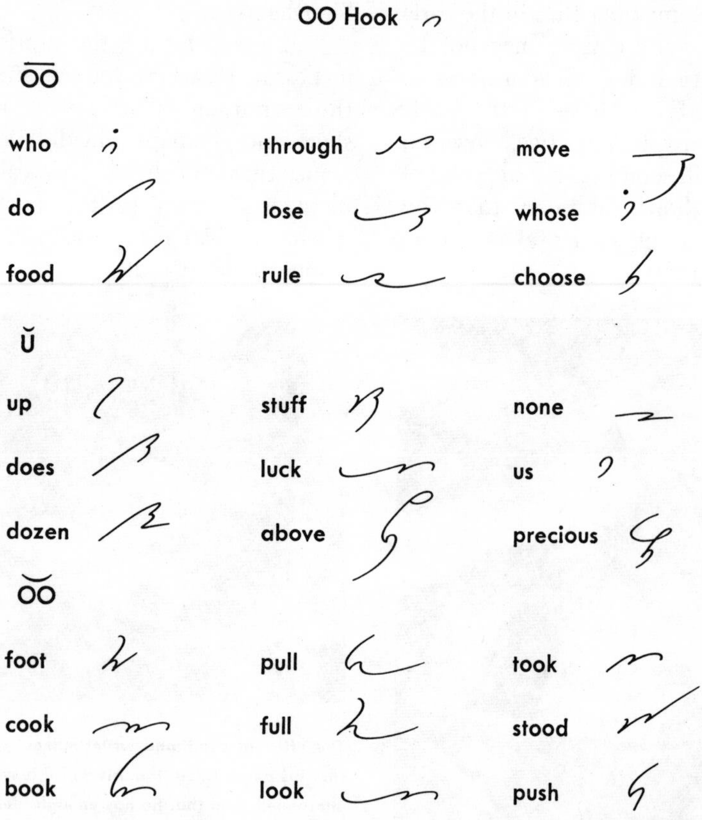
OO Hook
OO (long)
who
through
move
do
lose
whose
food
rule
choose
Ŭ
up
stuff
none
does
luck
us
dozen
above
precious
OO (short)
foot
pull
took
cook
full
stood
book
look
push

Did you notice that the *oo* hook has a slightly different slant when it follows *n* or *m*?

111. W, Sw. At the beginning of words *w* is represented by the oo hook; *sw*, by soo.

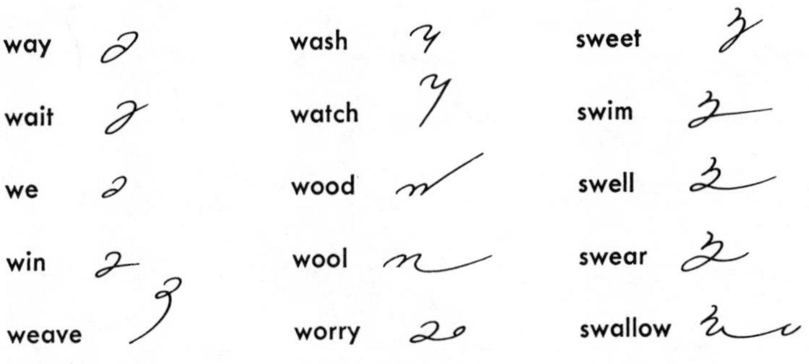
way
wash
sweet
wait
watch
swim
we
wood
swell
win
wool
swear
weave
worry
swallow

112. Wh. *Wh*, as in *while*, is pronounced *hw*; therefore, in shorthand we write the *h* first because we hear it first.

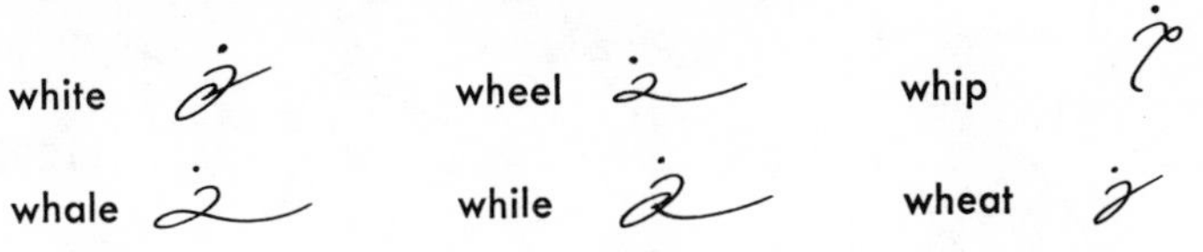
white
wheel
whip
whale
while
wheat

Reading and Writing Practice

113. Applied Vocabulary Study. *Irritating*, annoying, bothering, troubling. *Absorbs*, soaks up. *Cruising speed*, the speed at which a car or plane operates most efficiently and economically. *Business machines*, typewriters, adding machines, billing machines, etc.

114.

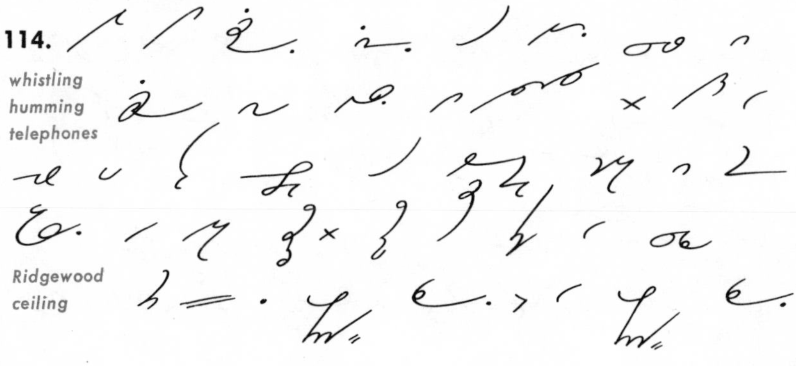
whistling
humming
telephones
Ridgewood
ceiling

irritating

truly

(129)

115.

Budd family

trial spin

(97)

116.

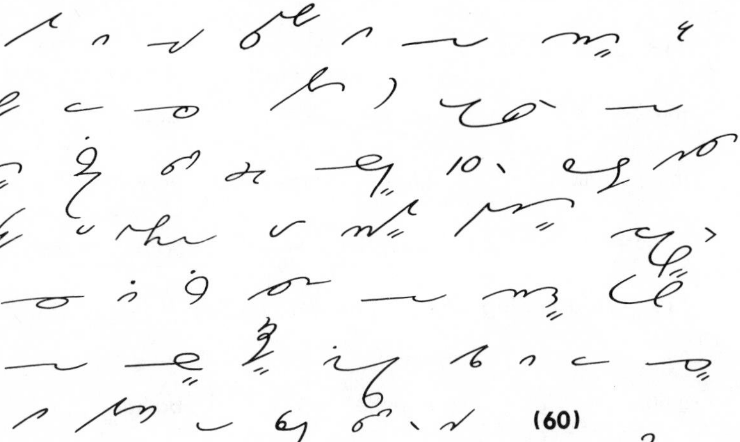

(60)

117.

we have had
truck

worry

(69)

LESSON **14**

118. Brief Forms

this	send	about
thing, think	glad	very
enclose	letter, let	worth

119. Word Ending -ther. The word ending *-ther* is represented by *th*.

neither	together	bother
gather	mother	leather
whether	brother	either
other	rather	farther

Reading and Writing Practice

120. Applied Vocabulary Study. *Ad,* a short form for *advertisement. Featuring,* emphasizing, stressing. *Pulls well,* brings in many sales or inquiries. *Leisurely,* taking plenty of time.

121.

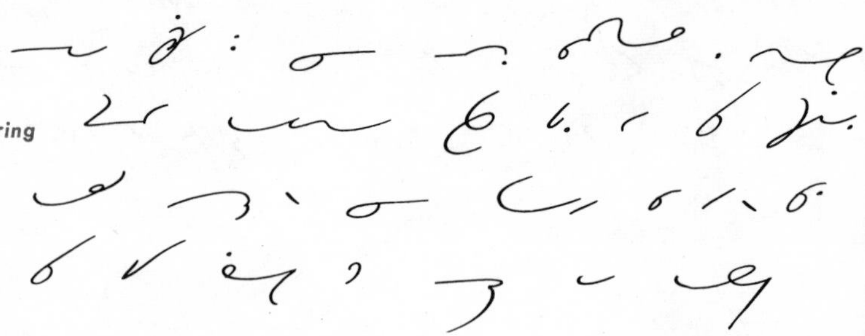

ad
featuring

wallets

well

repeat

so far

banner

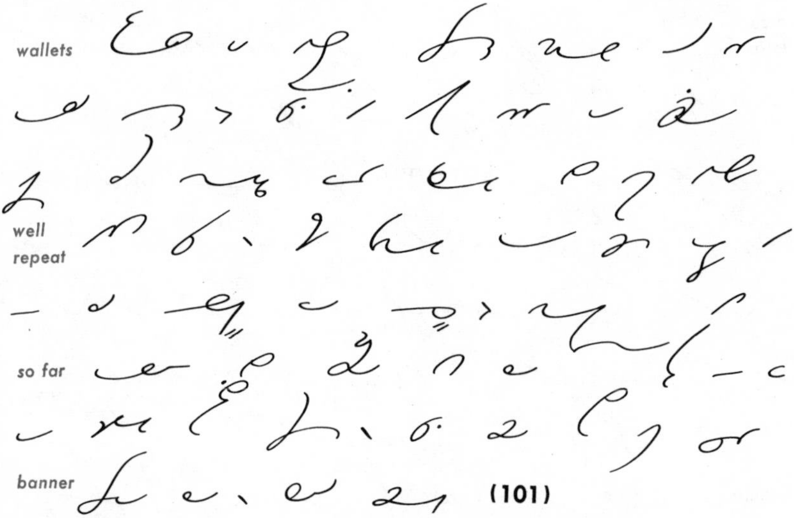

(101)

122.

appliance

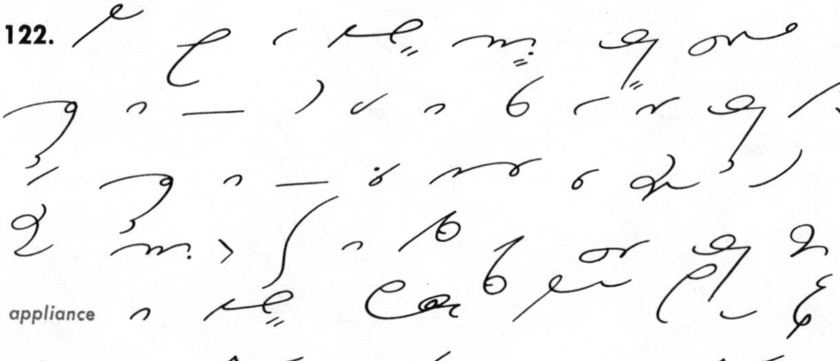

(90)

123.

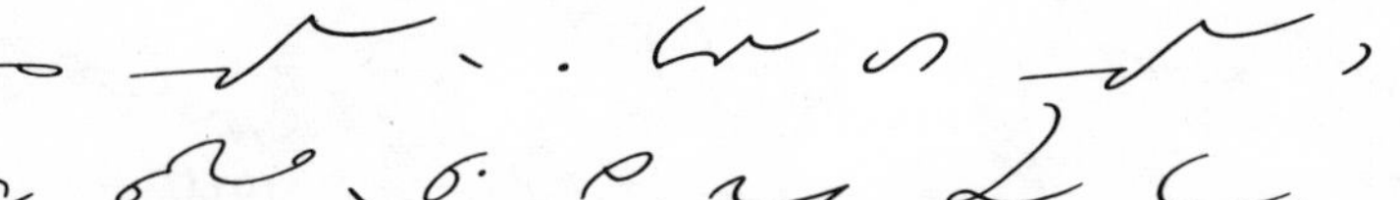

area
leisurely

(78)

124.

Retailing

production
to charge

(91)

125.

feet
shoes

(43)

126. W in the Body of a Word. When *w* occurs in the body of a word, it is represented by a short dash underneath the vowel.

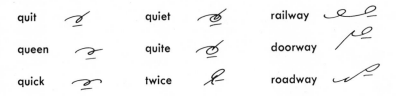

quit, quiet, railway, queen, quite, doorway, quick, twice, roadway

127. Ah, Aw. A dot is used for *a* in words that begin with *ah* and *aw*.

ahead, await, awoke, away, awake, aware

128. Y. Before *o* and *oo*, *y* is expressed by the small circle, as *y* is pronounced *e*. *Ye* is expressed by a small loop; *ya*, by a large loop.

yawn, youth, yarn, yacht, yellow, Yale

Reading and Writing Practice

129. Applied Vocabulary Study. *Affix* your *signature*, sign. *Annual quota*, the amount allowed or required for the year.

130.

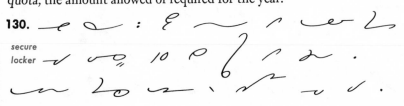

secure
locker

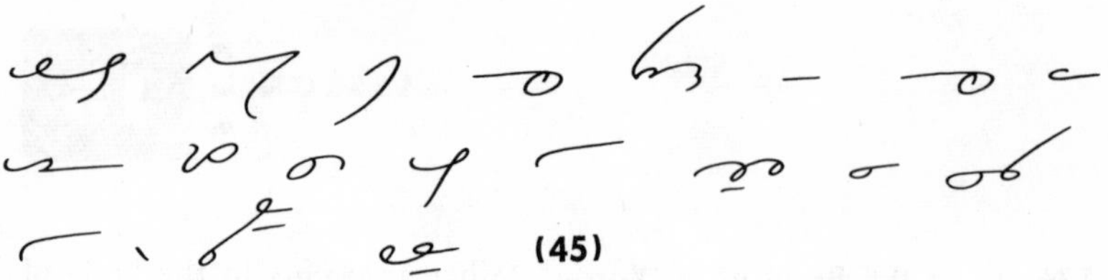

(45)

131.

Dwyer
Quill

girls

quota
register

fee

(107)

132.

weeds
lawn
yes

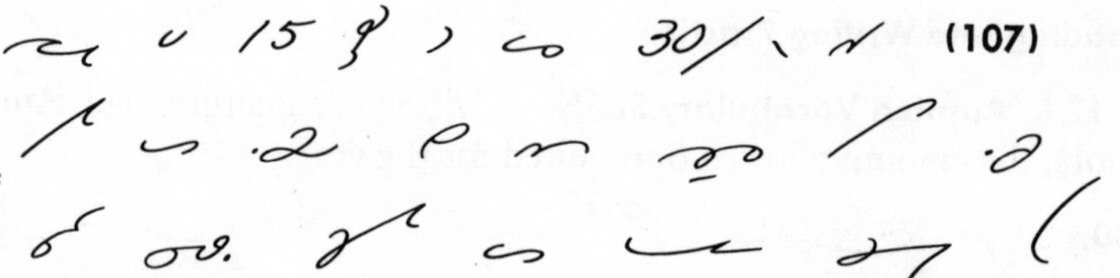

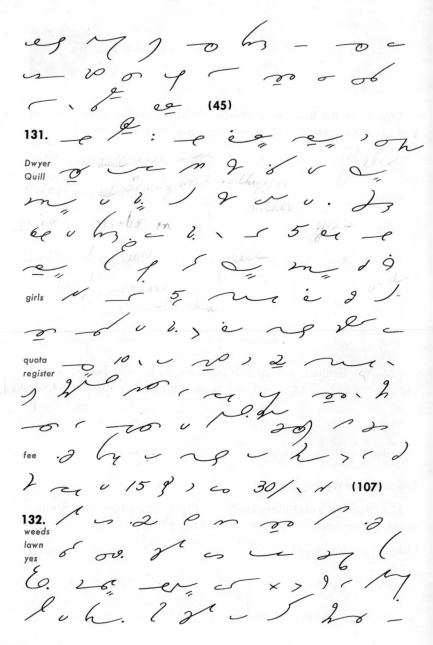

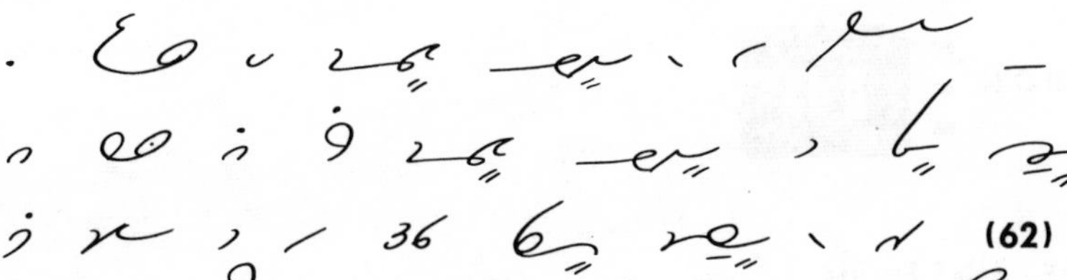

(62)

133.

adapt

annual

(79)

134.

affix
signature
premises

machine
quietly

fatigue
efficiency

(76)

LESSON 16

135. Brief Forms

necessary	believe, belief	deliver
doctor, during	satisfy, satisfactory	return
yet	next	work

136. Omission of Short U. In the body of a word, the sound of short *u* is omitted before *n*, *m*, or a straight downstroke.

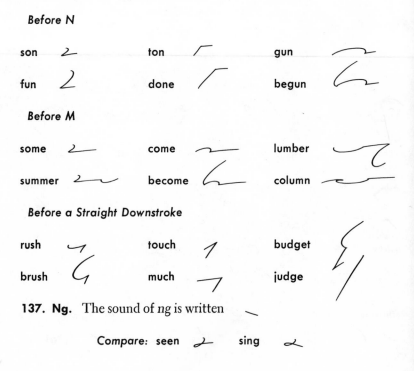

Before N

son	ton	gun
fun	done	begun

Before M

some	come	lumber
summer	become	column

Before a Straight Downstroke

rush	touch	budget
brush	much	judge

137. Ng. The sound of *ng* is written

Compare: seen sing

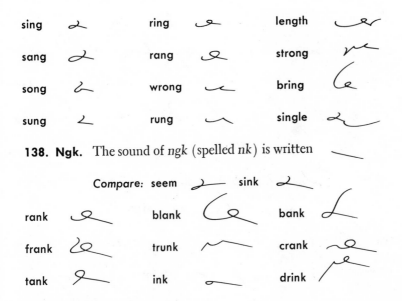

sing	ring	length
sang	rang	strong
song	wrong	bring
sung	rung	single

138. Ngk. The sound of *ngk* (spelled *nk*) is written

Compare: seem sink

rank	blank	bank
frank	trunk	crank
tank	ink	drink

Reading and Writing Practice

139. Applied Vocabulary Study. *Bank teller,* the one concerned with the direct handling of money received and paid out by a bank. *Cage,* barred enclosure within which the teller works. *Script,* the typewritten copy from which a movie is produced.

140.

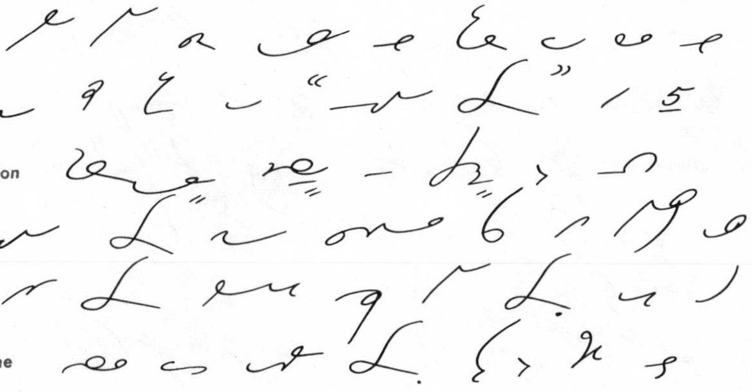

Jackson

routine

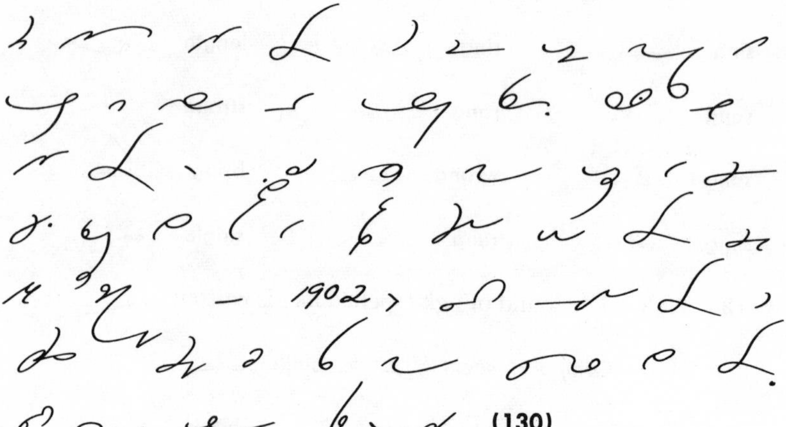

(130)

141.

campaigns
summary

script

satisfactorily

(116)

142.

Halifax
Bangor
deliveryman
depot

(100)

143.

description
and the

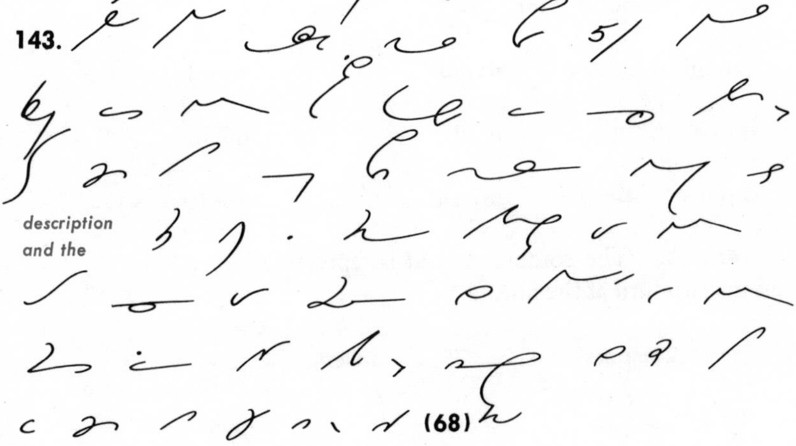

(68)

LESSON 17

144. Brief Forms

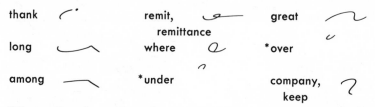

thank		remit, remittance		great	
long		where		*over	
among		*under		company, keep	

*The outlines for *under* and *over* are written above the following shorthand character. They may also be used as prefix forms, as in *underneath, overcome.*

145. Rd. The combination *rd* is represented by writing the *r* with an upward turn at the finish.

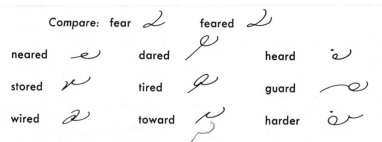

Compare: fear feared

neared	dared	heard
stored	tired	guard
wired	toward	harder

146. Ld. The combination *ld* is represented by writing the *l* with an upward turn at the finish.

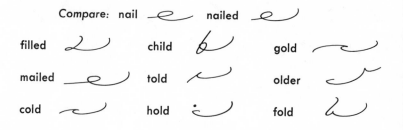

Compare: nail nailed

filled	child	gold
mailed	told	older
cold	hold	fold

Reading and Writing Practice

147. Applied Vocabulary Study. *"Live" list,* a list from which the names of people who have died or changed addresses have been removed. *Literature,* in business usage, any printed advertising matter. *Racks,* the stands on which clothes are displayed. *Scheduled,* planned.

148.

live

literature

accurately

(111)

149.

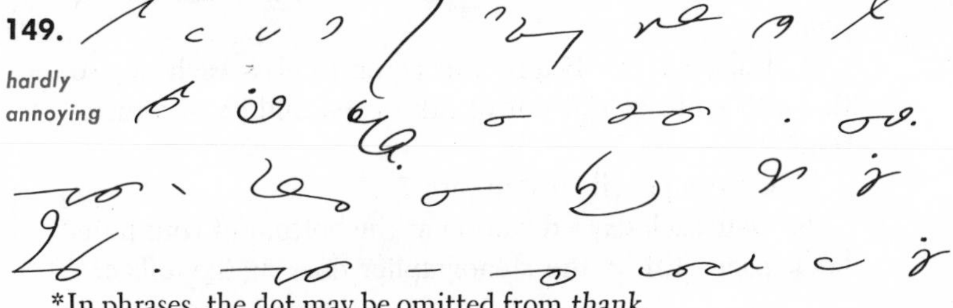

hardly

annoying

*In phrases, the dot may be omitted from *thank.*

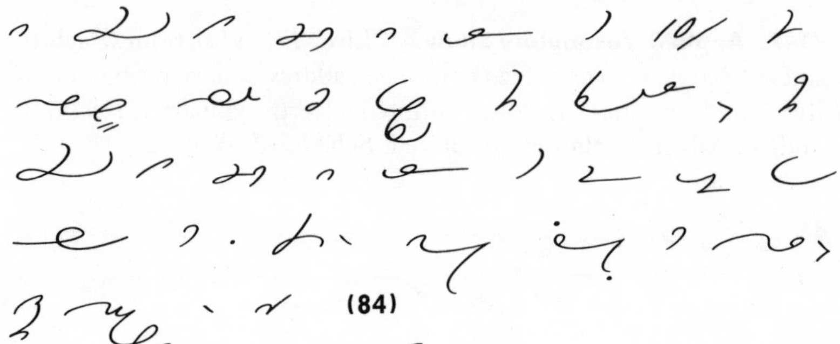

(84)

150.

patron
fur

Shorthand Writing Check List

When you write shorthand, do you

1. Use a fountain pen, preferably one with a stiff point?

2. Leave the cap off the pen when you are copying or taking dictation?

3. Place the cap back on the pen firmly when you are not actually writing so that the ink will not clot on the point?

4. Fill your pen before you come to class each day so that you will not run out of ink in the middle of a dictation?

5. Carry a pencil "just in case"?

6. Date each day's dictation at the bottom of your notebook page, just as the stenographer does in the office?

racks

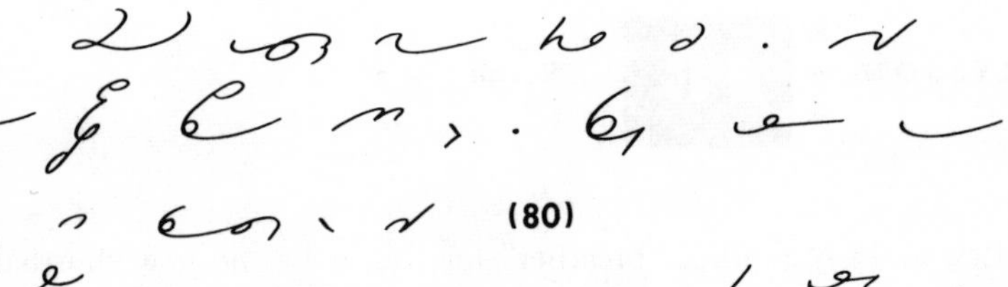

(80)

151.

scheduled

shopping

(69)

152.

young

(73)

LESSON 18 **Recall**

Lesson 18 is another "breather" for you; it has no new shorthand devices for you to learn. In this lesson you will find: (1) the last of the principles of joining of Gregg Shorthand, (2) another chart that will give you a quick overview of all the shorthand devices you have studied thus far, and (3) a number of Aesop's Fables that you may have read when you were younger and that you will enjoy rereading in the shorthand version.

Principles of Joining

153. The oo hook is written on its side after *n, m.*

noon  smooth  famous 

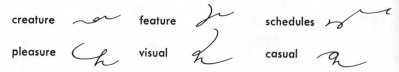

154. The word endings *-ure, -ual* are represented by *r* and *l* except after downstrokes.

creature  feature  schedules 

pleasure  visual  casual 

155. At the beginning of a word and after *k, g,* or a downstroke, the combination *us* is written without an angle.

husky  discuss 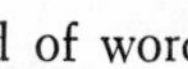 just 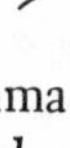

156. At the beginning and end of words, the comma *s* is used before and after *f, v, k, g;* the left *s,* before and after *p, b, r, l.*

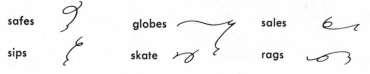

safes  globes  sales 

sips skate rags

157. The comma s is used before *t, d, n, m, o*; the left s is used after those characters.

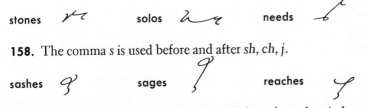

stones  solos  needs 

158. The comma s is used before and after *sh, ch, j*.

sashes  sages  reaches 

159. The comma s is used in words consisting of s and a circle vowel or s and *th* and a circle vowel.

see  these  seethe 

160. Recall Chart. This chart contains all the brief forms in Chapter 3 and one or more illustrations of all the shorthand devices you have studied in Chapters 1, 2, and 3. Read each word aloud. If you cannot immediately read a word, spell it.

This chart contains 84 words and phrases. Can you read the entire chart in 8 minutes or less?

Brief Forms

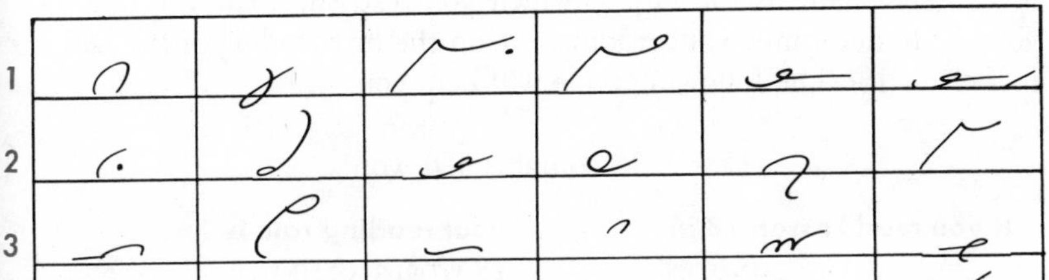

Phrases

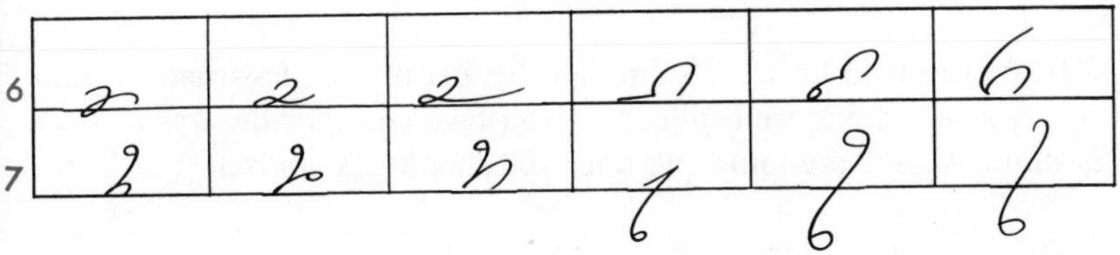

Words

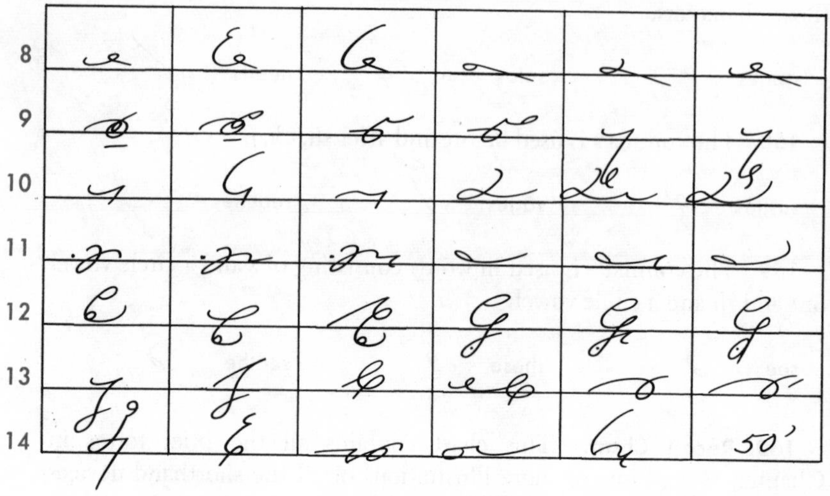

Reading and Writing Practice

Reading Scoreboard. One of the factors in measuring your progress in shorthand is the rate at which you read shorthand. Wouldn't you like to determine your reading rate on the *first reading* of the fables in Lesson 18? The following table will help you.

Lesson 18 contains 380 words.

If you read Lesson 18 in	**your reading rate is**
15 MINUTES	25 WORDS A MINUTE
17 MINUTES	22 WORDS A MINUTE
19 MINUTES	20 WORDS A MINUTE
21 MINUTES	18 WORDS A MINUTE
23 MINUTES	17 WORDS A MINUTE
25 MINUTES	15 WORDS A MINUTE

If you can read Lesson 18 through the first time in less than 15 minutes, you are doing well indeed. If you take considerably longer than 25 minutes, here are some questions you should ask yourself:

1. Am I spelling each outline I cannot immediately read?

2. Am I jotting down on a card or slip of paper any outline that the spelling does not give me?

3. Should I perhaps reread the directions for reading shorthand on pages 32 and 33?

After you have determined your reading rate, make a record of it in some convenient place. You can then watch your reading rate grow as you time yourself on the Reading Scoreboards in later lessons.

161. Applied Vocabulary Study. *Lurking,* lying hidden or moving secretly. *Deceived,* misled, fooled. *Pious,* religious.

162. The Wolf in Sheep's Clothing

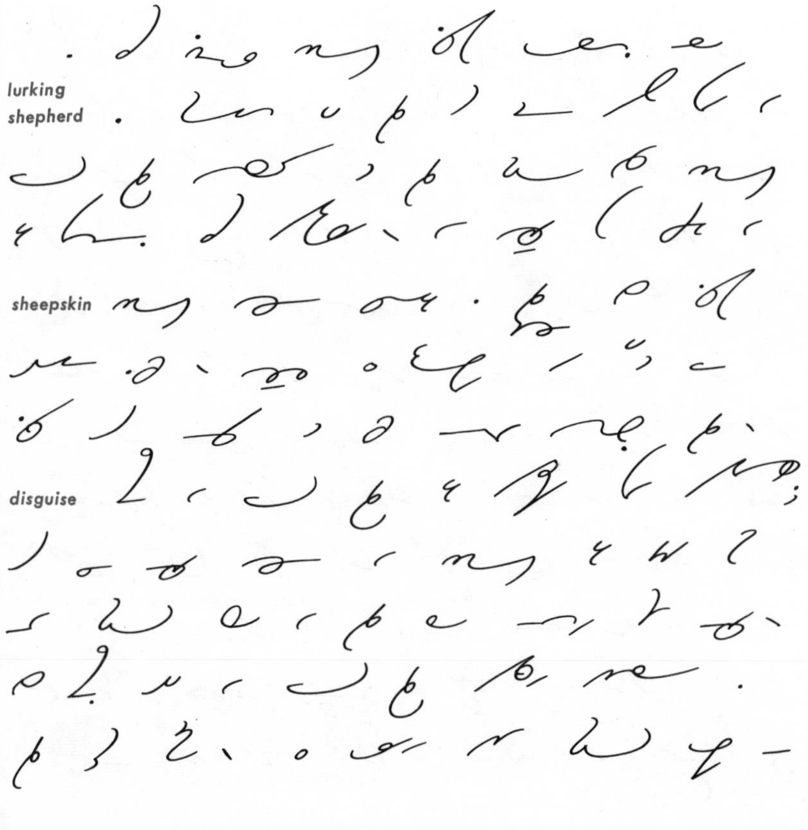
lurking
shepherd
sheepskin
disguise

seized
guessed

(148)

163. The Farmer and the Stork

cranes
stolen

birds
stork

greedy
pious

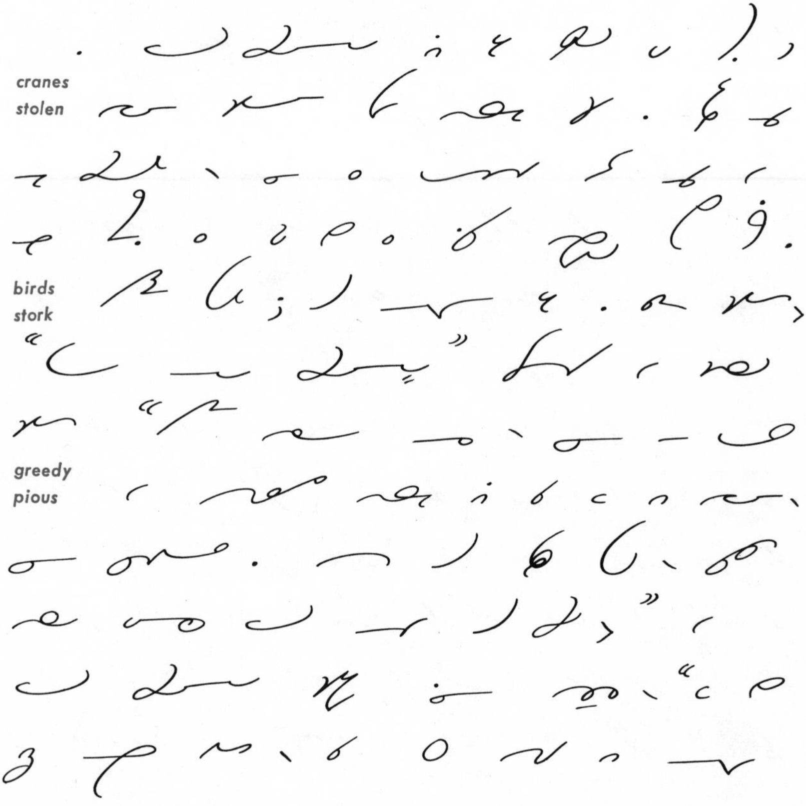

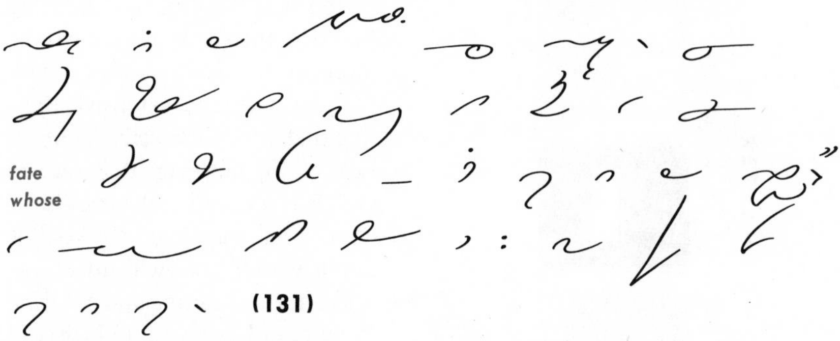

fate
whose

(131)

164. The Swallow's Advice

sowing
swallow
beware

cord
end

(101)

CHAPTER 4

The Importance of Reading

As you have no doubt noticed, each lesson that you have studied thus far contains a Reading and Writing Practice consisting of a number of business letters or articles. Have you stopped to consider the many important things that each Reading and Writing Practice is contributing to your shorthand skill development?

To begin with, each Reading and Writing Practice is helping to fix in your mind the shorthand devices that are presented in the lesson. For example, in Lesson 19, which you will study soon, you will take up the shorthand stroke for *ow*. In the Reading and Writing Practice of that lesson there are twenty-three words in which *ow* is used. After you have completed that Reading and Writing Practice, the stroke for *ow* will be more firmly fixed in your mind.

Even with the extensive practice that you will receive on *ow* in Lesson 19, however, it is safe to say that you will not have "mastered" that shorthand stroke. But don't worry; you will meet *ow* again in the Reading and Writing Practice of Lesson 20, and you will meet it in the Reading and Writing Practice of *every single lesson thereafter*. Some lessons after you were first introduced to *ow*, you will suddenly discover that *ow* is an old friend!

The same is true of all the other shorthand devices that you will study. You will meet them again and again in the lessons that follow and so will eventually master them even though you did not completely grasp them in the lessons in which they were first presented.

In addition to helping you fix the shorthand devices in your mind, each Reading and Writing Practice reviews many times the brief forms and phrases that you have previously studied. Each Reading and Writing Practice is helping you to stock your mind with joinings of shorthand characters and with the shapes of individual characters, so that, when you eventually take new dictation, your mind will quickly be able to form an outline for any words that are dictated.

The efficient stenographer is the one who can read shorthand easily and rapidly. To become a rapid shorthand reader, read all the shorthand you can. Remember, too, that the more shorthand you read, the more rapid shorthand *writer* you will become.

In Chapter 3 your shorthand practice material included not only business letters but also a number of Aesop's Fables. In Chapter 4, your practice material will become even more interesting with the addition of articles and stories that will inform and entertain you as well as develop your shorthand skill.

What's Ahead?

In Chapter 4 you will take up six new alphabetic characters, all of which you should find very easy, as they are simply combinations of strokes you already know. After Chapter 4, you have only four more new alphabetic strokes to learn!

In addition, you will cover three more sets of brief forms, five extremely useful abbreviating devices, the days of the week and the months of the year, and a number of important cities and states.

A new feature in Chapter 4 is the Accuracy Practice, which you will find in Lesson 24. This Accuracy Practice will help you refine your shorthand writing style so that you will be able to read your notes with greater ease and facility.

TODAY'S SECRETARY

The more shorthand you read — from your textbook and from shorthand magazines — the more firmly will you fix the shorthand outlines in your mind and the more rapidly will your shorthand speed develop.

LESSON 19

165. Ū. The sound of ū is represented by

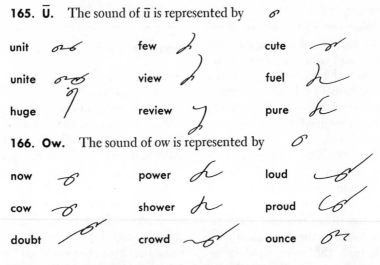

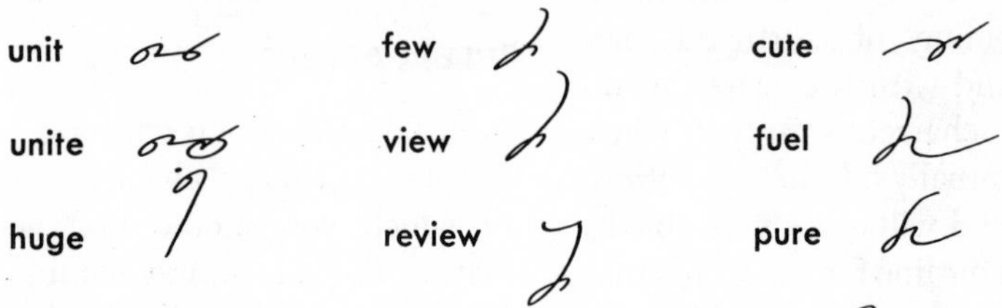
unit
few
cute
unite
view
fuel
huge
review
pure

166. Ow. The sound of ow is represented by

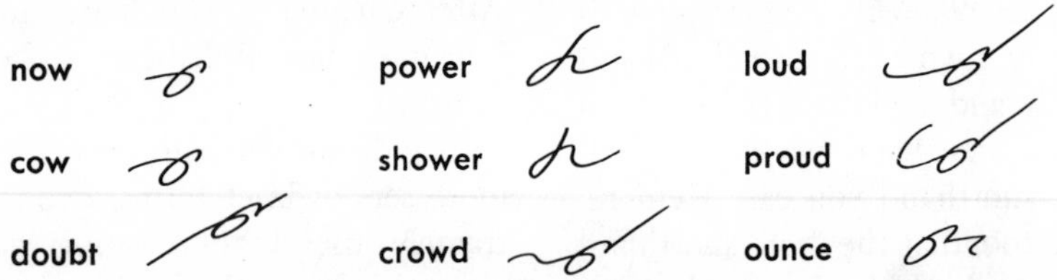
now
power
loud
cow
shower
proud
doubt
crowd
ounce

Be sure to keep the *e* in ū tiny; the *a* in *ow* large.

167. Brief Forms. When you have learned the brief forms in this paragraph, you will have covered more than half the brief forms of Gregg Shorthand.

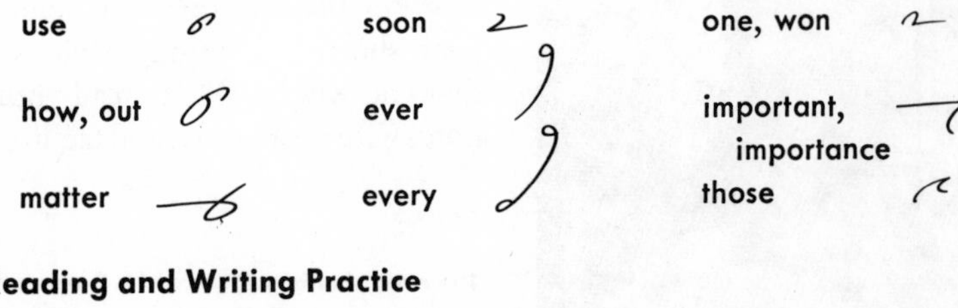
use
soon
one, won
how, out
ever
important, importance
matter
every
those

Reading and Writing Practice

168. Applied Vocabulary Study. *Review,* examination. *Grooming,* neatness, smartness. *Outcome,* result. *Unique,* the only one of its kind. It is therefore incorrect to say "very unique" or "most unique."

169.

hobby
flowers

without

prepared
outlining

(119)

170.

aside

(87)

171.

beauty
grooming

letters
pennies

(70)

172.

bookkeeper

outcome
handy

unique

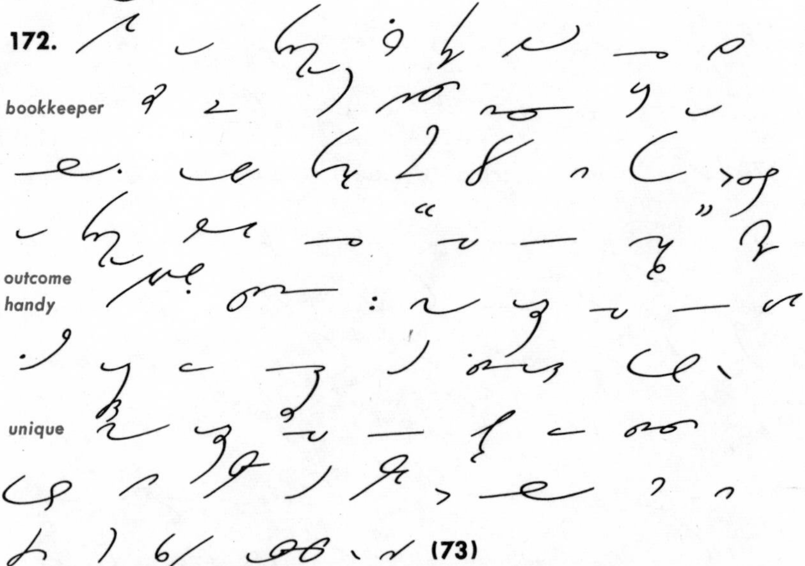

(73)

*The special joining of the *s* is used in the word *letters* to distinguish it from the word *lease*.

LESSON 20

173. Brief Forms

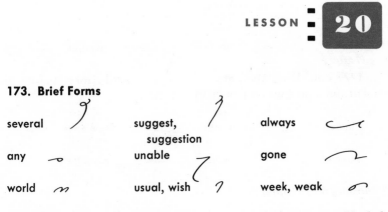

several	suggest, suggestion	always
any	unable	gone
world	usual, wish	week, weak

174. Ted. The combination *ted* is represented by joining *t* and *d* into one long upward stroke.

Ted

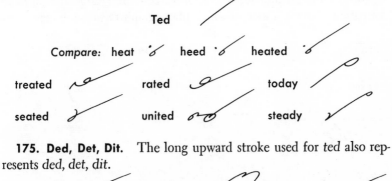

Compare: heat heed heated

treated	rated	today
seated	united	steady

175. Ded, Det, Dit. The long upward stroke used for *ted* also represents *ded, det, dit.*

traded	deduction	credit
needed	detail	editor

176. Men, Mem. The combinations *men, mem* are represented by joining *m* and *n* into one long forward stroke.

Men, Mem

Compare: knee me many

men — Mount meant — memory

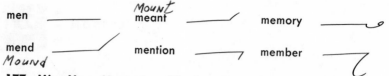

mend — mention — member

Mound

177. Min, Mon, Mun, etc. The long forward stroke used for *men, mem* also represents *min, mon, mun,* etc.

minute — month — summons

examine — money — manage

Reading and Writing Practice

178. Applied Vocabulary Study. *Credit bureau,* a central office in which information is kept on the credit and financial responsibility of companies and individuals. *Detailed,* containing a great deal of information. *Album,* a case in which phonograph records are kept.

179.

Bureau
usually

lets
easier
secret

(196)

Tues.

180.

welcome
album
world's
Club
anyway

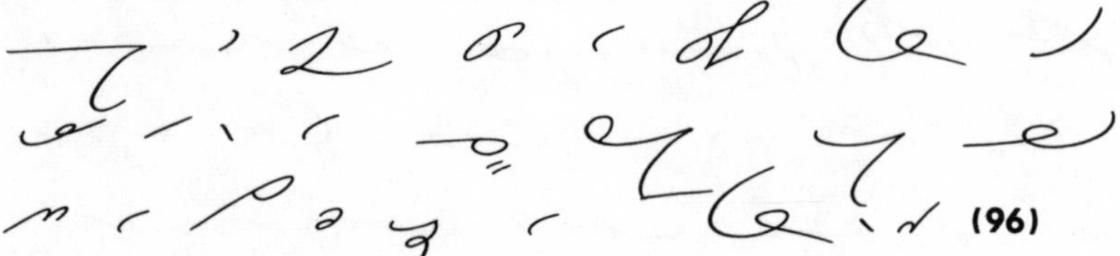

(96)

181.

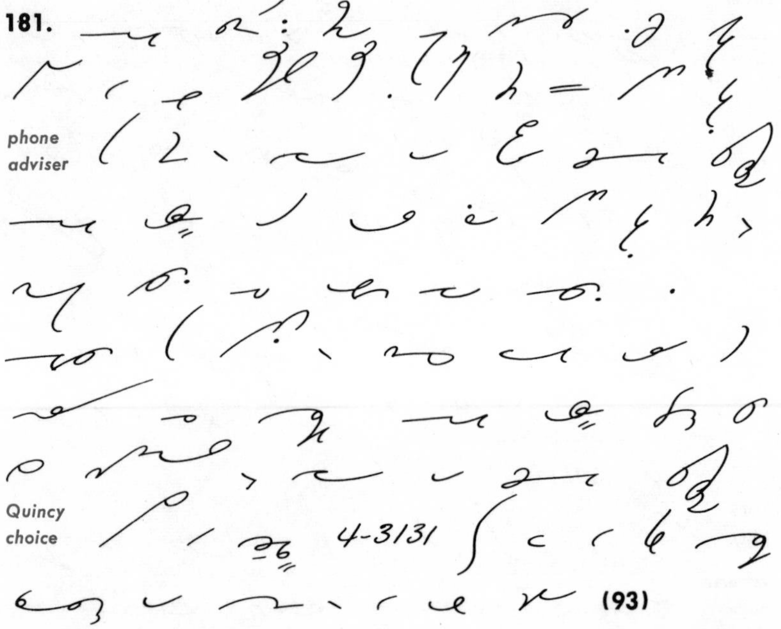

phone adviser
Quincy choice
4-3131

(93)

Up and Down Check List

Do you always write the following strokes *upward?*

1. And-end   their-there
2. It-at   would

Do you always write the following strokes *downward?*

1. Is-his   for   have
2. Shall-ship   which

LESSON 21

182. Nd. The shorthand strokes for *n-d* are joined without an angle to represent *nd*. You are already familiar with this stroke, as it represents the brief form *and-end*.

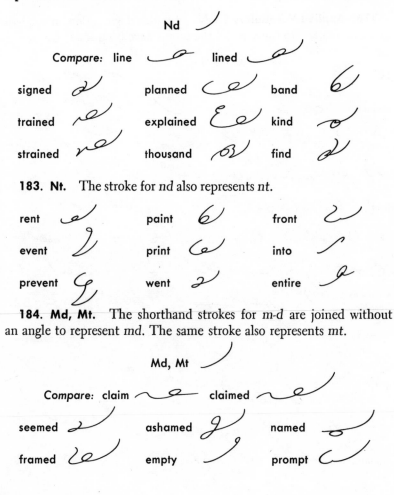

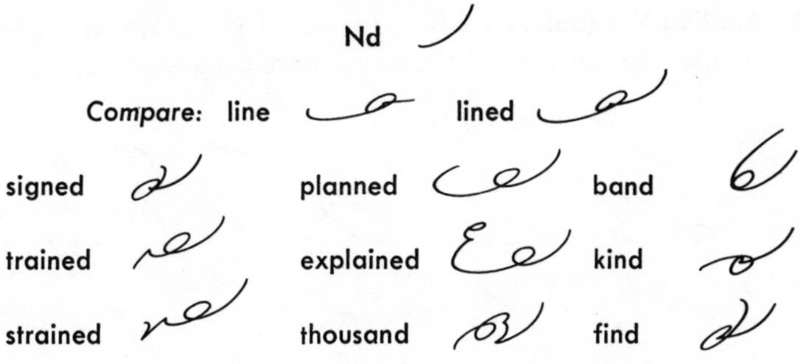
Nd
Compare: line
lined
signed
planned
band
trained
explained
kind
strained
thousand
find

183. Nt. The stroke for *nd* also represents *nt*.

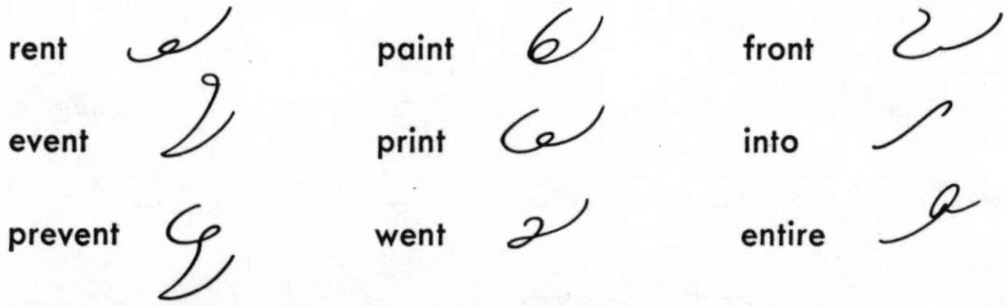
rent
paint
front
event
print
into
prevent
went
entire

184. Md, Mt. The shorthand strokes for *m-d* are joined without an angle to represent *md*. The same stroke also represents *mt*.

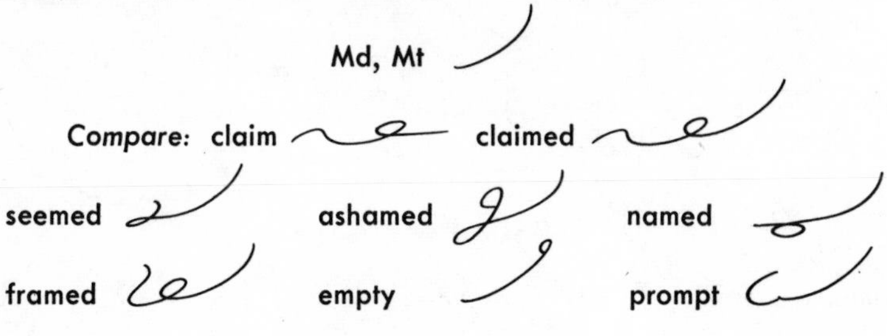
Md, Mt
Compare: claim
claimed
seemed
ashamed
named
framed
empty
prompt

185. Brief Forms

did, date; individual; opportunity; morning; office; general; want; got; big

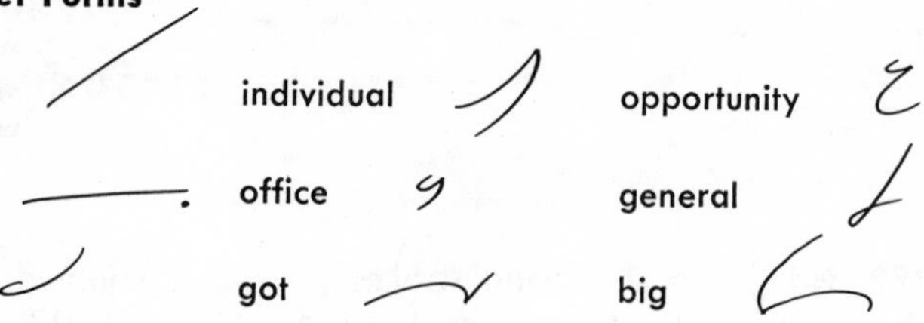

Reading and Writing Practice

186. Applied Vocabulary Study. *Rendered,* gave. *Puncture,* a hole in a tire. *Booked to capacity,* all the rooms have been reserved.

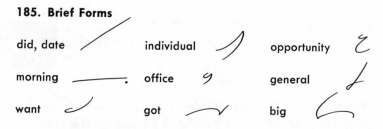

187.

pleasant

client

eventually

from his

thereafter

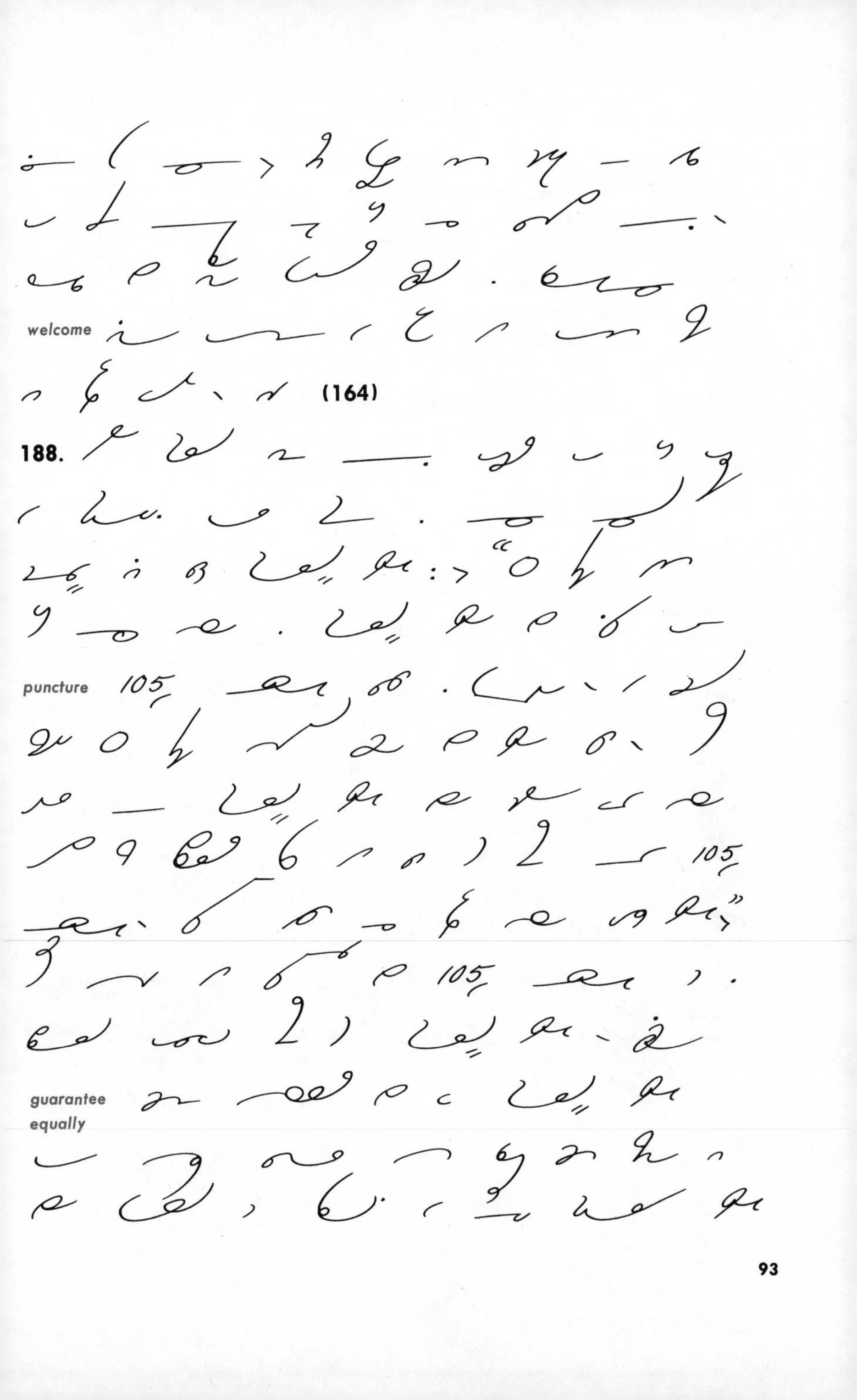

welcome

(164)

188.

puncture

guarantee

equally

equip

(157)

189.

seeking
thorough

acquainted
talented

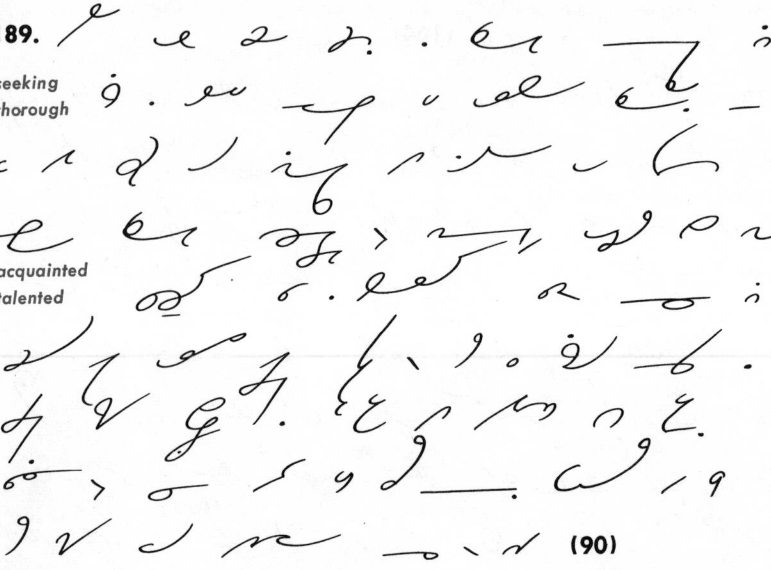

(90)

190.

booked
capacity

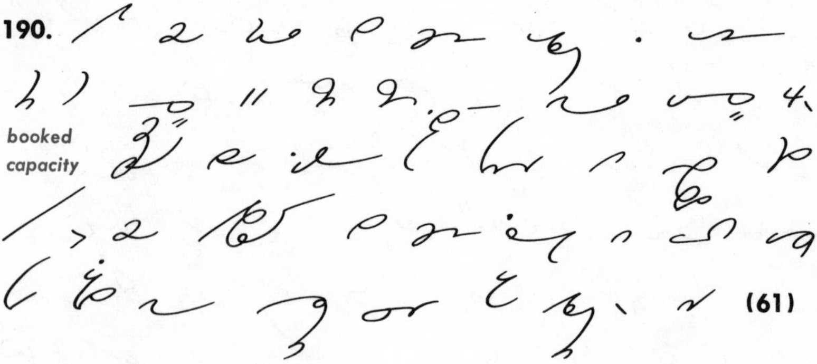

(61)

LESSON 22

191. Omission of Minor Vowels. When vowels come together, the minor vowel may often be omitted.

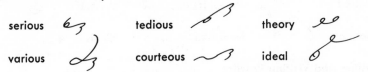

serious		tedious		theory	
various		courteous		ideal	

192. Ū Represented by OO. The oo hook is often used to represent the sound of ū.

new		avenue		reduce	
due		amuse		issue	

193. Days of the Week

Sunday		Wednesday	 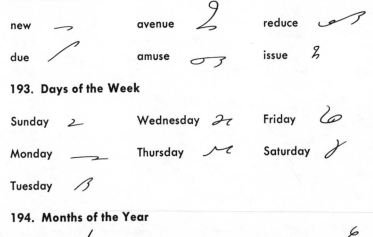	Friday	
Monday		Thursday		Saturday	
Tuesday					

194. Months of the Year

January		May		September	
February		June		October	
March		July		November	
April		August		December	

195. Cities and States. The stenographer must be able to write the common place names rapidly and accurately. Here are a few important cities and states.

New York	Philadelphia	Pennsylvania
Chicago	Los Angeles	California
Detroit	Memphis	Missouri
Boston	Nebraska	Illinois

Reading and Writing Practice

196. Applied Vocabulary Study. *Unusual,* uncommon, rare. *Manuscript,* the author's original typewritten copy of a book. *Current,* present.

197.

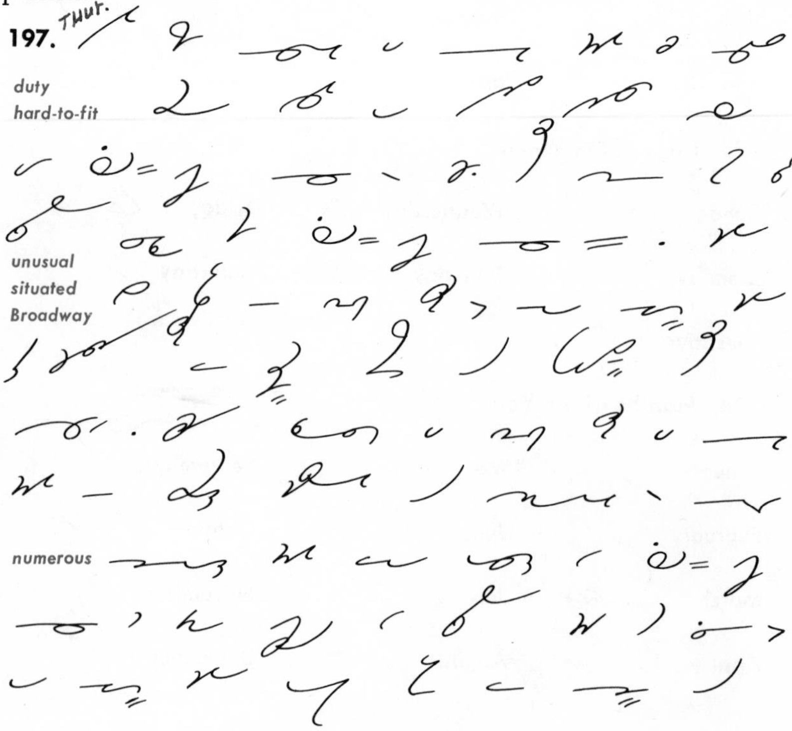

duty
hard-to-fit
unusual
situated
Broadway
numerous

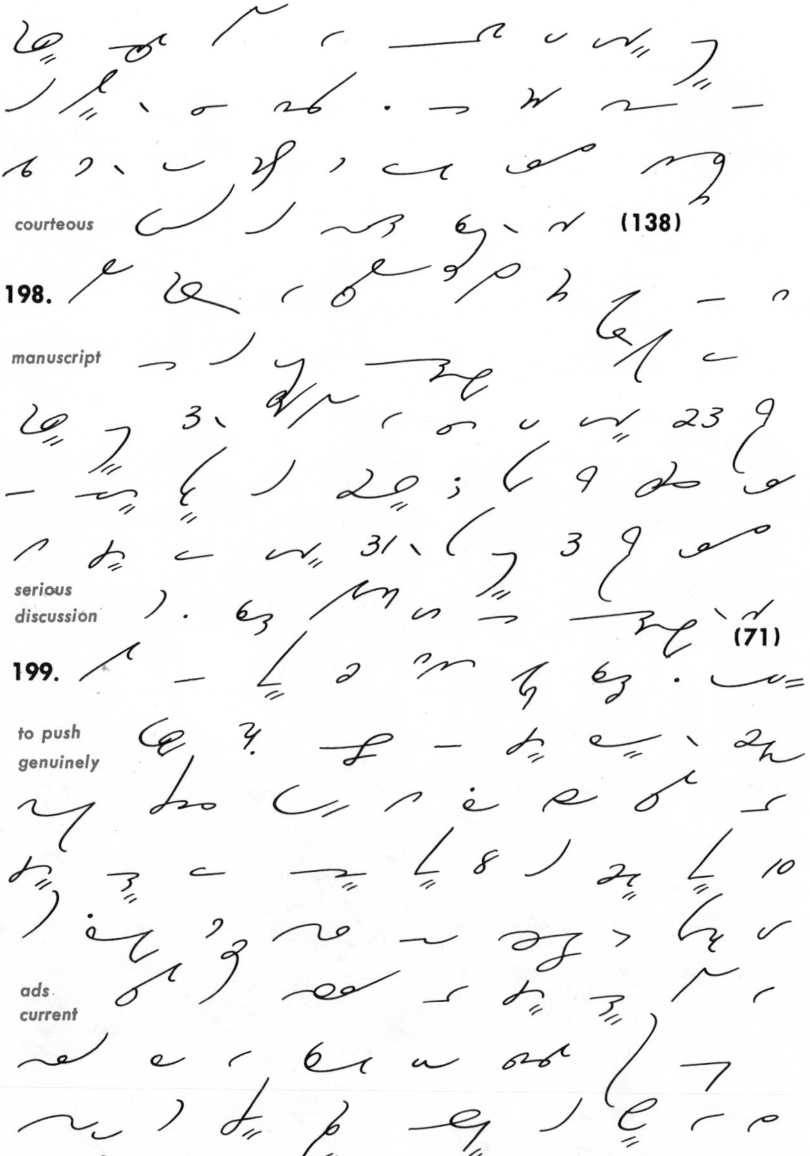
courteous
(138)
198.
manuscript
serious
discussion
(71)
199.
to push
genuinely
ads
current

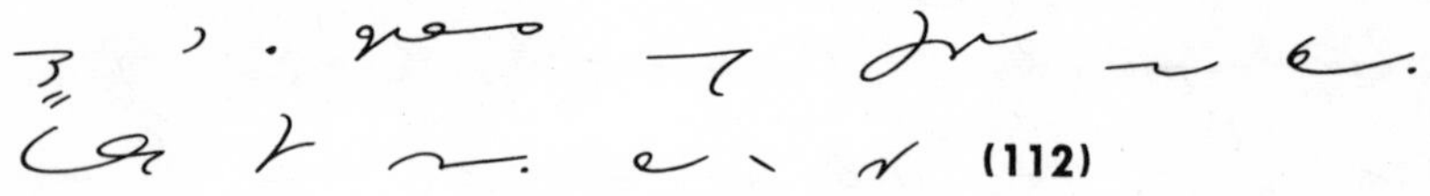

(112)

200.

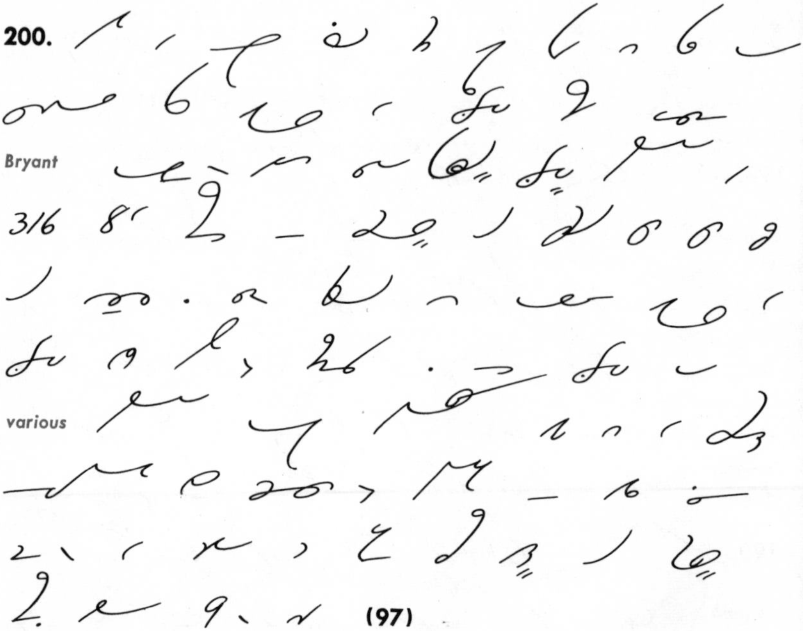

Bryant

316 8

various

(97)

201.

Club

416 8

genuine

(71)

LESSON 23

202. Omission of Ow before N. In the body of a word, *ow* is omitted before *n*.

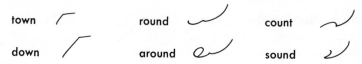

town		round		count	
down		around		sound	

203. Omission of Ow between N-N. When *ow* is omitted between *n-n*, a jog is used to indicate the omission.

announce		announces		renounce	

204. Omission of Ow in Moun. *Moun* is represented by the *men* blend.

mount		amount		dismount	

205. Word Beginnings Per-, Pur-, Pro-. The word beginnings *per-*, *pur-*, *pro-* are represented by *pr*.

permit		purple		promote	
person		pursue		provision	
perfume		pursued		proper	

206. Word Ending -ment. The word ending *-ment* is represented by *m*.

excitement		payment		experimented	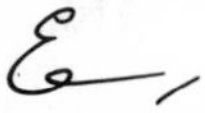
moment		agreement		experimental	

207. Word Ending -ble. The word ending *-ble* is represented by *b*.

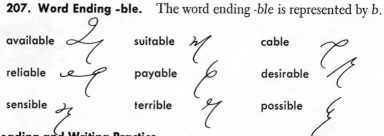

available, suitable, cable, reliable, payable, desirable, sensible, terrible, possible

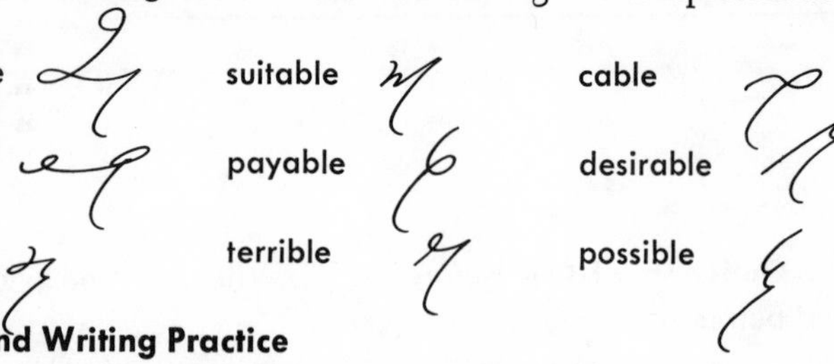

Reading and Writing Practice

208. Applied Vocabulary Study. *Equitable,* just, fair. *Perplexing,* puzzling, disturbing. *Garment,* article of clothing. *Reliable,* trustworthy. *Reputable,* enjoying a good reputation.

209.

acceptable

equitable

worry

perplexing

(99)

210.

judgment

flies

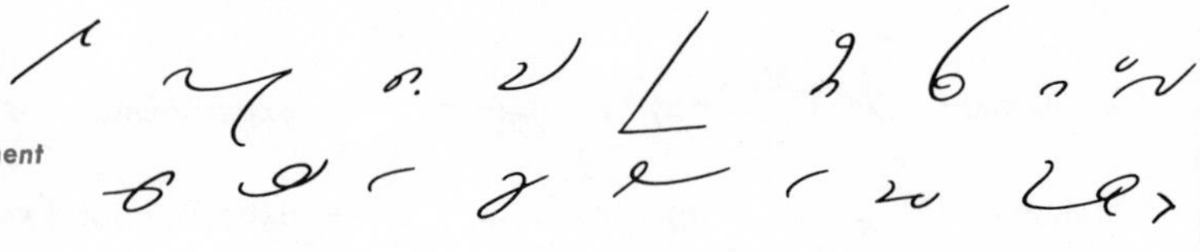

easy-payment

(90)

211.

lawyer routine

not found

(107)

212.

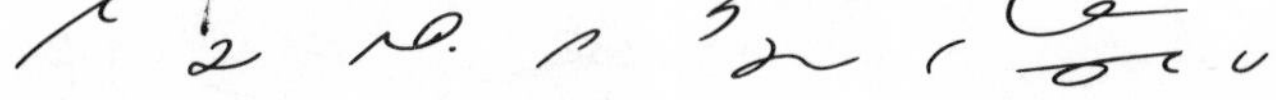

reputable

zipper

documents

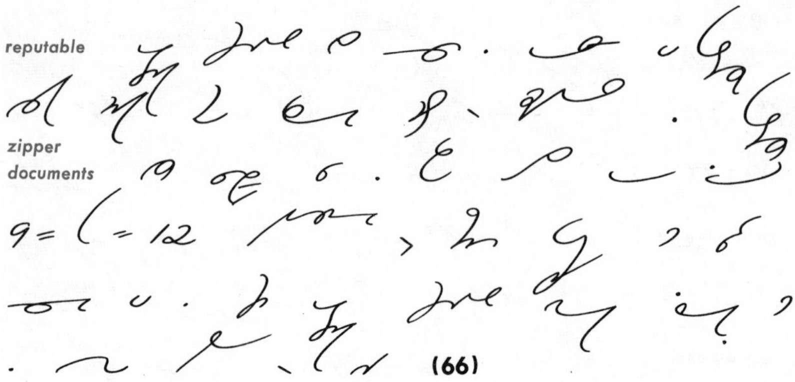

(66)

213.

approval

(73)

214.

(52)

LESSON 24 Recall

In Lesson 24 you will have no new shorthand devices to learn; you will have a little time to "digest" the devices that you have studied in previous lessons. In Lesson 24 you will find a new feature — Accuracy Practice — that will help you improve your shorthand writing style.

Be sure to read carefully the articles in the Reading and Writing Practice. These articles contain many tips that will be of value to you on your first job as an office worker.

Accuracy Practice

The speed and accuracy with which you will be able to transcribe your shorthand notes will depend on how well you write them. If you follow the suggestions given in this lesson when you work with each Accuracy Practice, you will soon find that you can read your own notes with greater ease and facility.

So that you may have a clear picture of the proper shapes of the shorthand strokes that you are studying, enlarged models of the alphabetic characters and of the typical joinings are given, together with a short explanation of the things that you should keep in mind as you practice.

To get the most out of each Accuracy Practice, follow this simple procedure:

a. Read the explanations carefully.

b. Study the model to see the application of each explanation.

c. Write the first outline in the Practice Drill.

d. Compare what you have written with the enlarged model.

e. Write three or four more copies of the outline, trying to improve your outline with each writing.

f. Repeat this procedure with the remaining outlines in the Practice Drill.

215. **R** **L** **K** **G**

To write these strokes accurately:

a. Start and finish each one on the same level of writing.

b. Make the *beginning* of the curve in *r* and *l* deep. Make the *end* of the curve in *k* and *g* deep.

c. Make the *l* and *g* considerably longer than *r* and *k*.

Practice Drill

Are-our-hour; will-well; can, go-good.
Air, lay, ache, gay.

216. **Kr** **Rk** **Gl**

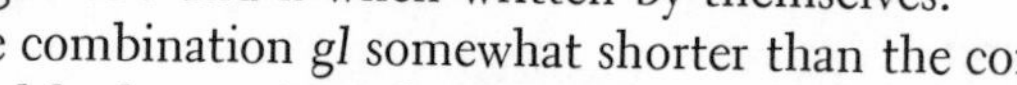

To write these combinations accurately:

a. Make the curves rather flat.

b. Make the combinations *kr* and *rk* somewhat shorter than the combined length of *r* and *k* when written by themselves.

c. Make the combination *gl* somewhat shorter than the combined length of *g* and *l* when written by themselves.

Practice Drill

Cream, crate, maker, mark, dark.
Gleam, glean, glare, eagle.

217. Recall Chart. This chart contains all the brief forms in Chapter 4 and one or more illustrations of all the shorthand devices you have studied in Chapters 1 through 4.

The chart contains 84 words. Can you read the entire chart in 7 minutes or less?

Words

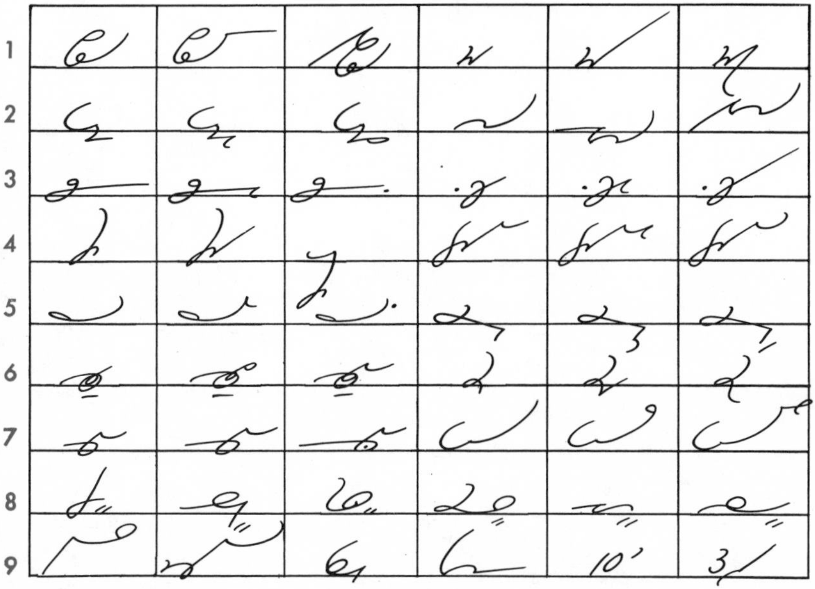

Brief Forms

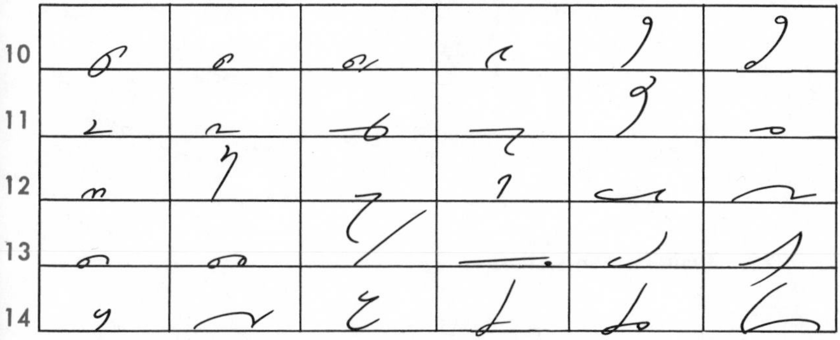

Reading and Writing Practice

218. Applied Vocabulary Study. *Survey,* a study to get exact information. *Bored,* tired from dullness or lack of interest. *Occasional,* occurring now and then. *Lucky stars.* It was once believed that certain stars watched over each person, some lucky and some unlucky for that person.

219. Tips for the Beginning Secretary

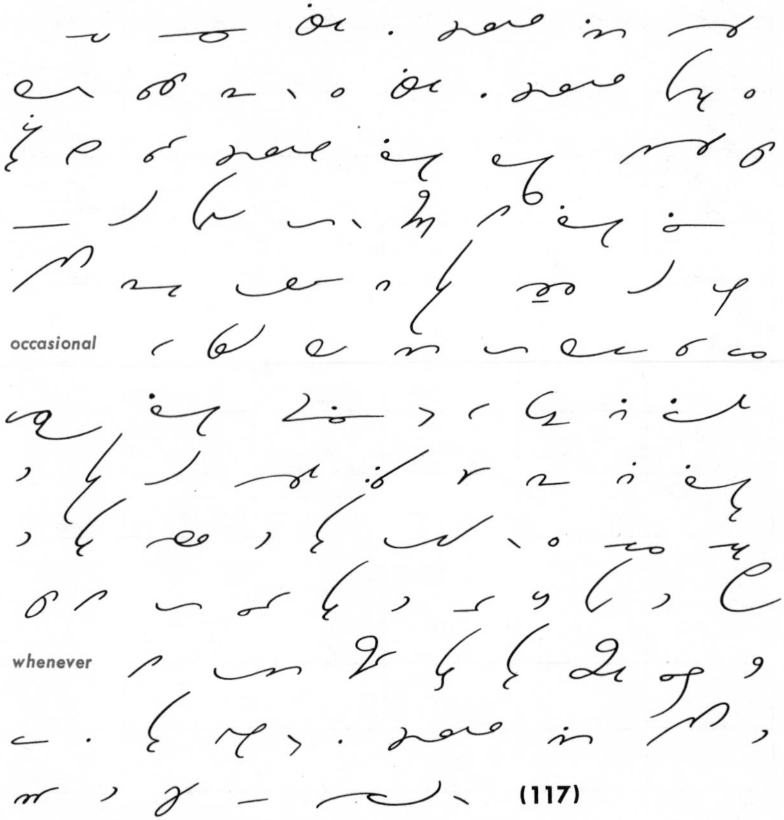
occasional
whenever

(117)

220. Businessmen's Likes

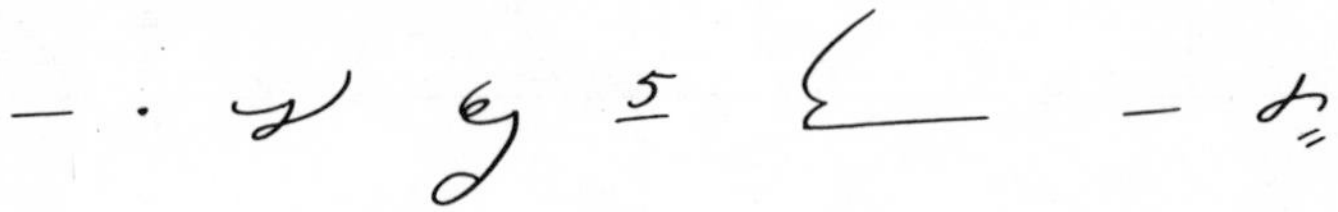

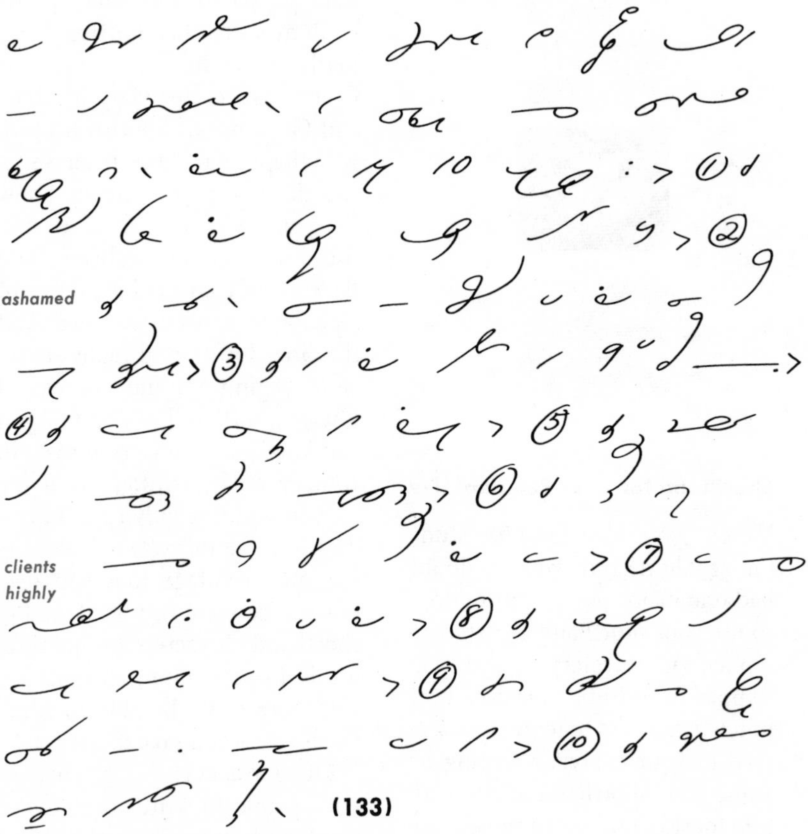

ashamed

clients
highly

(133)

221. The Pleasure of Work

busy
movies

(49)

CHAPTER 5

Shorthand for Your Personal Use

When you decided to study Gregg Shorthand, you no doubt had one major purpose in mind—to use your shorthand as a stenographer or secretary. Have you stopped to consider, however, how much time and energy you can save in your everyday writing by using your shorthand as a substitute for slow and much more cumbersome longhand?

Many great men have used their shorthand as a personal tool. Samuel Pepys wrote his famous diary in shorthand. George Bernard Shaw did all his composing in shorthand and then his secretary transcribed his notes. Former President Woodrow Wilson was very proud of his shorthand ability and used to draft all his state papers in shorthand. James F. Byrnes used his shorthand regularly while he was a Supreme Court Justice, Secretary of State, and Governor of South Carolina.

Perhaps you have been using the shorthand you already know for your personal notes. If not, this is a good time to begin. You have already covered all but four alphabetic strokes, well over half the brief forms, and many useful word beginnings and endings of Gregg Shorthand. Why not put this knowledge to work for you in your everyday writing? By doing so, you will not only save a great deal of time, but you will also derive an advantage that you may not realize—you will be fixing the shorthand characters and joinings firmly in your mind so that you will more easily be able to recall them when you take dictation.

Of course, at this stage you will not be able to write all words in shorthand; but write in shorthand those words for which you can recall the outline and write all other words in longhand.

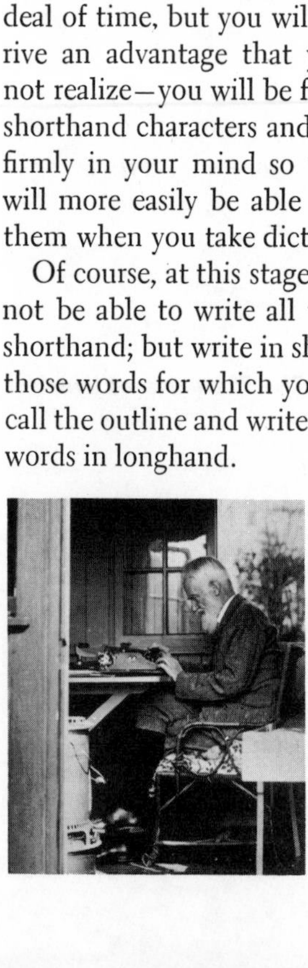

George Bernard Shaw at his typewriter.

How can you use your shorthand as a personal tool? Here are a few suggestions:

1. When your teachers give you instructions for homework to be done, see how much of them you can write in shorthand.

2. When you have a composition or report to write, make your first draft in shorthand. You can do all the scratching out and revising that you wish with the minimum loss of time.

3. When you write to a friend who knows shorthand, write him in shorthand. It is always a thrill to a shorthand writer to receive a letter in shorthand.

4. If you keep a diary, the more of the entries you make in shorthand, the more difficult will it be for those who do not know shorthand to learn your secrets!

What's Ahead?

Chapter 5 contains only two new alphabetic strokes, after which but two more remain. This chapter is devoted largely to useful word beginnings and word endings for combinations that, if written in full, would be long and sometimes difficult to write. There are four word beginnings and ten word endings.

Lesson 28 contains four advanced phrasing principles. If you can write without hesitation the common phrases written under these principles, you will greatly increase the ease with which you will be able to take dictation.

You will be interested to know that after you have completed Chapter 5, you will have only twenty lessons to study in which there are new shorthand devices —and they are the easiest lessons, too!

Shorthand is a very useful personal tool. Do you use it every day to take down homework assignments, to draft reports, or to correspond with friends who know shorthand?

LESSON 25

222. Word Ending -ship. The word ending *-ship* is represented by a disjoined *sh*.

friendship		apprenticeship		ownership	
township		steamships	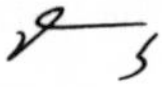	membership	

223. Word Endings -cal, -cle. The word endings *-cal, -cle* are represented by a disjoined *k*.

physical		practical		critical	
technical		radical		article	

224. Word Endings -self, -selves. The word ending *-self* is represented by a joined *s*; *-selves*, by a joined *ses* blend.

yourself		herself		themselves	
myself		itself		ourselves	
himself		oneself		yourselves	

Did you notice that we use the *ses* blend in *itself* and *oneself?* By doing so, we get a positive distinction between *itself* and *its, oneself* and *once*.

225. Word Beginning After-. The word beginning *after-* is represented by *af*.

afternoon		afterthought		aftermath	

Reading and Writing Practice

226. Applied Vocabulary Study. *Gesture,* act of courtesy. *Recreation,* play. *Adapted,* made suitable, adjusted. *Mail meter,* a machine that prints the amount of postage on envelopes and packages, making stamps unnecessary.

227.

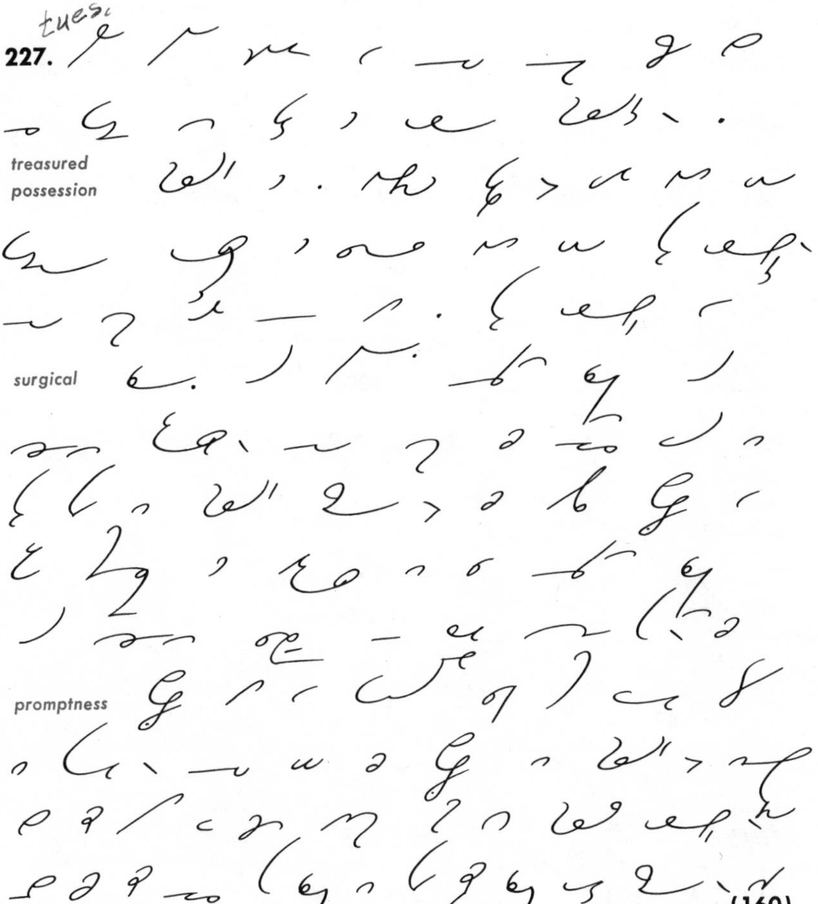

treasured possession

surgical

promptness

(160)

228.

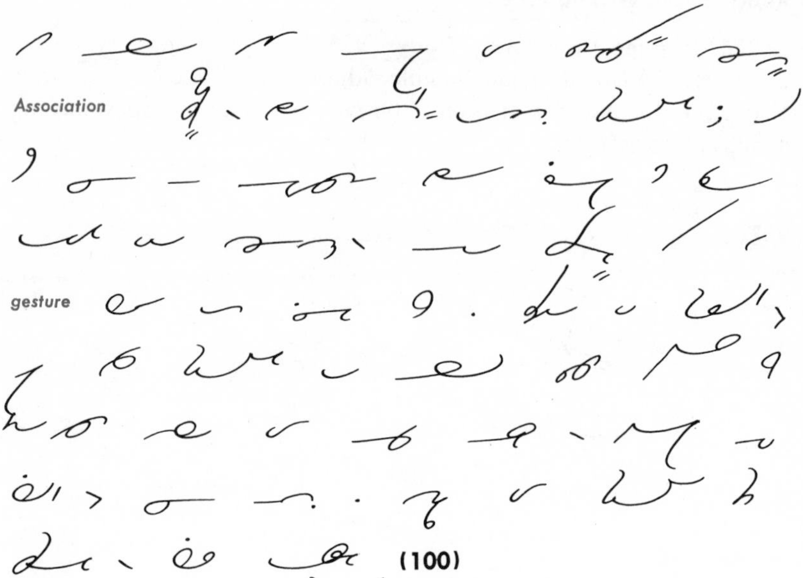

Association

gesture

(100)

229.

physical
indulge
recreation

choice
adapted

(134)

230.

double

budget

County

(98)

231.

mechanical

56

250

(53)

LESSON 26

232. Brief Forms

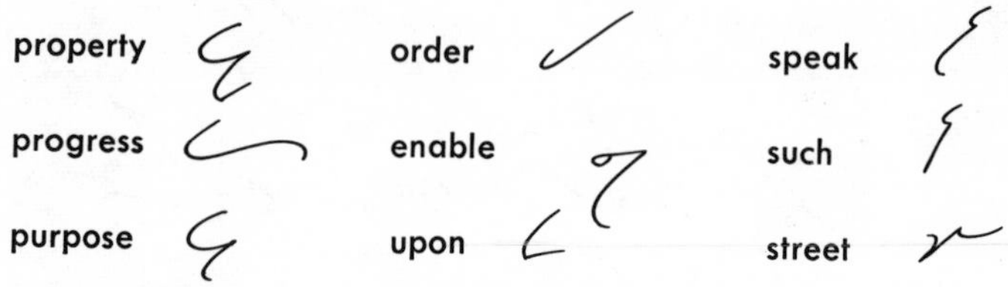

property	order	speak
progress	enable	such
purpose	upon	street

233. Jent, Jend. By rounding off the angle between *j* and *nt, nd,* we obtain the fluent *jent, jend* blend.

Jent, Jend 

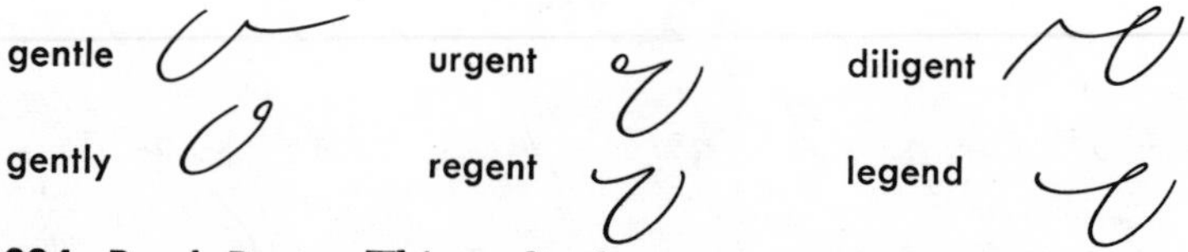

gentle	urgent	diligent
gently	regent	legend

234. Pend, Pent. This stroke also represents *pend, pent.*

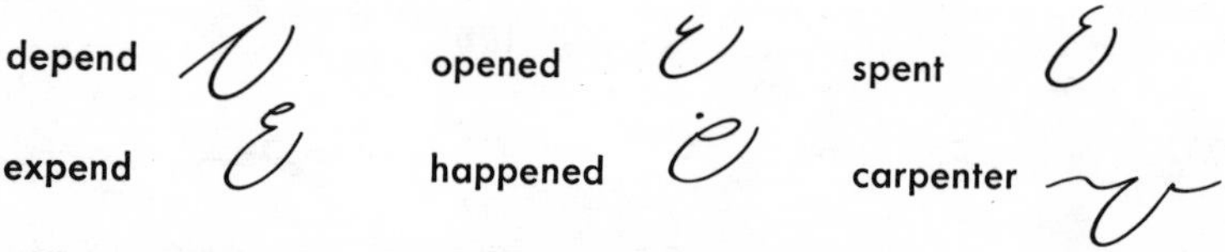

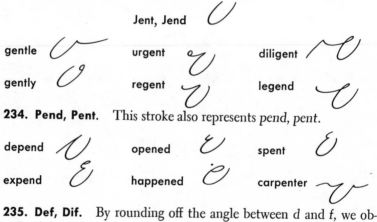

depend	opened	spent
expend	happened	carpenter

235. Def, Dif. By rounding off the angle between *d* and *f,* we obtain the *def, dif* blend.

Def, Dif 

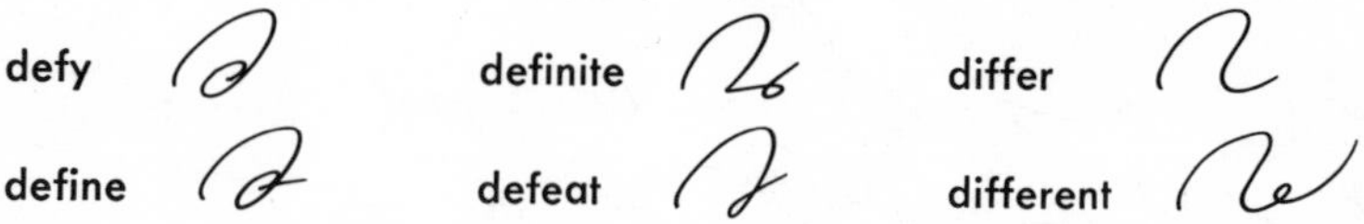

defy	definite	differ
define	defeat	different

236. Div, Dev. This stroke also represents *div* and *dev.*

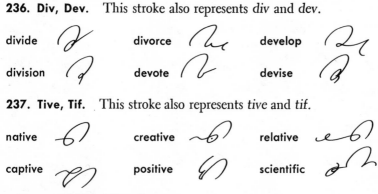

divide  divorce  develop 

division  devote  devise 

237. Tive, Tif. This stroke also represents *tive* and *tif.*

native  creative  relative 

captive  positive  scientific 

Reading and Writing Practice

238. Applied Vocabulary Study. *Urgently,* calling for immediate attention. *Progressive,* forward-looking, constantly moving ahead. *Bargain,* a purchase made at a low price. *Millionaires,* those who possess a million dollars or more.

239.

destroy
urgently

positive
won't

(130)

240.

he seemed
intelligent
progressive

resell
figured

(119)

241.

Proportion Check List

As you copy from the Reading and Writing Practice, do you

1. Keep the a circles large, the e circles tiny?
2. Keep the straight strokes very straight and the curves very deep?
3. Keep the o and oo hooks deep and narrow?
4. Make the short strokes, such as *t* and *n*, very short and the long strokes, such as *ted* and *men*, very long?

speedily
regain

(66)

242.

piece
downtown

(138)

243.

millionaires

executives

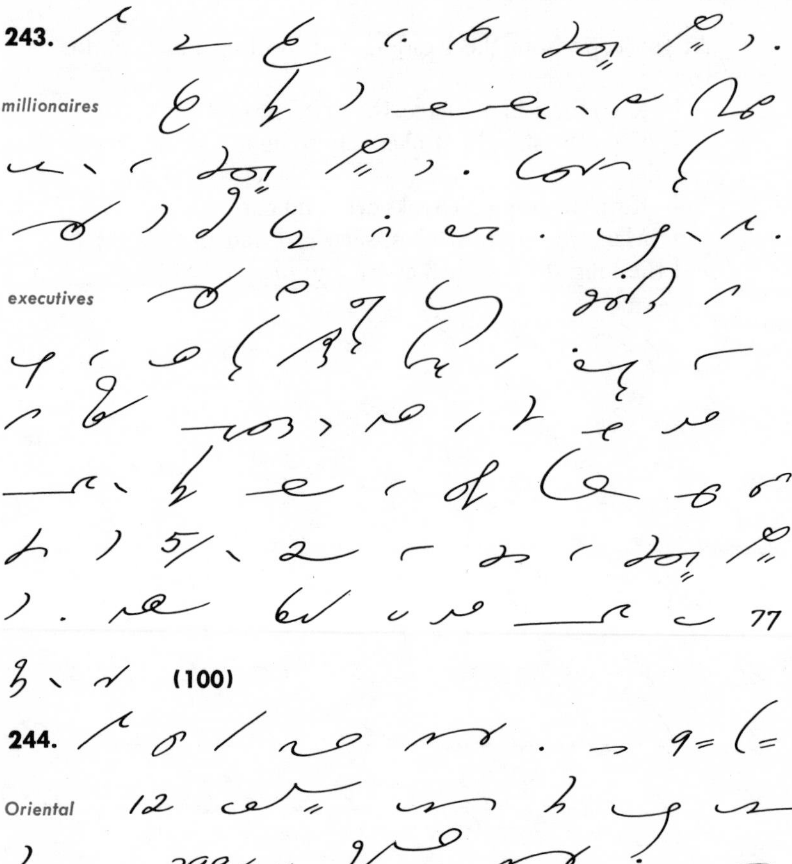

(100)

244.

Oriental

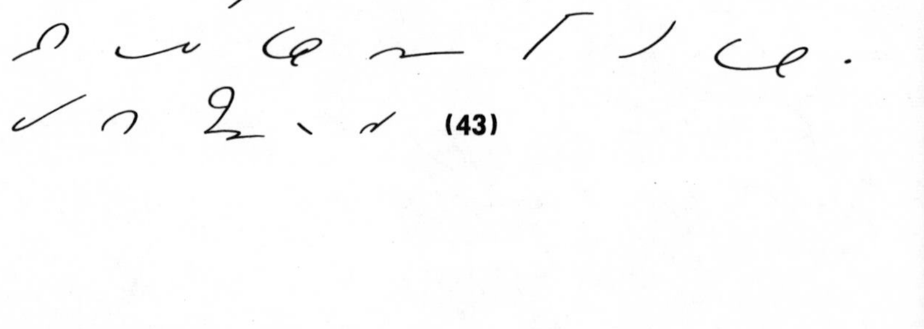

(43)

LESSON 27

245. Word Beginning Electr-. The word beginning *electr-* is represented by disjoined *el* placed above the following character.

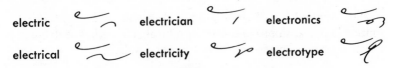

electric  electrician  electronics 

electrical  electricity  electrotype 

246. Electric. The word *electric* when followed by a noun is represented by disjoined *el* placed above the following character.

electric light  electric fan  electric clock 

electric wire  electric motor  electric razor 

247. Word Beginnings Inter-, Intro-. The word beginnings *inter-*, *intro-* are represented by a disjoined *n* placed above the following character.

interfere  interrupt  introduce 

interfered  interruption  introduces 

international  internal  introduction 

248. Enter-, Entr-. This stroke also represents *enter-*, *entr-*.

enter entered  entrance 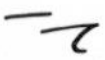

entering  enterprise  entrances 

249. Word Beginnings Short-, Ship-. The word beginnings *short-*, *ship-* are represented by a disjoined *sh* placed above the following character.

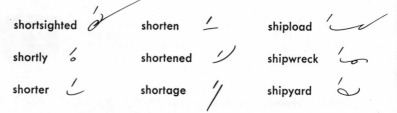

shortsighted		shorten		shipload	
shortly		shortened		shipwreck	
shorter		shortage		shipyard	

Reading and Writing Practice

250. Applied Vocabulary Study. *Introduced,* brought in. *Interruption,* a break, stoppage caused by a break. *Expanding,* enlarging. *Renewal,* an extension or a new start. *Interior,* inside.

251.

Electrical

millions
feature

disappointing
interruptions

shortages

(197)

252.

expiration
typical

hereafter

anyone
money's

(137)

253.

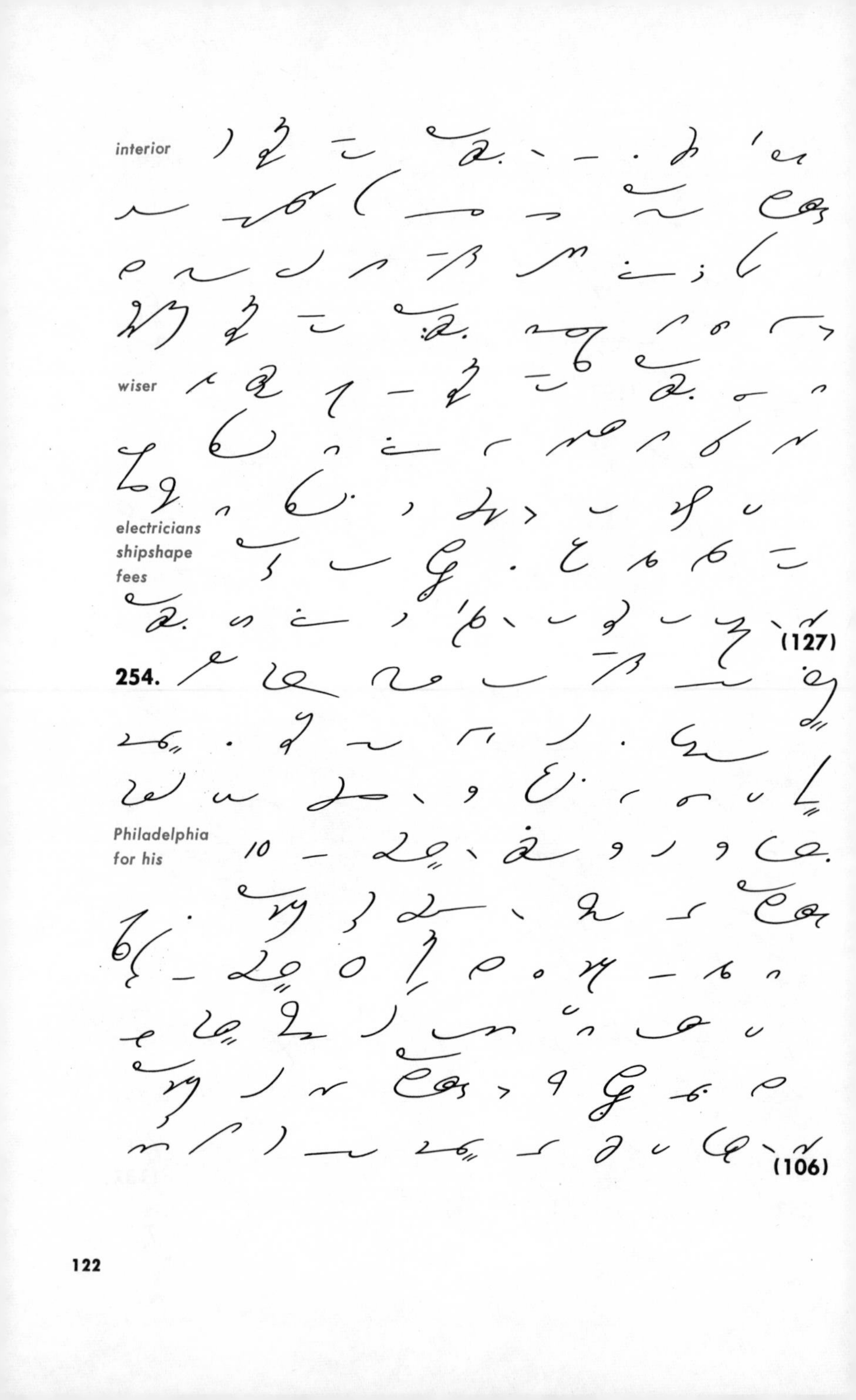

interior

wiser

electricians
shipshape
fees

(127)

254.

Philadelphia
for his

10

(106)

LESSON 28

255. Useful Business Phrases. Because of the frequency of the following phrases, a slight modification is made in the outlines for some words in the phrases. Learn these phrases as you would learn brief forms, but do not attempt to extend these modifications to similar phrases.

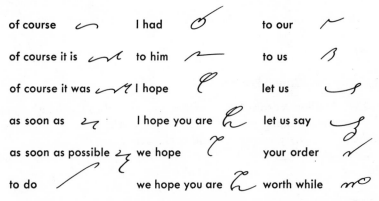

of course	I had	to our
of course it is	to him	to us
of course it was	I hope	let us
as soon as	I hope you are	let us say
as soon as possible	we hope	your order
to do	we hope you are	worth while

256. *Is Not, Was Not* in Phrases. The *nt* blend is used to add *not* to *was* and to *is* when the left *s* is used for *is*. The apostrophe is used to show the contracted forms.

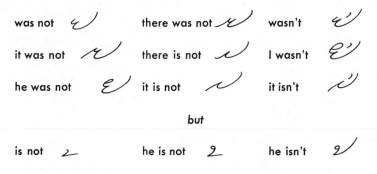

was not	there was not	wasn't
it was not	there is not	I wasn't
he was not	it is not	it isn't

but

is not	he is not	he isn't

257. Ago in Phrases. In expressions of time, *ago* is represented by g.

days ago — weeks ago — months ago

years ago — minutes ago — long ago

258. *Want* in Phrases. The hook is omitted from *want* when *want* is phrased after a pronoun.

I want — he wants — do you want

you want — who wants — I wanted

we want — they want — if you want

Reading and Writing Practice

259. Applied Vocabulary Practice. *Equipped to do the work,* has the necessary training for the work. *Principal,* the head or chief; *principle,* rule. *Traits,* qualities of mind or character.

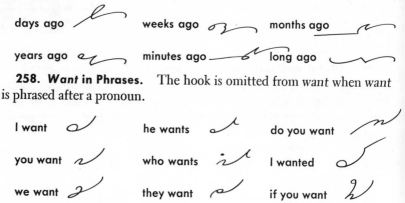

260.

season

aware

scholarship

traits

(136)

261.

apparently

(105)

262.

unique

Los Angeles

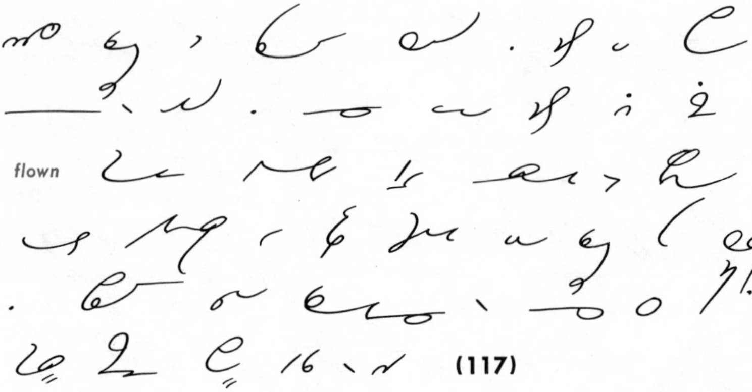

flown

(117)

263.

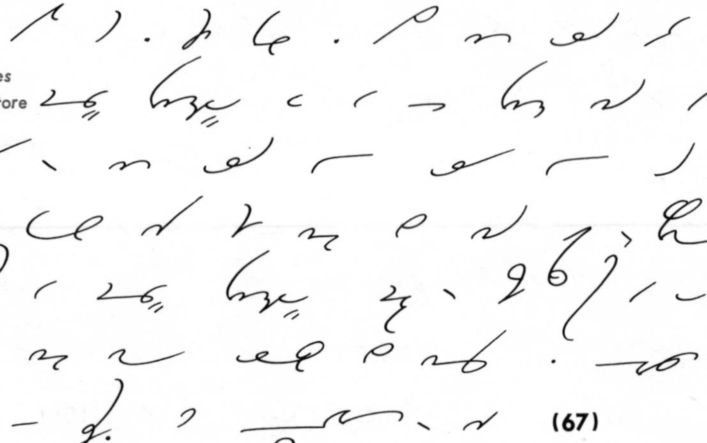

pennies

Bookstore

(67)

264.

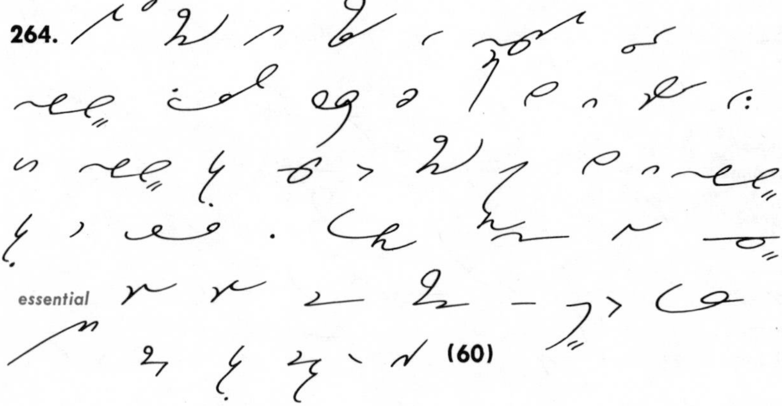

essential

(60)

LESSON 29

265. Word Ending -ful. The word ending *-ful* is represented by a joined *f*.

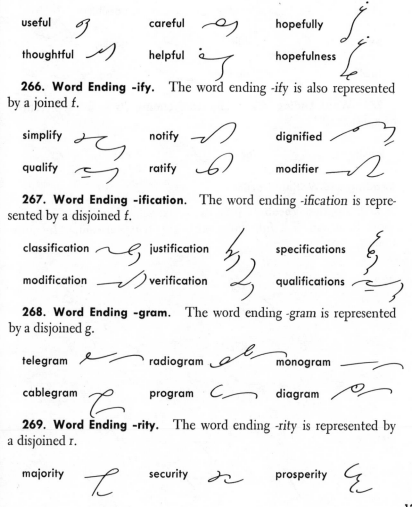

useful
careful
hopefully
thoughtful
helpful
hopefulness

266. Word Ending -ify. The word ending *-ify* is also represented by a joined *f*.

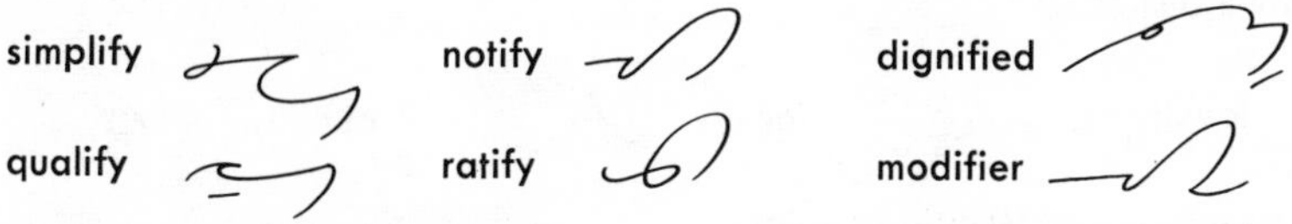
simplify
notify
dignified
qualify
ratify
modifier

267. Word Ending -ification. The word ending *-ification* is represented by a disjoined *f*.

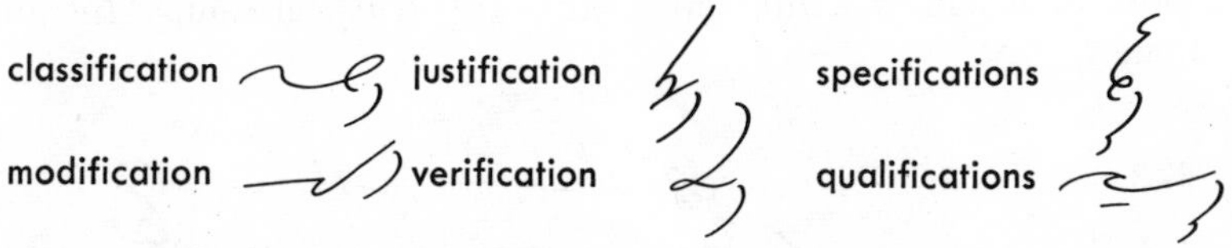
classification
justification
specifications
modification
verification
qualifications

268. Word Ending -gram. The word ending *-gram* is represented by a disjoined *g*.

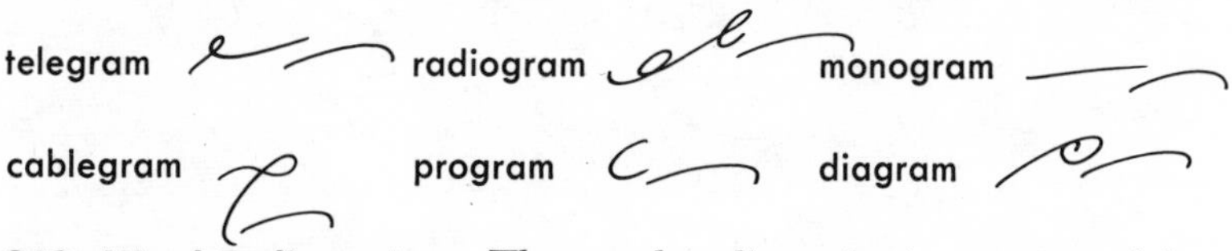
telegram
radiogram
monogram
cablegram
program
diagram

269. Word Ending -rity. The word ending *-rity* is represented by a disjoined *r*.

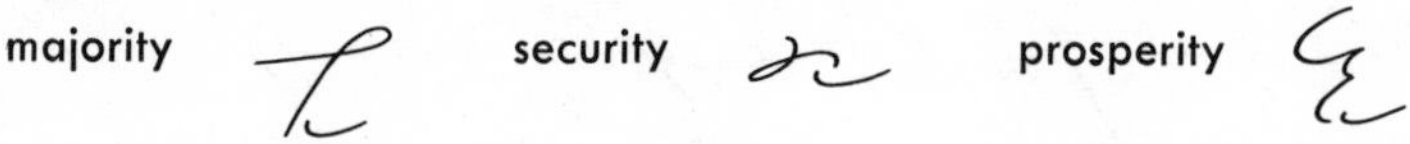
majority
security
prosperity

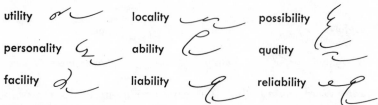

authority sincerity minority

charity maturity familiarity

270. Word Ending -lity. The word ending *-lity* is represented by a disjoined *l.*

utility locality possibility

personality ability quality

facility liability reliability

271. Word Ending -lty. The word ending *-lty* is also represented by a disjoined *l.*

loyalty faculty penalty

Reading and Writing Practice

272. Applied Vocabulary Study. *Manual,* a handbook. *Majority,* more than half. *Tactful,* thoughtful. *Terrifying,* alarming. *Integrity,* honesty.

273.

manual

patrons

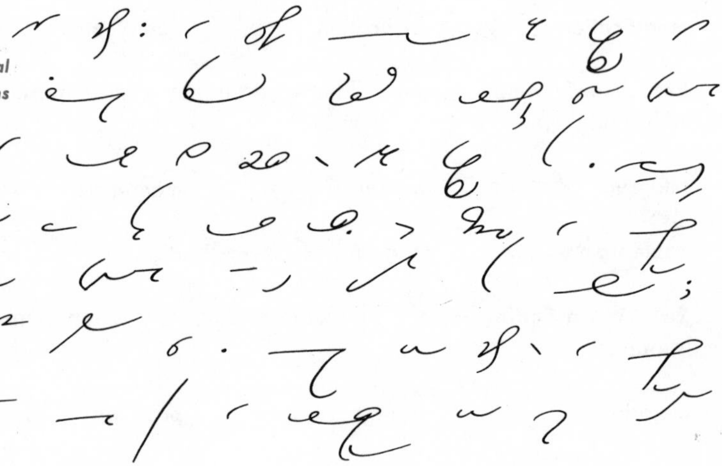

quality
tactful

ring
sincerity

desirability

(185)

274.

destroyed
terrifying

shadow
integrity

(134)

275.

(70)

276.

article

urgent

(90)

LESSON 30 Recall

After studying the word beginnings, word endings, and phrases in Lessons 25 through 29, you have earned a breathing spell! Therefore, you will have no new shorthand devices to learn in this lesson.

In this lesson you will find an Accuracy Practice devoted to the curved strokes of Gregg Shorthand, a recall chart, and a story by Andrew Carnegie that you will like.

Accuracy Practice

To get the most benefit from these accuracy drills, be sure to follow the practice procedure suggested on page 103.

277. B V P F S

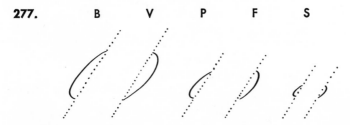

To write these strokes accurately:

a. Give them approximately the slant indicated by the dotted lines.

b. Make the curve deep at the *beginning* of v, f, comma s; make the curve deep at the *end* of b, p, left s.

Practice Drill

Puts, spare, business, bares, stairs, sphere, leaves, briefs.

278. Pr Pl Br Bl

To write these combinations accurately:

a. Write each without a pause between the first and second letter of each combination.

b. Watch your proportions carefully.

Practice Drill

Press, pray, prim, plan, plate, place. Brim, brief, bread, blame, blast.

279. Fr Fl

To write these combinations accurately:

a. Write them with one sweep of the pen, with no stop between the *f* and the *r* or *l*.

Practice Drill

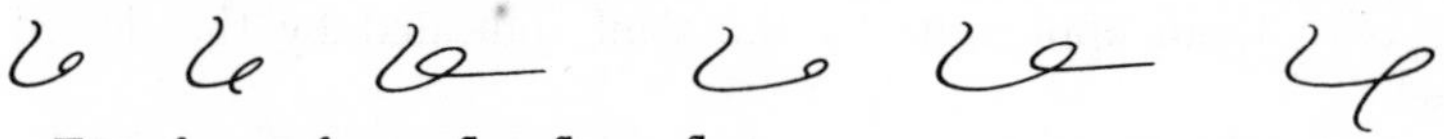

Free, freeze, frame, flee, flame, flap.

280. Recall Chart. This chart contains all the brief forms in Chapter 5 and one or more illustrations of all the shorthand devices you have studied in Chapters 1 through 5.

As you read the words in this chart, you won't forget to spell each word that you cannot read immediately, will you?

Can you read the 96 words and phrases in this chart in 7 minutes or less?

Words

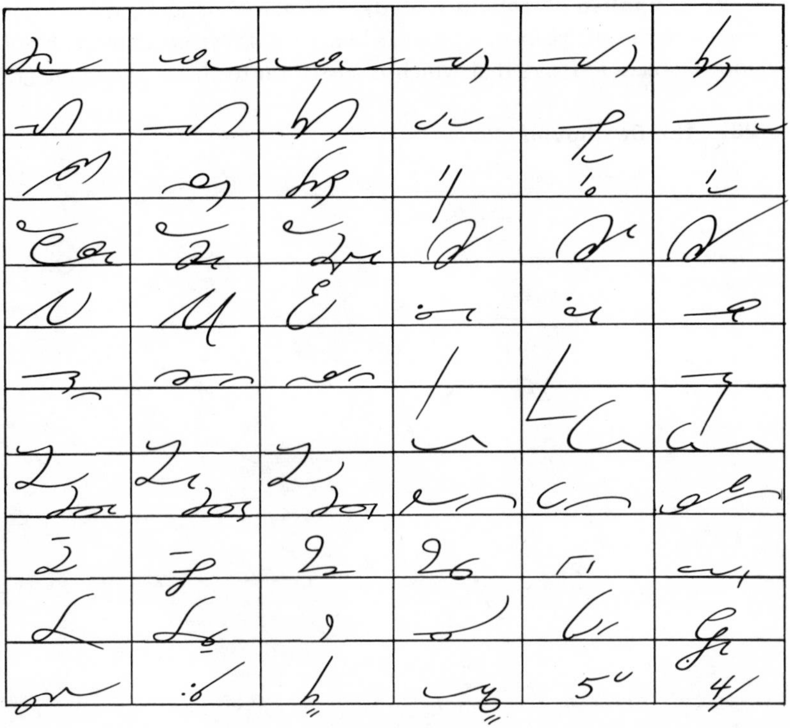

1
2
3
4
5
6
7
8
9
10
11

Brief Forms

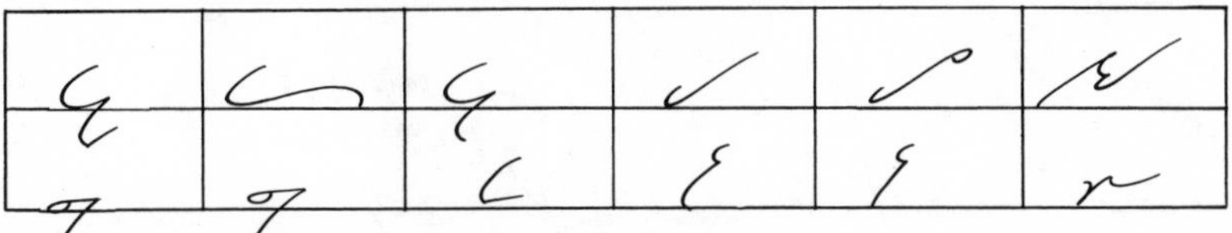

12
13

Phrases

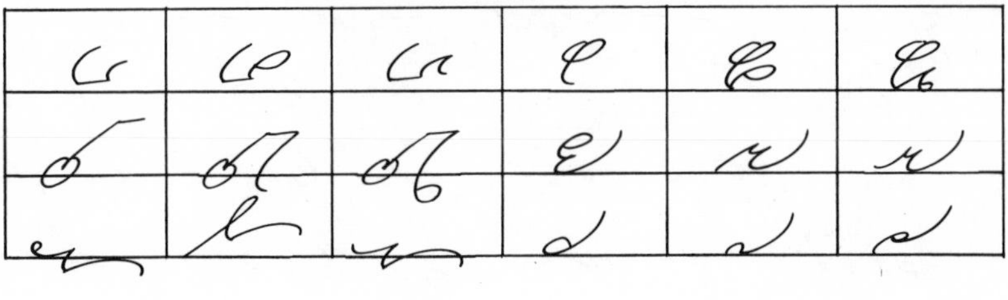

14
15
16

Reading and Writing Practice

281. Applied Vocabulary Study. *Hazards,* dangers, risks. *Declining days,* the last years of a person's life. *Vicious,* wicked, savage. *Flabby,* soft, feeble. *Heritage,* that which is passed on to those who come after.

282. The Deerhound

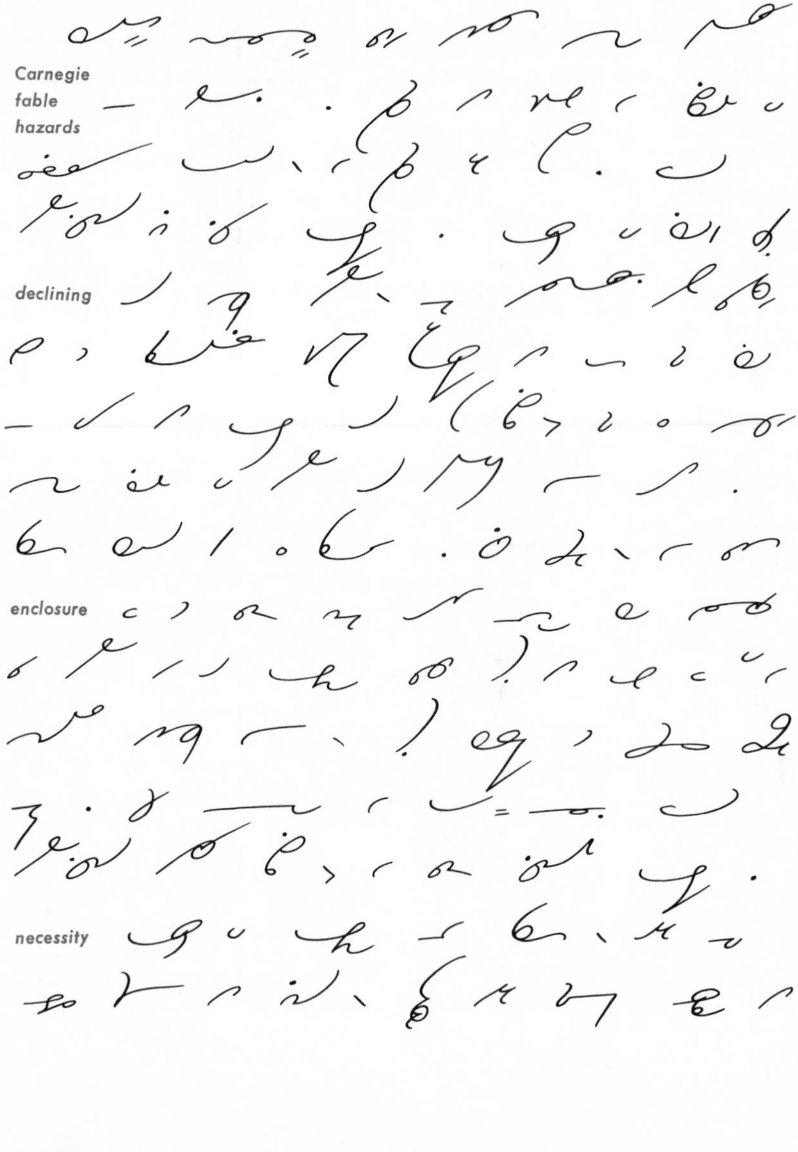

Carnegie
fable
hazards
declining
enclosure
necessity

vicious
flabby
prey
disease
heritage

(314)

CHAPTER 6

Spelling and Punctuation

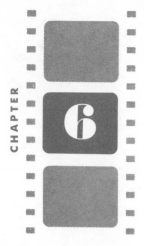

To be a successful stenographer or secretary, you must be able to do more than write shorthand rapidly and accurately; you must be able to spell and punctuate, so that you can turn out a transcript that your employer will have no hesitation in accepting. To make sure that you will be able to spell and punctuate accurately when you have completed your shorthand course, we shall, from this point on, give special attention to these factors in each Reading and Writing Practice.

In Chapter 6, beginning with Lesson 31, you will review three of the more common uses of the comma—parenthetical, series, and apposition. Each time one of these uses of the comma occurs in the Reading and Writing Practice, the comma will appear encircled in the shorthand, thus calling it to your attention. At the left of the column, you will find a brief "marginal reminder" explaining why the comma has been used.

Also in the marginal reminders you will find a number of words that have been selected from the Reading and Writing Practice for special spelling study; they are words that stenographers and secretaries often misspell.

To get the greatest benefit from these marginal reminders, you should observe the following procedure:

1. Read the full explanation of

The businessman insists that his letters be correctly punctuated and that they contain no spelling errors. This secretary has taken her employer's dictation and checked the spelling of any words about which she was in doubt when she transcribed. Her employer is obviously pleased with the letter!

the marginal reminders on page 138, to be sure that you understand just how and when commas parenthetical, series, and apposition are used. Do not try to memorize these principles, but be sure that you understand them. Illustrations of these principles will occur again and again in your Reading and Writing Practice, so that eventually you will acquire the "knack" of applying the principles correctly.

2. Continue to read and copy each Reading and Writing Practice as you have done. You will, however, add these three easy steps:

a. Each time that you meet an encircled comma as you read the shorthand, glance in the left margin of the page to be sure that you know why the comma has been used.

b. As you copy the Reading and Writing Practice, insert the commas in your own shorthand notes, encircling them as in the book.

c. As you meet each spelling word in the margin, spell it once, preferably aloud.

What's Ahead?

You are rapidly approaching the home stretch in your study of shorthand. You are making such rapid progress, in fact, that with the completion of Lesson 31 you will have covered the entire alphabet of Gregg Shorthand. If you had to, you could construct a satisfactory outline for any word in the English language after completing Lesson 31.

In Chapter 6 you will also study two more groups of brief forms, leaving only six groups to learn. In addition, you will take up nine abbreviating and phrasing devices—and easy ones, too!

LESSON 31

Commas — Parenthetical, Apposition, Series

, parenthetical

A writer, in order to make his meaning clearer, sometimes inserts a comment or an explanation that could be omitted without changing the meaning of the sentence. These added comments and explanations are called parenthetical and are usually separated from the rest of the sentence by commas.

> I shall, of course, be glad to help you.
> Is the reason, Mr. Dix, for your failure to pay or notify us a shortage of funds?

A special type of parenthetical expression is called appositive and is explained here.

, apposition

Sometimes a writer mentions some person or thing and then, in order to make his meaning perfectly clear to the reader, says the same thing in different words.

> Your dealer, Mr. E. R. Teller, has figures to show you.
> The shipment we purchased on Monday, July 16, arrived this afternoon.

In many cases these constructions in apposition resemble the constructions in which the commas are used to set off parenthetical expressions. It is really immaterial whether the transcriber thinks he is using the commas to set off an apposition or to set off a parenthetical expression. The result is identical.

Some of the appositions occur at the end of a sentence, in which case only one comma is needed.

> The shipment arrived on Monday, July 16.

, series

When three or more similar expressions (words, phrases, or clauses) occur in a series with a conjunction before the last expression, a comma should be placed before the conjunction.

> We are going to face the problem sincerely, squarely, and intelligently.
> We had your business, your good will, and your friendship.
> He planted them in the grass, in the bushes, and in the hedge bordering the garden.

283. Den. By rounding off the angle between *d-n,* we obtain the fluent *den* blend.

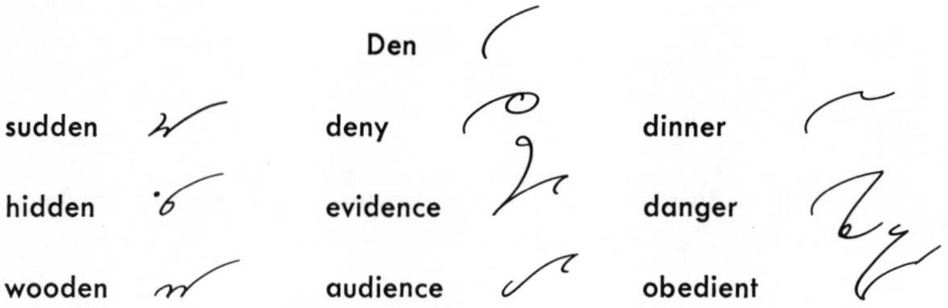
Den
sudden
deny
dinner
hidden
evidence
danger
wooden
audience
obedient

284. Ten. This same stroke represents *t-n.*

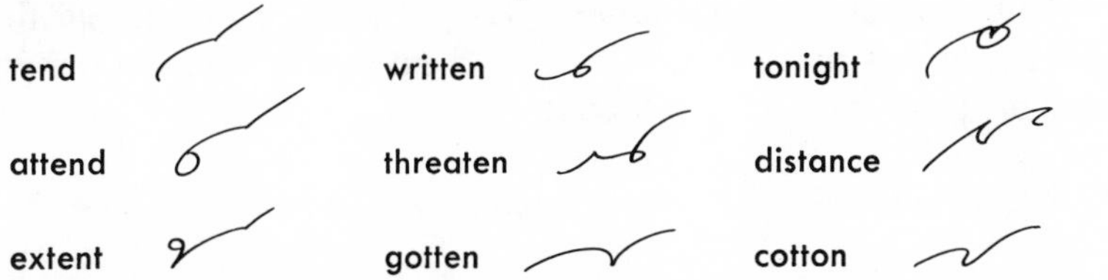
tend
written
tonight
attend
threaten
distance
extent
gotten
cotton

285. Tain. This same stroke represents the syllable *tain.*

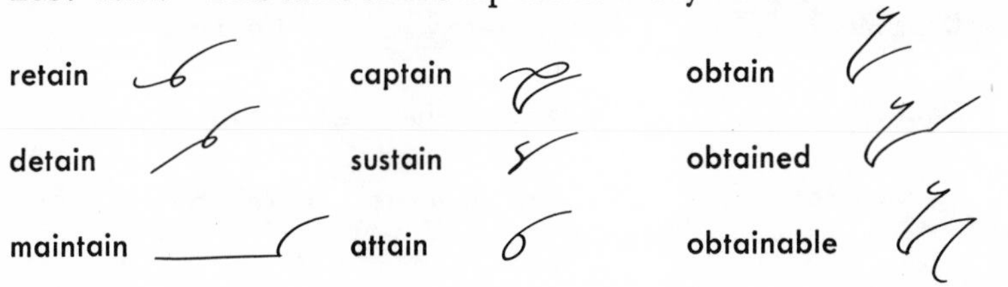
retain
captain
obtain
detain
sustain
obtained
maintain
attain
obtainable

286. Dem. By rounding off the angle between *d-m*, we obtain the fluent *dem* blend.

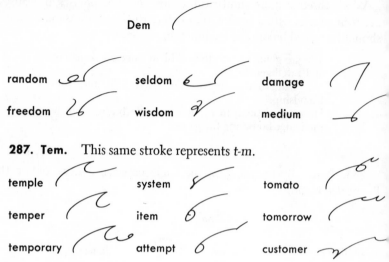

Dem

random **seldom** **damage**

freedom **wisdom** **medium**

287. Tem. This same stroke represents *t-m*.

temple **system** **tomato**

temper **item** **tomorrow**

temporary **attempt** **customer**

288. Useful Phrases. With the blends you have just studied, we form these useful phrases.

to me **to know** **to make**

289. Special Business Forms. Do not attempt to learn all these phrases at this time. You will master them as they occur in the practice matter of the following lessons.

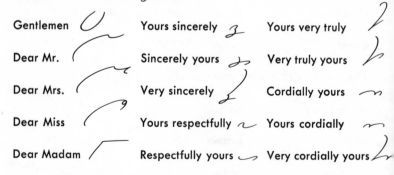

Gentlemen **Yours sincerely** **Yours very truly**

Dear Mr. **Sincerely yours** **Very truly yours**

Dear Mrs. **Very sincerely** **Cordially yours**

Dear Miss **Yours respectfully** **Yours cordially**

Dear Madam **Respectfully yours** **Very cordially yours**

Reading and Writing Practice

290. Applied Vocabulary Study. *Temporary*, for a short time. *Collection letter*, a letter intended to persuade someone to pay a debt. *Faculty*, teaching staff. *Guidance*, help, direction. *Finance*, money matters.

291.

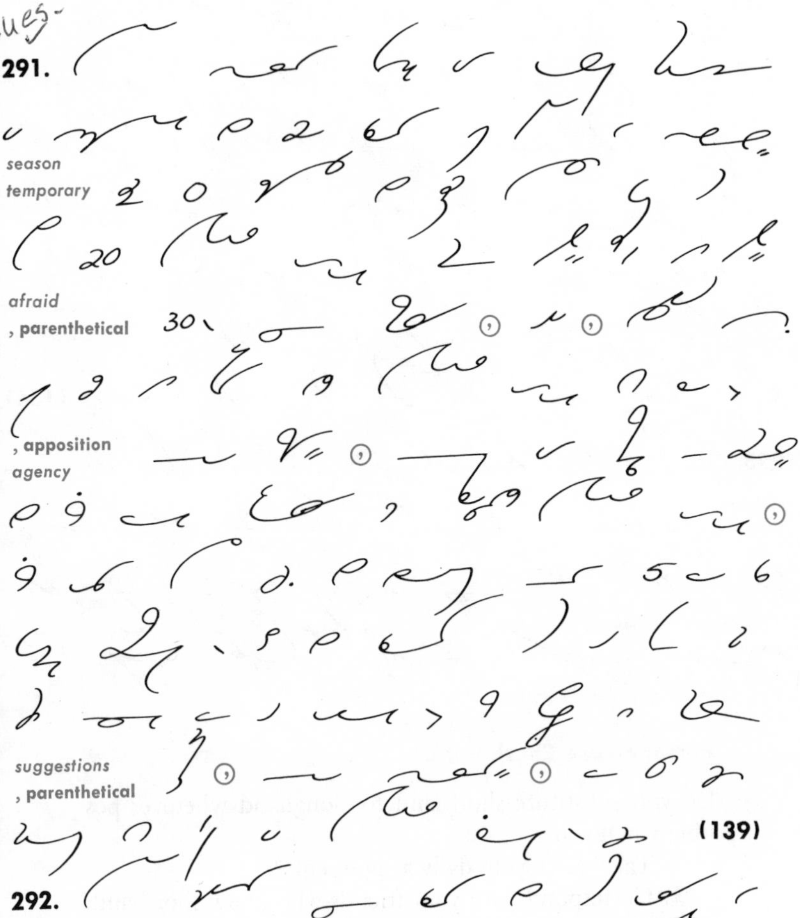
season
temporary
afraid
, parenthetical
, apposition
agency
suggestions
, parenthetical

(139)

292.

intelligently
, series
, parenthetical

(136)

293.

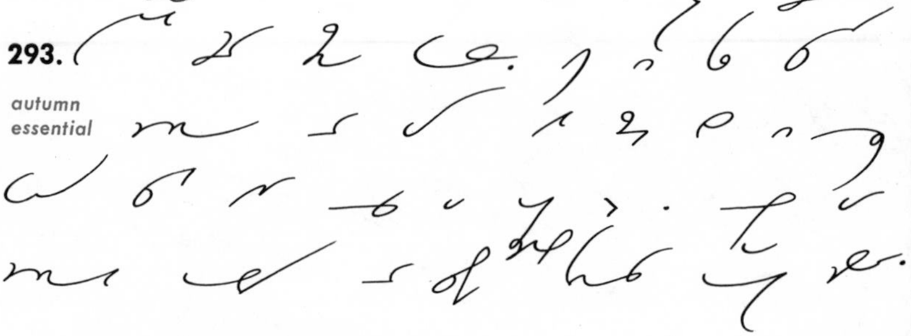
autumn
essential

Personal-Use Check List

Do you substitute shorthand for longhand wherever possible when you

1. Take down your daily assignments?
2. Correspond with your friends who know shorthand?
3. Draft compositions and reports?
4. Make entries in your diary?
5. Make notes to yourself on things to do, people to see, appointments to keep, etc.?

faculty
, series
guidance
, parenthetical

(102)

294.

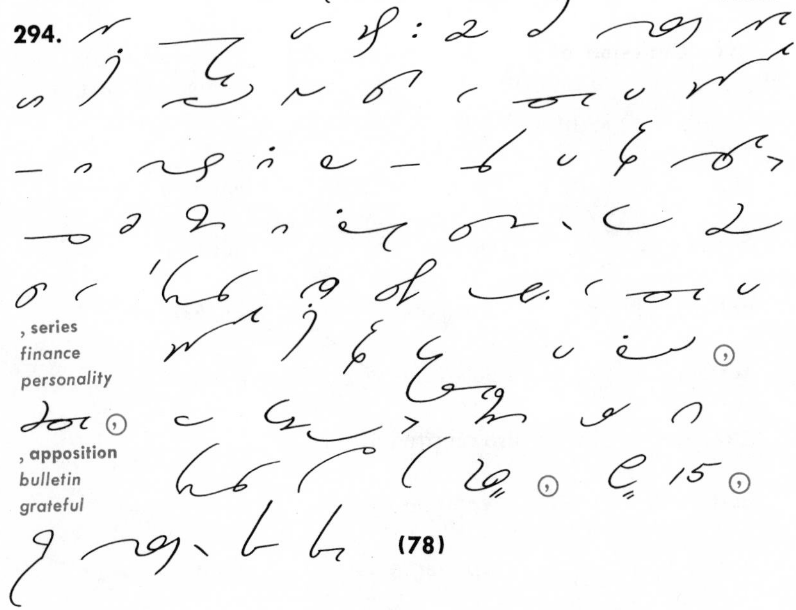

, series
finance
personality
, apposition
bulletin
grateful

(78)

LESSON 32

295. Brief Forms

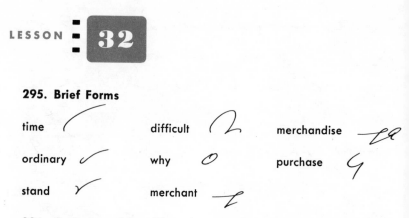

time	difficult	merchandise
ordinary	why	purchase
stand	merchant	

296. Omission of R. The *r* is omitted in *tern, term; dern, derm; thern, therm.* By omitting the *r*, we simply drop a sound that is not ordinarily stressed in speaking.

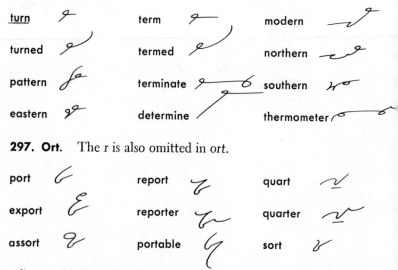

turn	term	modern
turned	termed	northern
pattern	terminate	southern
eastern	determine	thermometer

297. Ort. The *r* is also omitted in *ort.*

port	report	quart
export	reporter	quarter
assort	portable	sort

Reading and Writing Practice

298. Applied Vocabulary Study. *Assortment,* variety, collection. *Extraordinary,* remarkable. *Securely,* tightly, firmly. *Periodic,* now and then.

299.

, series
overcoat

, parenthetical
difficulty

, series
efficient

justification

, apposition
Sothern

(130)

300.

Stern's
extraordinary

, parenthetical
guarantee
article

, parenthetical

(147)

301.

, series

, parenthetical
some time

, parenthetical
naturally
eager

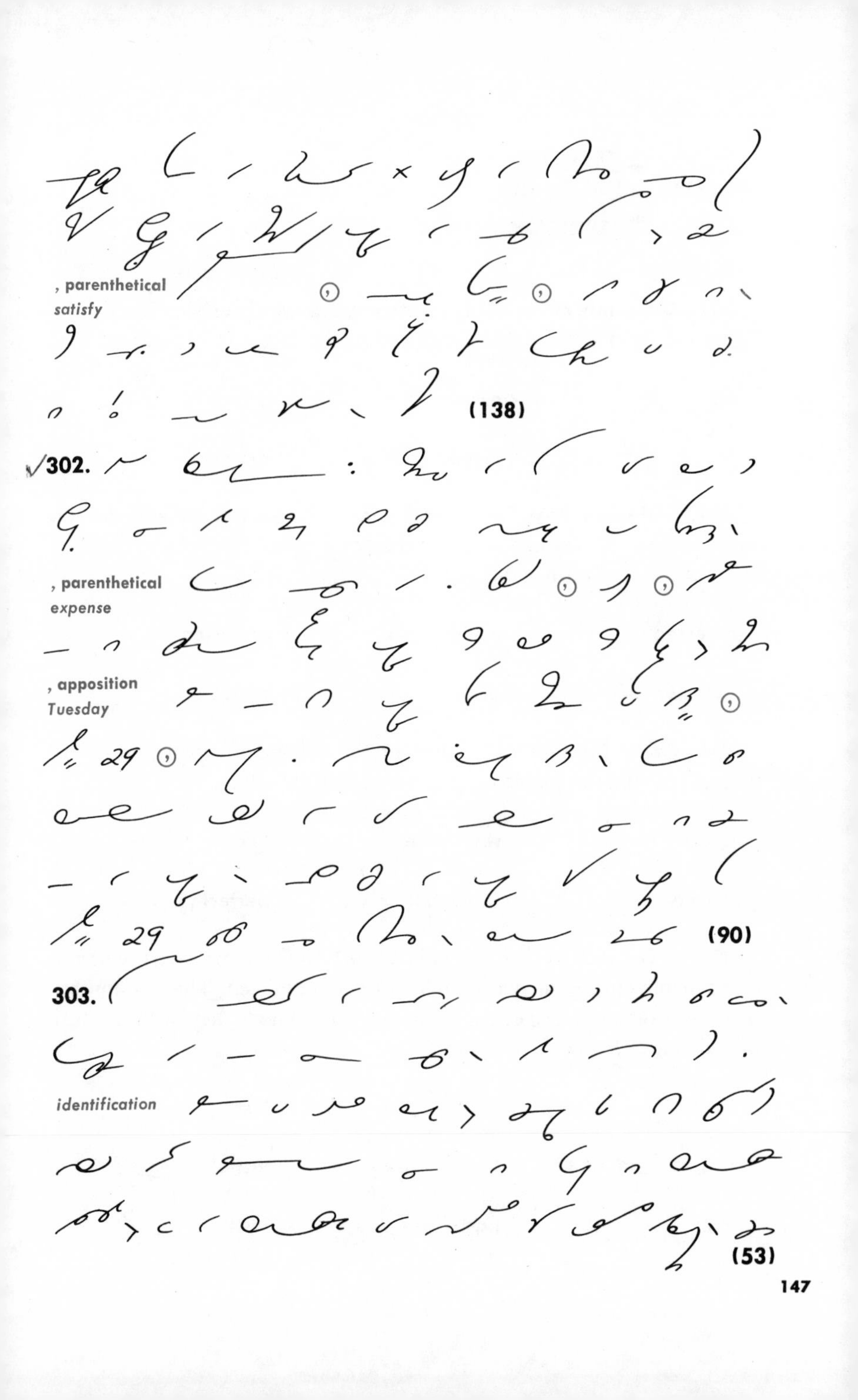

, parenthetical
satisfy

(138)

302.

, parenthetical
expense

, apposition
Tuesday

(90)

303.

identification

(53)

LESSON 33

304. Omission of T. *T* is omitted from words ending in *ct* (*kt*). Again we drop a letter that is not ordinarily stressed in speaking.

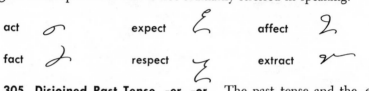

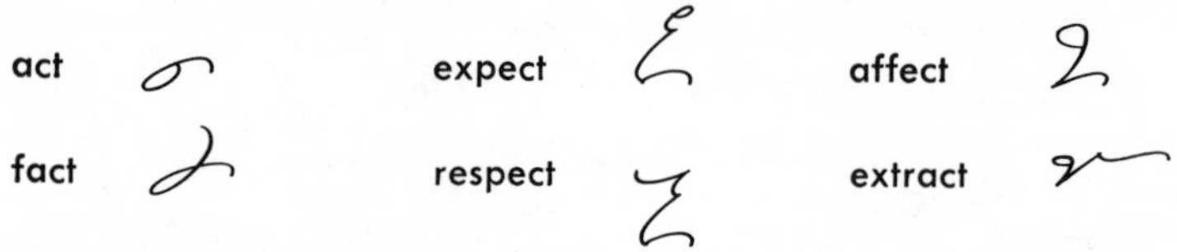
act
expect
affect
fact
respect
extract

305. Disjoined Past Tense, -er, -or. The past tense and the -er, -or derivatives are formed with the disjoined characters because the last letter of the root form is missing.

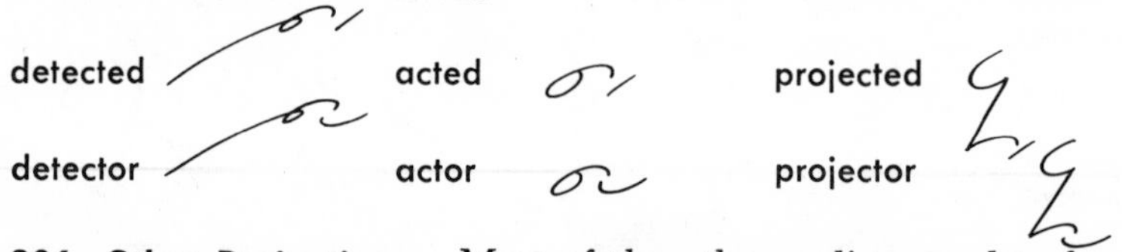
detected
acted
projected
detector
actor
projector

306. Other Derivatives. Most of the other endings used to form derivatives may be joined— *-ive, -ivity, -ful, -ly,* etc.

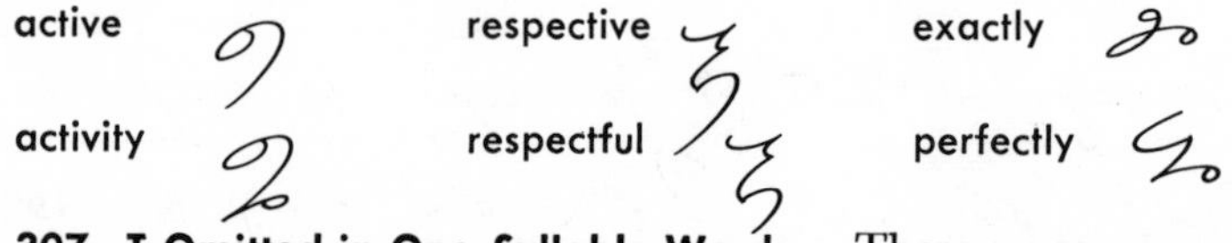
active
respective
exactly
activity
respectful
perfectly

307. T Omitted in One-Syllable Words. There are seven words of one syllable ending in *st* from which the *t* is omitted. The *t* is omitted in these words because of the frequency with which they occur in business dictation.

best
cost
last
rest
first
lasted
test
past
lasts

308. T Omitted in Words of More Than One Syllable. The final *t* is omitted in words of more than one syllable ending in *st* except as explained in Paragraph 309.

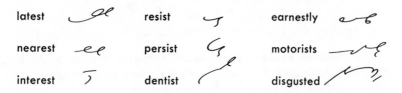

latest		resist		earnestly	
nearest		persist		motorists	
interest		dentist		disgusted	

309. Disjoined St to Represent -ist, -est. If the last letter of the root word is missing, or if the word ends in a vowel, a disjoined *st* is used to represent the endings *-ist, -est.*

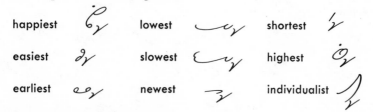

happiest		lowest		shortest	
easiest		slowest		highest	
earliest		newest		individualist	

Reading and Writing Practice

Reading Scoreboard. The previous Reading Scoreboard appeared in Lesson 18. If you have been studying each Reading and Writing Practice faithfully, no doubt there has been an increase in your reading speed. Let us measure that increase on the *first reading* of the letters in Lesson 33. The following table will help you:

Lesson 33 contains 518 words.

If you read Lesson 33 in	your reading rate is
18 MINUTES	29 WORDS A MINUTE
20 MINUTES	26 WORDS A MINUTE
22 MINUTES	24 WORDS A MINUTE
24 MINUTES	22 WORDS A MINUTE
26 MINUTES	20 WORDS A MINUTE
28 MINUTES	19 WORDS A MINUTE
30 MINUTES	17 WORDS A MINUTE

If you can read Lesson 33 in 18 minutes or less, you are doing well. If you take considerably longer than 30 minutes, perhaps you should review your homework procedures. For example, are you

1. Practicing in a quiet place at home?
2. Practicing without the radio on?
3. Spelling aloud any words that you cannot immediately read?

310. Applied Vocabulary Study. *Resistance,* opposition. *Protest,* complaint, objection. *Exhausted,* all gone. *Necessities,* things without which one could not get along. *Existing,* present.

311.

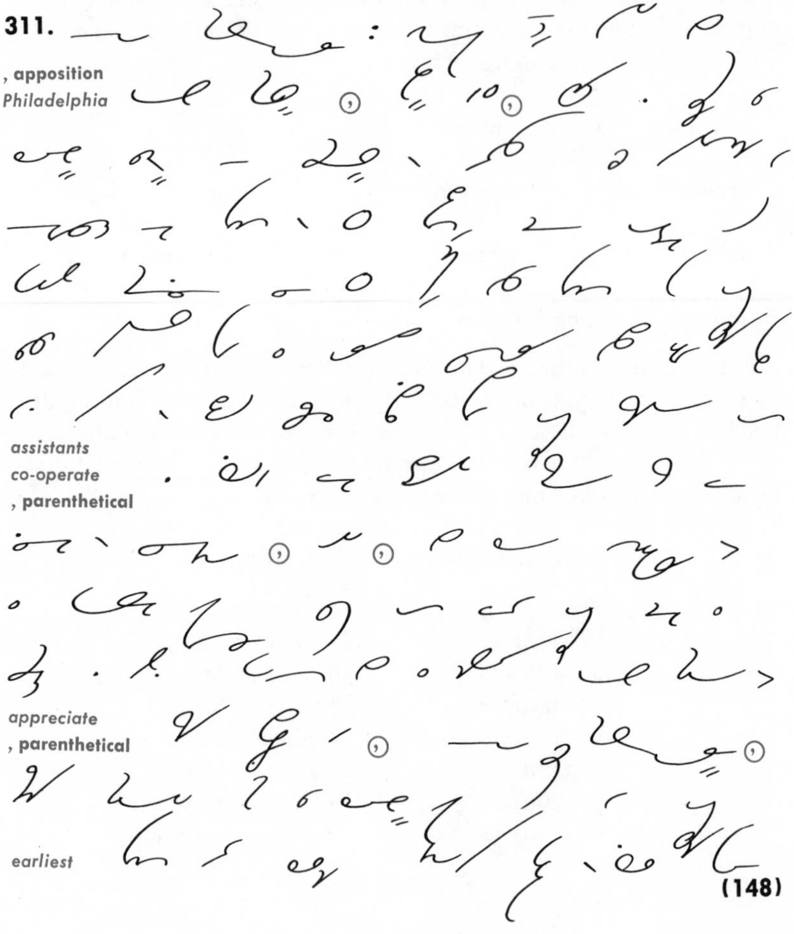

, apposition
Philadelphia
assistants
co-operate
, parenthetical
appreciate
, parenthetical
earliest

(148)

312.

, apposition
received

, parenthetical
justification

(90)

313.

, parenthetical
necessities
rising

, parenthetical
existing

earnestly
, parenthetical
, series

(100)

314.

, apposition
catalogue
, parenthetical
interested
, series
cherries

(96)

315.

official
letterhead
chemical
, series

(84)

316. Brief Forms

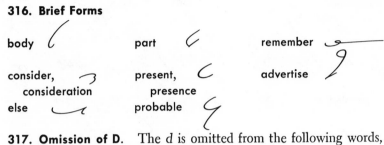

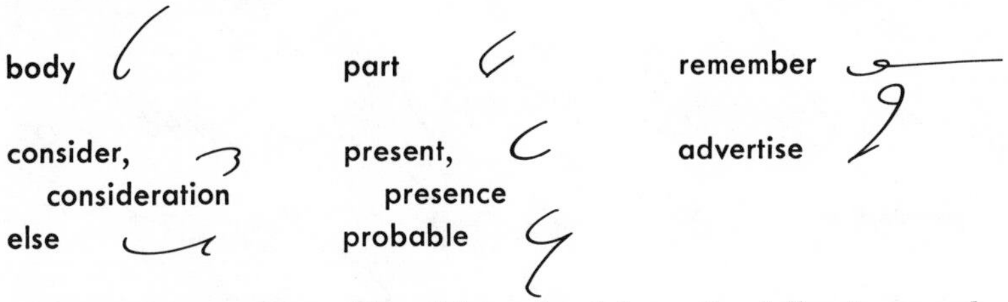
body
part
remember
consider, consideration
present, presence
advertise
else
probable

317. Omission of D. The *d* is omitted from the following words, which fall naturally into family groups.

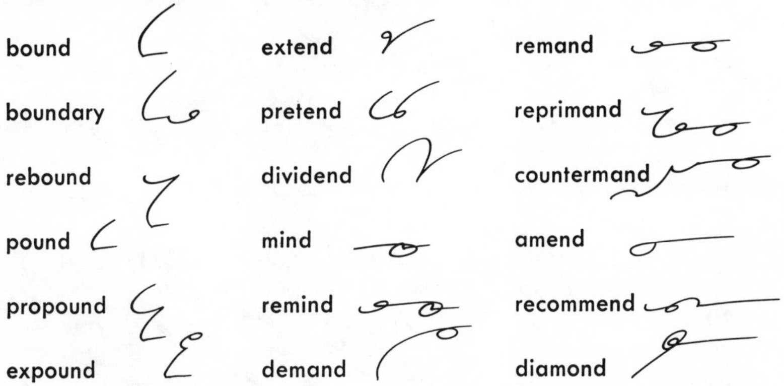
bound
extend
remand
boundary
pretend
reprimand
rebound
dividend
countermand
pound
mind
amend
propound
remind
recommend
expound
demand
diamond

Reading and Writing Practice

318. Applied Vocabulary Study. *Venture,* an undertaking that involves some risk or danger. *Quarterly,* a newspaper or magazine that appears four times a year. *Leads,* inquiries that may result in sales. *Personnel manager,* the one in charge of hiring employees. (Notice the double *n* in *personnel.*)

319. 

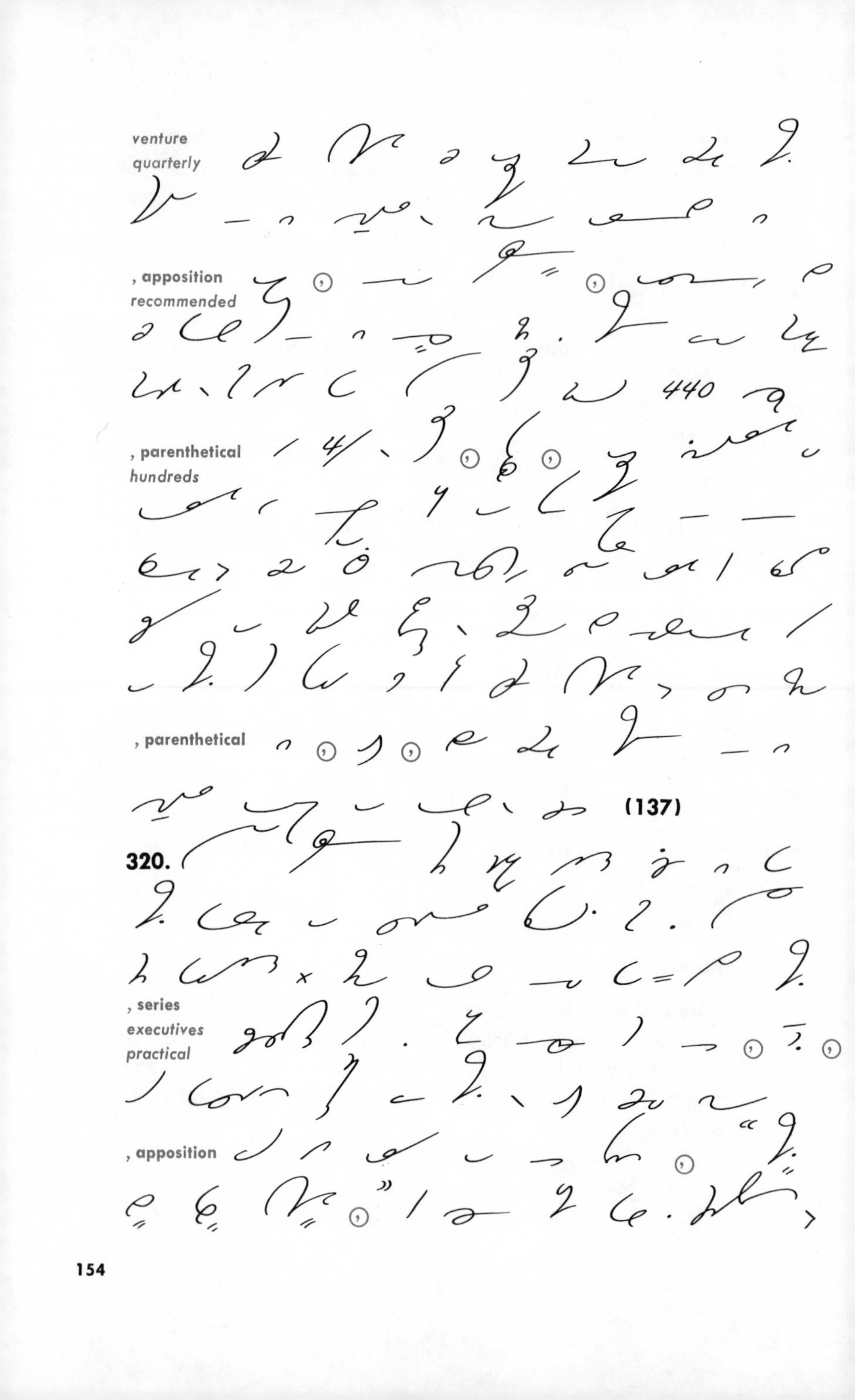

venture
quarterly

, apposition
recommended

440

, parenthetical
hundreds

, parenthetical

(137)

320.

, series
executives
practical

, apposition

Homework Check List

When you do your homework assignment each day,

1. Do you read the Applied Vocabulary Study before tackling the Reading and Writing Practice?
2. Do you read aloud each Reading and Writing Practice before copying it?
3. Do you spell each shorthand outline that you cannot immediately read?
4. Do you glance in the margin of the shorthand page each time you meet a comma so that you know the reason for its use?
5. Do you spell aloud all the spelling words in the marginal reminders?

Remember, nothing will build up your shorthand speed more rapidly than regular reading and writing of shorthand.

, parenthetical

enclosed

(137)

321.

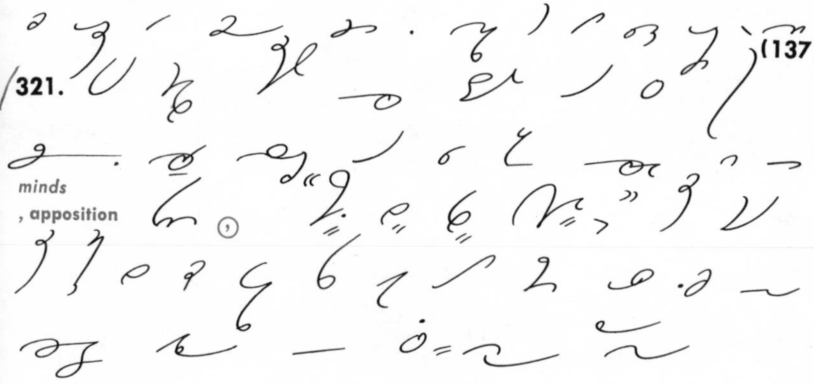

minds

, apposition

(95)

322.

career
recommend

previous
essential
, series

, apposition
personnel

assure
, parenthetical

(151)

LESSON 35

323. Word Beginning Incl-. The word beginning *incl-* is represented by a disjoined small circle placed above the following character.

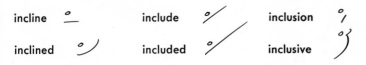

incline		include		inclusion	
inclined		included		inclusive	

324. Word Beginning Post-. The word beginning *post-* is represented by a disjoined *p* placed on the line of writing.

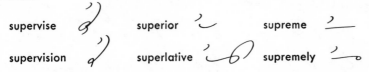

postage		postpone		post card	
postal		postponed		postman	

325. Word Beginnings Super-, Supr-. The word beginnings *super-*, *supr-* are represented by a disjoined comma *s* placed above the following character.

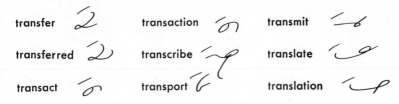

supervise		superior		supreme	
supervision		superlative		supremely	

326. Word Beginning Trans-. The word beginning *trans-* is represented by a disjoined *t* placed above the following character.

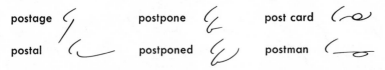

transfer		transaction		transmit	
transferred		transcribe		translate	
transact		transport		translation	

Reading and Writing Practice

327. Applied Vocabulary Study. *In transit,* while being shipped. *Transmitted,* sent. *Tracer,* inquiry started to learn what has happened to a shipment that has not arrived. *Hustling,* active, full of energy. *Cash reserve,* money kept on hand.

328.

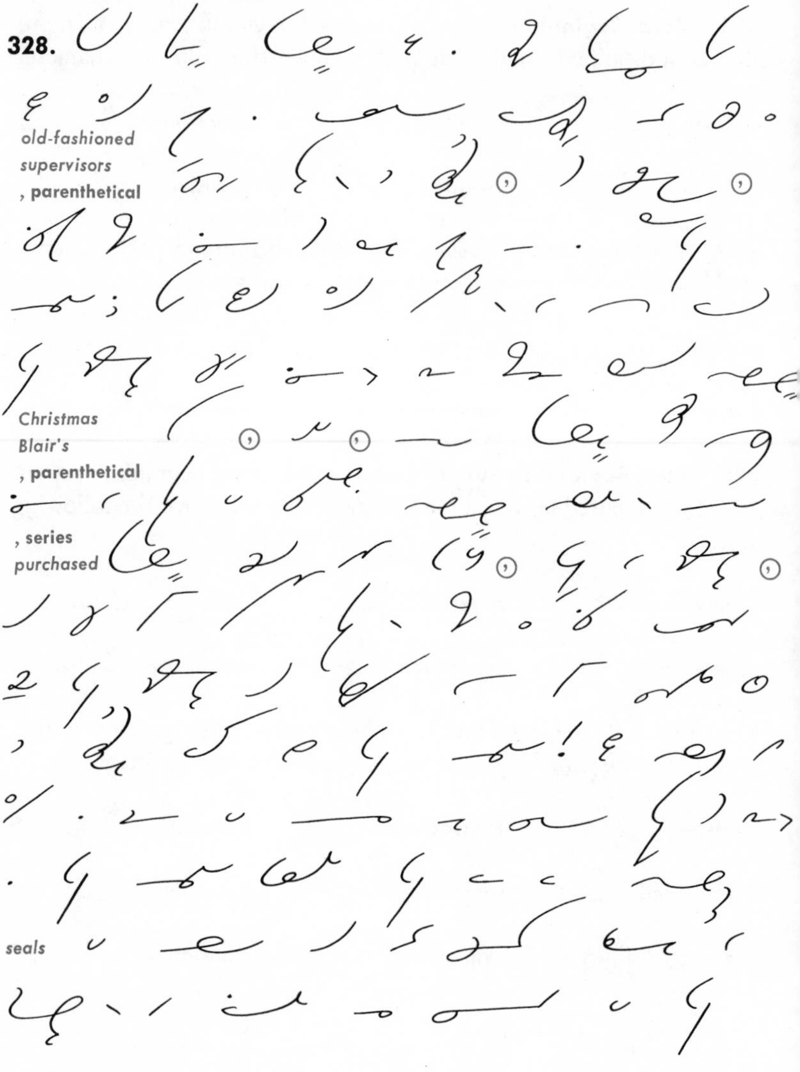
old-fashioned
supervisors
, parenthetical
Christmas
Blair's
, parenthetical
, series
purchased
seals

descriptive
booklet

(204)

329.

cloth
, apposition

, apposition
notifies
Thursday

transferred
receipt

transit
freight

tracer
, parenthetical

(133)

330.

Transcript

superior
support

clothes
, series

personnel
, apposition

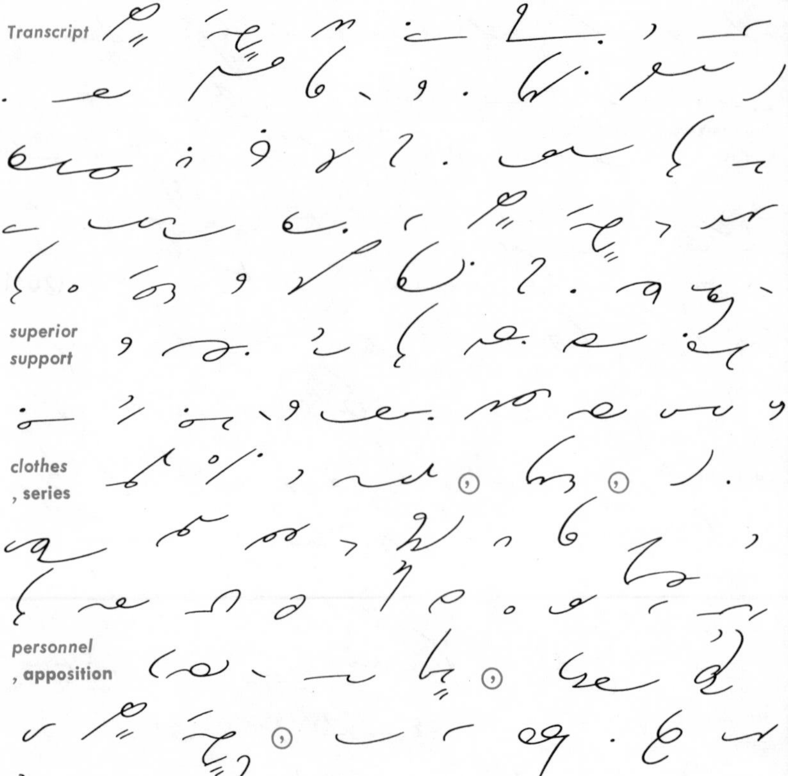

(135)

331.

, parenthetical

, parenthetical
lawyer
, apposition
legal

(178)

LESSON 36 Recall

This lesson is one that you should especially enjoy. First, it contains no new shorthand devices for you to learn. Second, it contains, in addition to the Accuracy Practice and a recall chart, an amusing tale about Mr. Smith's unruly chickens and how they were finally subdued!

Accuracy Practice

332. O On Sho

To write these combinations accurately:

a. Keep the o hook narrow, being sure that the beginning and end are on the same level of writing, as indicated by the dotted line.

b. Keep the o in *on* and *sho* parallel with the consonant, as indicated by the dotted line.

c. Avoid a point at the curved part indicated by the arrows.

Practice Drill

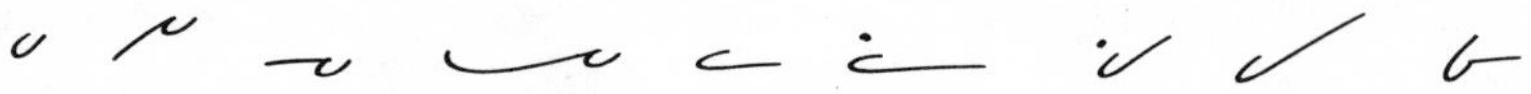

Of, tow, know, low, own, home, hot, odd, shown.

333. Non Kor

To write these combinations accurately:

a. Make the beginning of the o retrace the preceding character.

b. Avoid a point at the curved part of the o indicated by the arrows.

Practice Drill

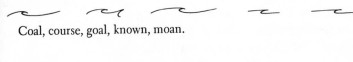

Coal, course, goal, known, moan.

334. OO Noo Noom

To write these combinations accurately:

a. Keep the *oo* hook narrow and deep.

b. Keep the beginning and end of the hook on the same level of writing.

c. In the words *new* and *numb*, keep the hook parallel with the straight line that precedes it.

d. In the word *numb*, retrace the *m* on the bottom of the *oo* hook.

e. Avoid a point at the places indicated by arrows.

Practice Drill

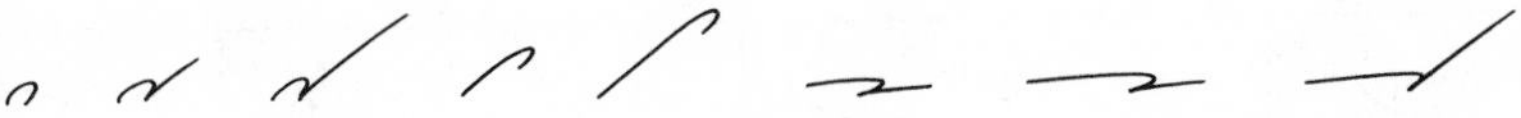

You-your, yours truly, you would, to-too-two, do, noon, moon, mood.

335. Hard Hailed

To write these combinations accurately:

a. Give the end of the *r* and of the *l* a lift upward.

b. Do not lift the end too soon, or the strokes may resemble the *nd*, *md* combinations.

Practice Drill

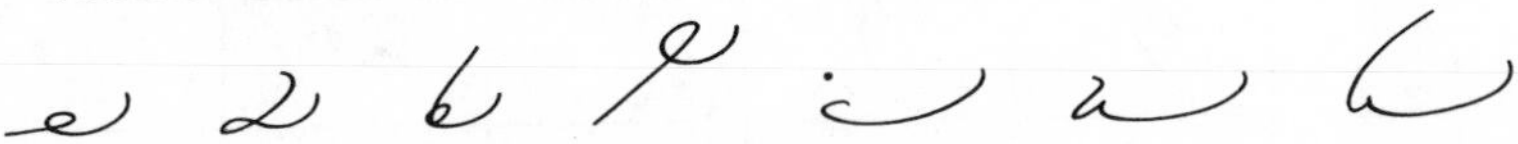

Neared, feared, cheered, dared, hold, sold, bold.

336. Recall Chart. This chart contains all the brief forms in Chapter 6. It also contains a complete recall of the phrasing principles you have studied thus far. There are 108 brief forms and phrases in the chart.

Because you have seen most of these phrases many times, do you think you can read through the chart in 7 minutes?

Phrases

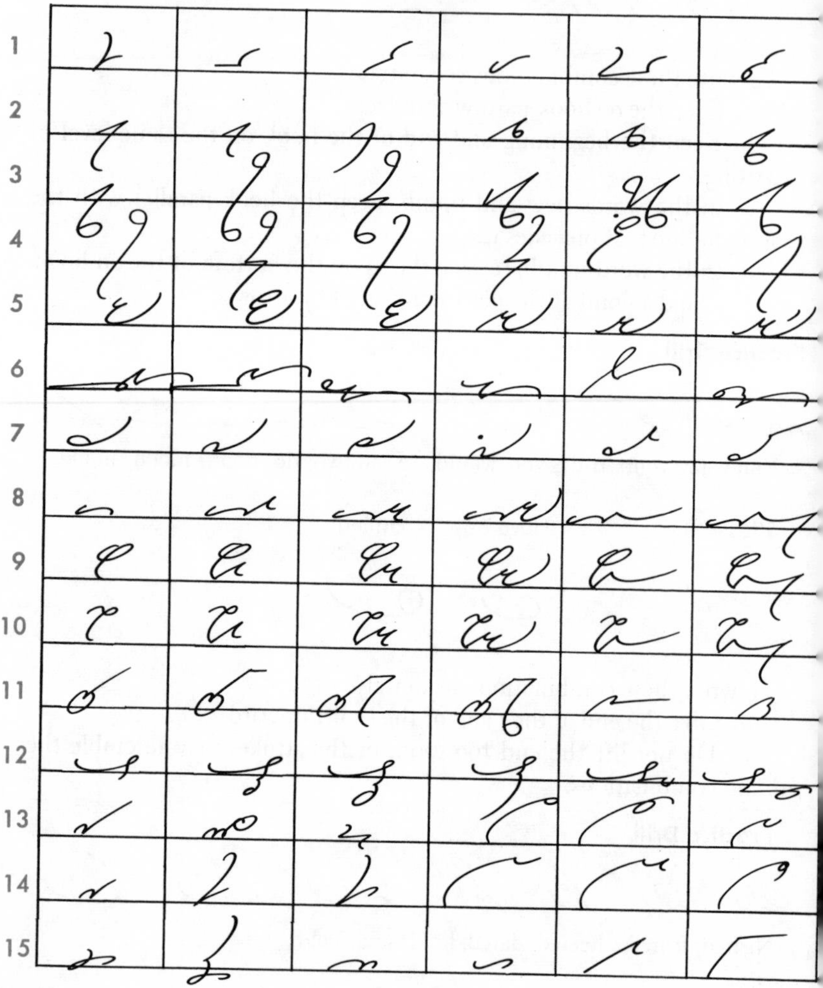

Brief Forms

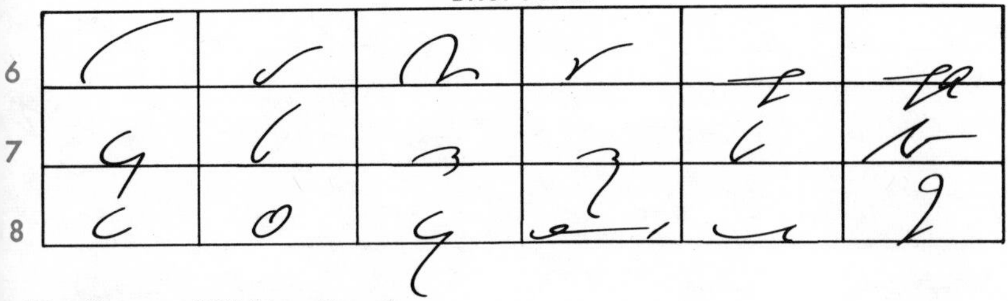
6
7
8

Reading and Writing Practice

337. Applied Vocabulary Study. *Run at will,* as they liked, without control. *Hedge,* shrubbery, especially when planted as a boundary.

338. Mr. Smith's Chickens

occasion
, parenthetical
, parenthetical
won't

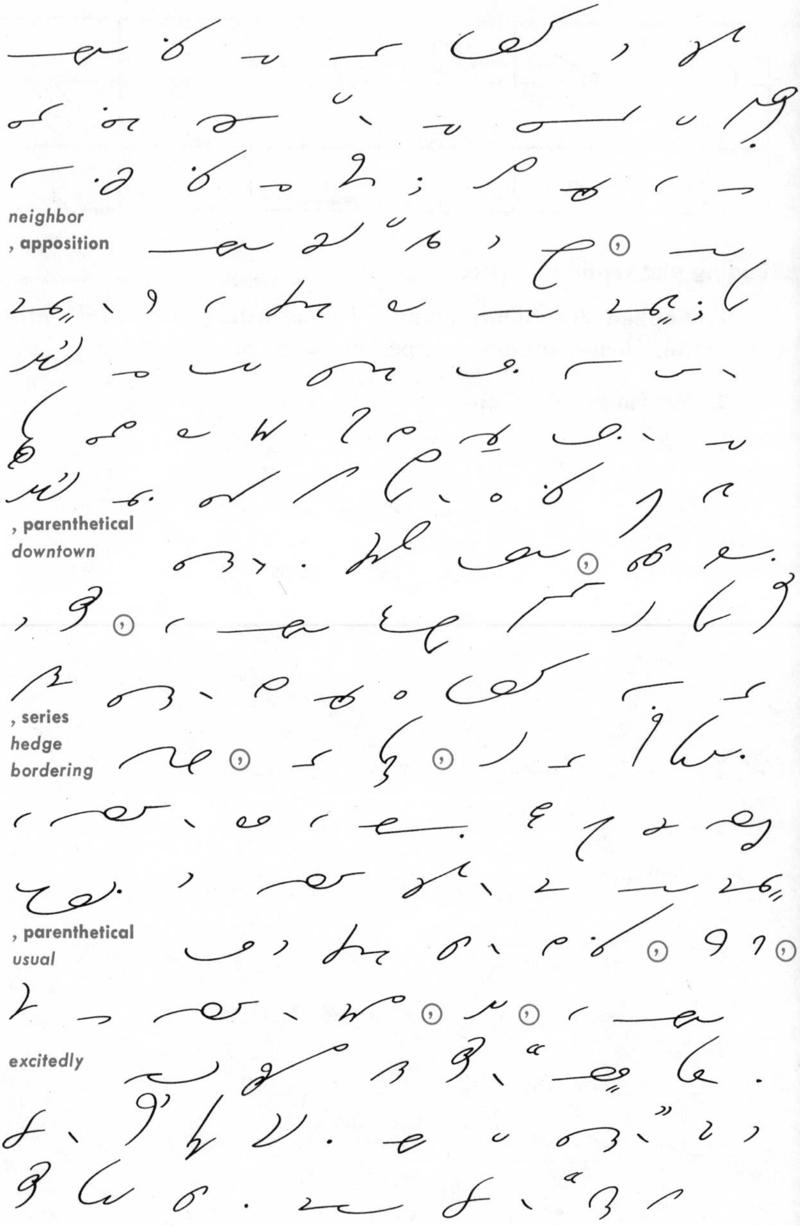

neighbor
, apposition
, parenthetical
downtown
, series
hedge
bordering
, parenthetical
usual
excitedly

visitor

, apposition

nothing

, parenthetical

, parenthetical

(421)

CHAPTER 7

More About Commas

In Chapter 6 you reviewed the easiest points of punctuation—commas parenthetical, apposition, and series. In each Reading and Writing Practice in Chapter 6 you encountered many illustrations of these uses of the comma, and perhaps you are already beginning to get the "knack" of them. You may even have reached the point where you can determine why a comma is used when it appears in the Reading and Writing Practice so that you don't have to look in the margin for the reason.

Here is a word of caution, however: if there is the slightest doubt in your mind about the reason for the use of a comma, don't fail to look in the margin. If necessary, reread the full explanations that appear on page 138.

If commas parenthetical, apposition, and series have not yet "sunk in," don't worry; you will meet these uses of the comma again and again in every Reading and Writing Practice.

In Chapter 7 you will take up another use of the comma—with introductory words, phrases, and clauses. Before you begin your work on the Reading and Writing Practice in Lesson 37, read the full explanations given on pages 170 and 171 so that you will thoroughly understand when and why introductory commas are used.

To be sure that you are deriving the greatest benefit from the marginal reminders, let's review briefly the procedure you should follow.

1. Read the full explanation of the new marginal reminders on pages 170 and 171.
2. Each time you meet a comma in a circle, as you read the shorthand in the Reading and Writing Practice, glance in the margin for the reason for the use of the punctuation.
3. As you copy the Reading and Writing Practice, insert the commas in your notes, encircling them.
4. Spell aloud each spelling word in the marginal reminders.

The attention you give to the marginal reminders in your shorthand class will, of course, do much to improve your ability to spell and punctuate correctly. Your improvement, however, will be much more rapid if you pay equal attention to correct spelling and punctuation in *all* the writing you do—your compositions in English, your reports in social studies, your personal longhand or typewritten correspondence.

Remember, correct spelling and punctuation are marks of an educated person!

What's Ahead?

Chapter 7 is devoted entirely to new shorthand abbreviating devices that will enable you to write more rapidly and easily. In addition to a number of word beginnings and word endings that apply to large families of words, you will take up the abbreviating principle, which shows you how to handle long words that do not fall into any particular family group.

Only eight lessons left in which there are new shorthand devices!

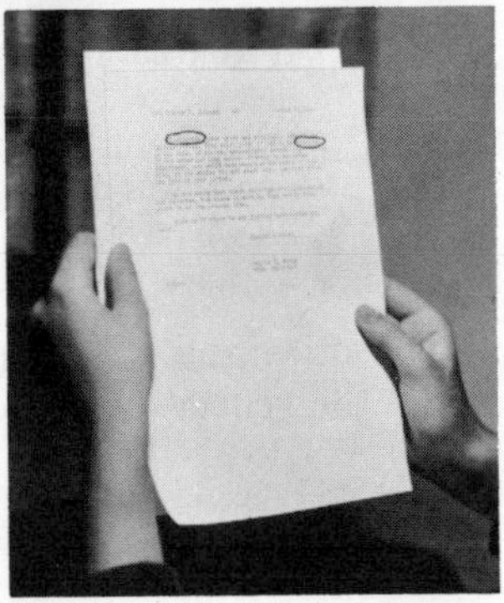

This businessman is not at all pleased with the letter his secretary has handed him. The reason? The spelling errors in it. By not verifying her spelling, the secretary will have to retype the letter, thus wasting her employer's time, her time, and the company's money.

LESSON 37

Commas — with Introductory Expressions

, *if* clause
, *when* clause
, *as* clause
, introductory

One of the most frequent errors made by the beginning transcriber is the failure to make a complete sentence. In most cases the incomplete sentence is a dependent or subordinate clause introduced by *if, when,* or *as*. The dependent or subordinate clause deceives the transcriber because it is a complete sentence, except that it is introduced by a word such as *if* and therefore requires another clause to complete the thought. If . . . *what?* When . . . *what?*

The dependent or subordinate clause signals its coming with a relative pronoun or a subordinate conjunction. The relative pronouns are *that, who, what, which, whoever, whatever, whichever.* The commonest subordinating conjunctions are *if, though, although, whether, unless, as, because, when, since, while, where, after, wherever, until, before, how, however.*

In this text each *if* clause, *when* clause, and *as* clause that precedes the main clause has been marked as such in the margin because these are by far the three commonest subordinating conjunctions found in business correspondence.

> If you have any suggestions, please submit them to me.
> When your letter arrived some days afterward, your stencil was no longer in our files.
> As we have not heard from you, we feel that perhaps we have not explained our plan adequately.

The other and less frequent dependent clauses have been grouped under the general marginal reminder ", introductory."

The principle covering the group of introductory dependent clauses, however, is that a comma is used to separate a subordinate clause from a *following* main clause. If the main clause comes first, no comma is required. A comma was placed in the preceding sentence after the subordinate clause (*if the main clause comes first*) because that clause came before the main clause. No comma would be required if the position of the two clauses were reversed so that the sentence would read: *No comma is required if the main clause comes first.*

Thus, the comma is required when the subordinate clause introduces the main clause. Similarly, a comma is required after other introductory or explanatory expressions such as *on the contrary, in brief, for instance.*

> Supplementing the annual report, I have occasionally written to the members of our company.
> For your convenience in returning this form, we are enclosing a prepaid envelope.

The second example just given shows the use of the comma after the introductory or explanatory expression *for your convenience in returning this form.* When a similar expression is used at the end of the sentence, no comma is required.

> A self-addressed envelope is enclosed for your convenience in returning this form.

You will find it safe to use a comma after any introductory or explanatory expression or after any element of a sentence used at the beginning of the sentence out of its natural word order. The writer whose judgment has been formed by constant practice will often prefer to omit the comma after a short introductory expression that seems to flow into the rest of the sentence without a break.

The constant observation of good models is the best and surest way to become proficient in punctuation.

339. Word Beginnings Con-, Com-. The word beginnings *con-* and *com-* are represented by *k* before a consonant other than *r* or *l*.

Con-

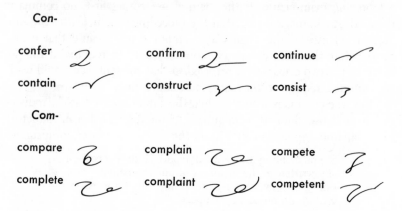

confer 	confirm 	continue 
contain 	construct 	consist 

Com-

compare 	complain 	compete 
complete 	complaint 	competent 

340. Con-, Com- Followed by Vowel or R or L. When *con-, com-* are followed by a vowel or *r* or *l*, these word beginnings are represented by *kn* or *km*.

connect 	committee 	Conrad 
connection 	commerce 	comrade 

341. Word Beginnings En-, In-, Un-. The word beginnings *en-, in-, un-* are represented by *n* before a consonant.

En-

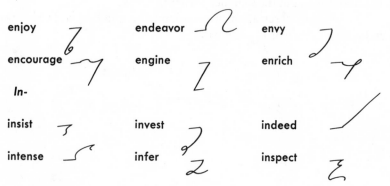

enjoy 	endeavor 	envy 
encourage 	engine 	enrich 

In-

insist 	invest 	indeed 
intense 	infer 	inspect 

Un-

unfair  **unwritten**  **unlucky** 

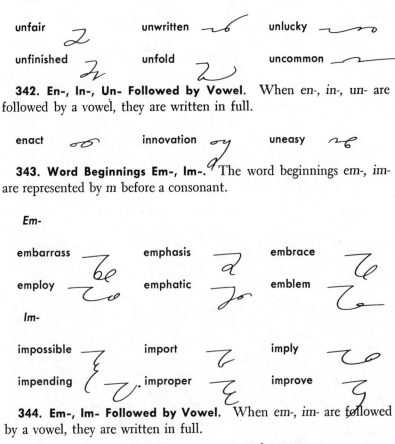

unfinished  **unfold**  **uncommon** 

342. En-, In-, Un- Followed by Vowel. When *en-*, *in-*, *un-* are followed by a vowel, they are written in full.

enact  **innovation** 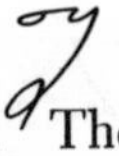 **uneasy** 

343. Word Beginnings Em-, Im-. The word beginnings *em-*, *im-* are represented by *m* before a consonant.

Em-

embarrass  **emphasis**  **embrace** 

employ  **emphatic**  **emblem** 

Im-

impossible 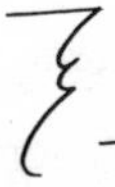 **import**  **imply** 

impending  **improper** 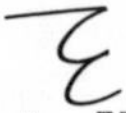 **improve** 

344. Em-, Im- Followed by Vowel. When *em-*, *im-* are followed by a vowel, they are written in full.

emotion  **immodest**  **imitate** 

Reading and Writing Practice

345. Applied Vocabulary Study. *Endeavors*, tries. *Inviting claims*, tempting claims. *Constructive*, helpful. *Ensuing year*, following year, the year ahead. *Contemplating*, considering, planning.

346.

, as clause
accomplishes
constructive

basis
competitor's

, introductory
impressively

, introductory
ensuing

, parenthetical
emphasize

(174)

347.

, as clause
commercial
operating

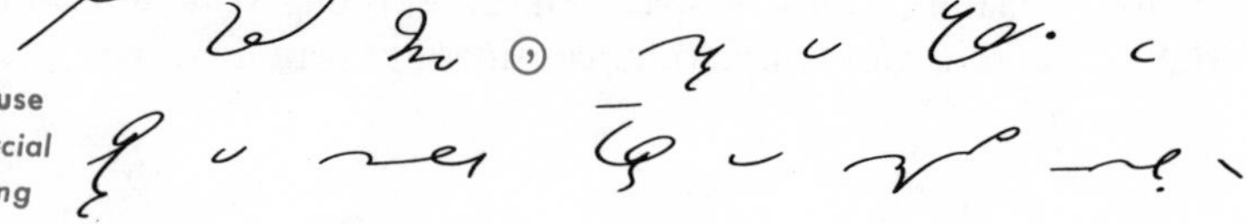

, when clause
unnecessary

, parenthetical

effect
, apposition

desirable
, introductory

(118)

348.

excellent
, introductory

, when clause
trial

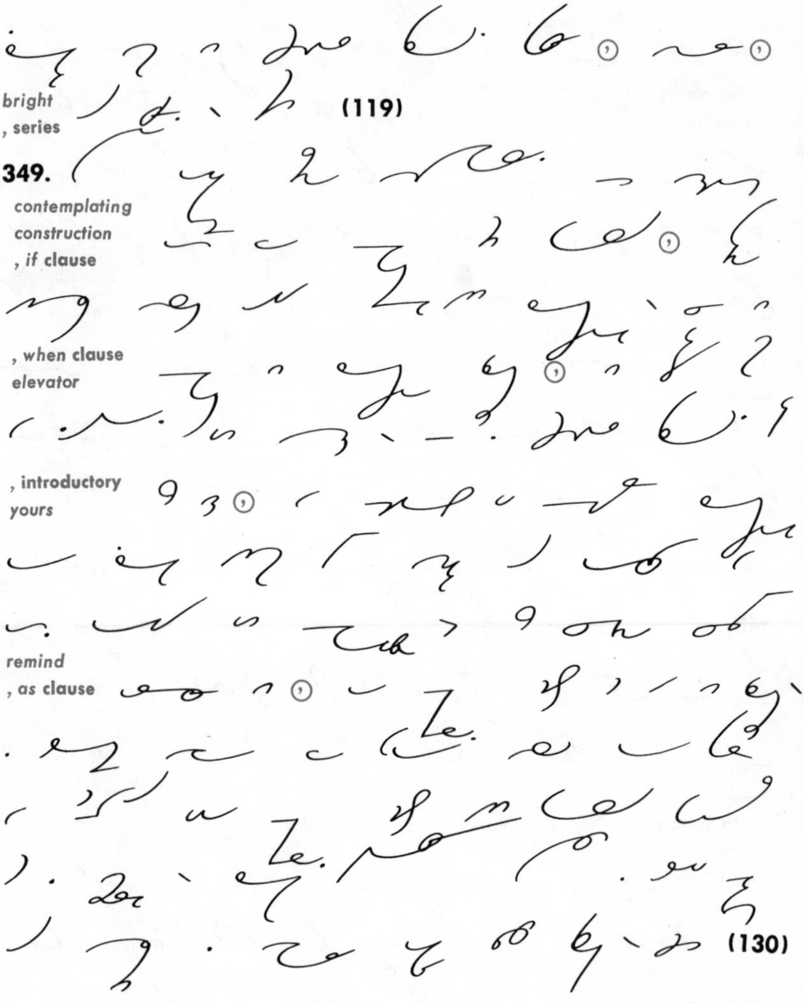

bright
, series

(119)

349.

contemplating
construction
, if clause
, when clause
elevator
, introductory
yours
remind
, as clause

(130)

LESSON 38

350. Word Beginnings For-, Fore-. The word beginnings *for-*, *fore-* are represented by *f*. The *f* is joined with an angle to *r* or *l* to indicate that it represents a word beginning. The *f* is disjoined if the following character is a vowel.

forget  force  forerunner 

forgive  enforce  forlorn 

form  effort  forever 

conform  fortune  forearm 

351. Word Beginning Fur-. The word beginning *fur-* is also represented by *f*.

furnace  furnish  further 

furniture  furnished  furlough 

352. Word Beginning Al-. The word beginning *al-* is represented by *o*.

also  alternate  almost 

although  alternative 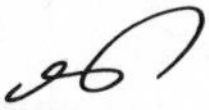 already 

353. Word Beginning Sub-. The word beginning *sub-* is represented by *s*.

submit  subdue  suburb 

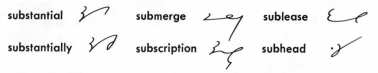

substantial	submerge	sublease
substantially	subscription	subhead

354. Ul. *Ul* is represented by the oo hook before a forward or upward stroke.

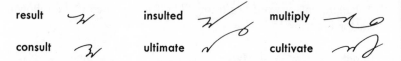

result	insulted	multiply
consult	ultimate	cultivate

355. Word Ending -hood. The word ending *-hood* is represented by a disjoined *d*.

boyhood	manhood	childhood
neighborhood	womanhood	girlhood

356. Word Ending -ward. The word ending *-ward* is also represented by a disjoined *d*.

homeward	afterward	forward
onward	upward	reward

357. Compound Word Beginnings. Compound word beginnings are joined naturally in the order in which they occur.

uncontested	undisputed	indispensable
uninterrupted	unemployed	misinterpret

Reading and Writing Practice

358. Applied Vocabulary Study. *Suburbs,* residential districts, usually on the outskirts of a city. *Impartial,* not favoring one side more than another. *Awkward,* embarrassing. *Ultimate,* eventual, final.

359.

, introductory
subscription

, as clause
suburbs

(120)

360.

awkward
, apposition

, introductory
searching
already

canceled
stencil

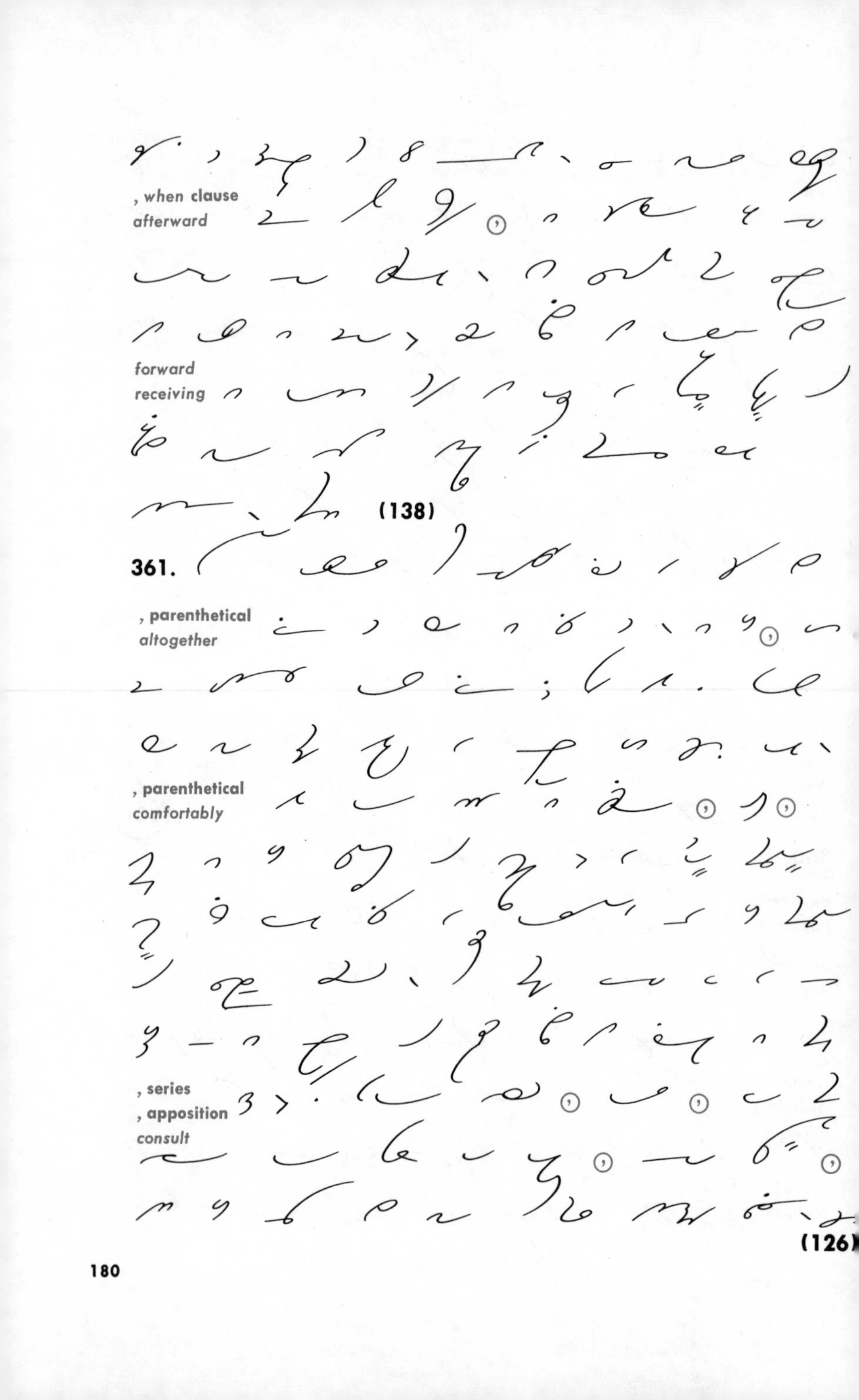

, when clause
afterward

forward
receiving

(138)

361.

, parenthetical
altogether

, parenthetical
comfortably

, series
, apposition
consult

(126)

362.

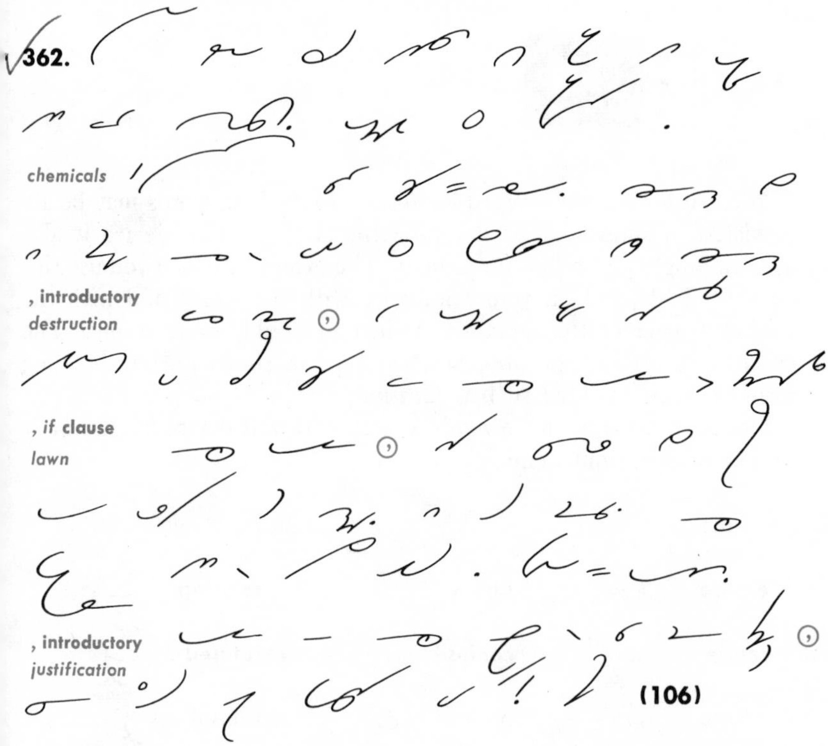
chemicals
, introductory
destruction
, if clause
lawn
, introductory
justification

(106)

Pretranscription Check List

Are you getting the full benefit from the spelling and punctuation reminders in the Reading and Writing Practice by

1. Encircling all punctuation in your notes as you copy each Reading and Writing Practice?
2. Looking in the margin of the shorthand to be sure that you understand the reason for the use of each punctuation mark?
3. Spelling aloud at least once the spelling words in the margin?

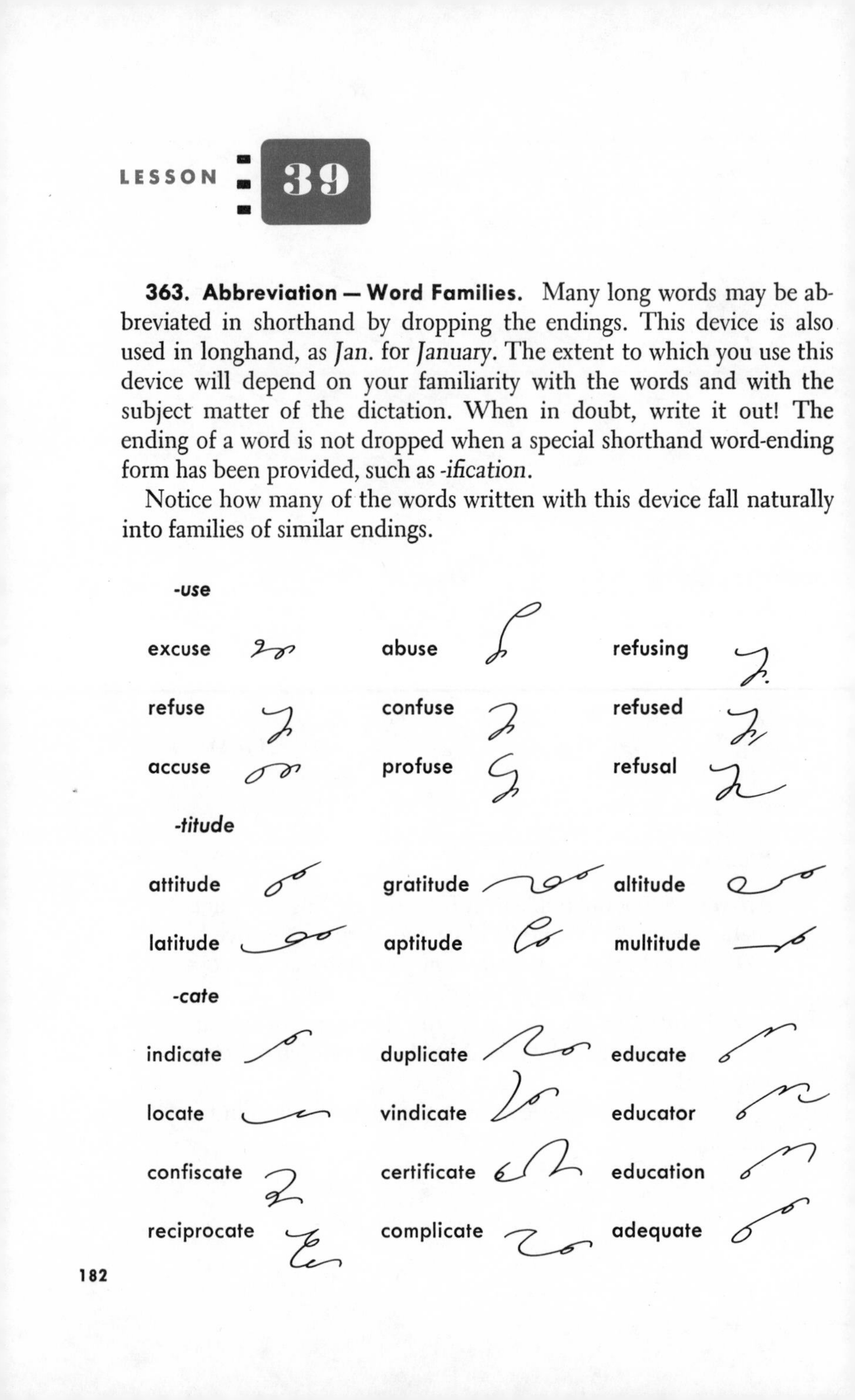

LESSON 39

363. Abbreviation — Word Families. Many long words may be abbreviated in shorthand by dropping the endings. This device is also used in longhand, as *Jan.* for *January*. The extent to which you use this device will depend on your familiarity with the words and with the subject matter of the dictation. When in doubt, write it out! The ending of a word is not dropped when a special shorthand word-ending form has been provided, such as *-ification*.

Notice how many of the words written with this device fall naturally into families of similar endings.

-use

excuse	abuse	refusing
refuse	confuse	refused
accuse	profuse	refusal

-titude

attitude	gratitude	altitude
latitude	aptitude	multitude

-cate

indicate	duplicate	educate
locate	vindicate	educator
confiscate	certificate	education
reciprocate	complicate	adequate

-gate

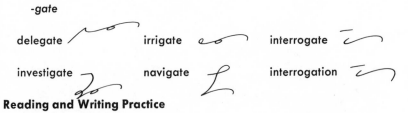

delegate  irrigate  interrogate 

investigate  navigate  interrogation 

Reading and Writing Practice

364. Applied Vocabulary Study. *Adequate,* sufficient, enough. *Reciprocate,* to return a favor or kindness. *Potential,* possible. *Aptitude tests,* tests designed to find out what special ability a person may have. *Aggregating,* adding up to, totaling.

365.

gratitude
adequate

, as clause
various

reciprocate
, if clause

(119)

366.

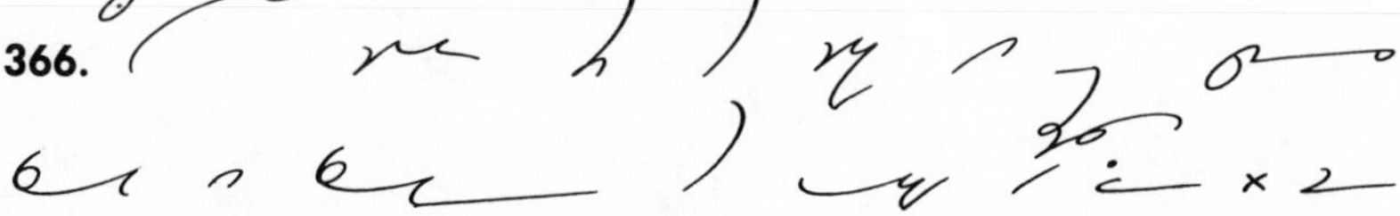

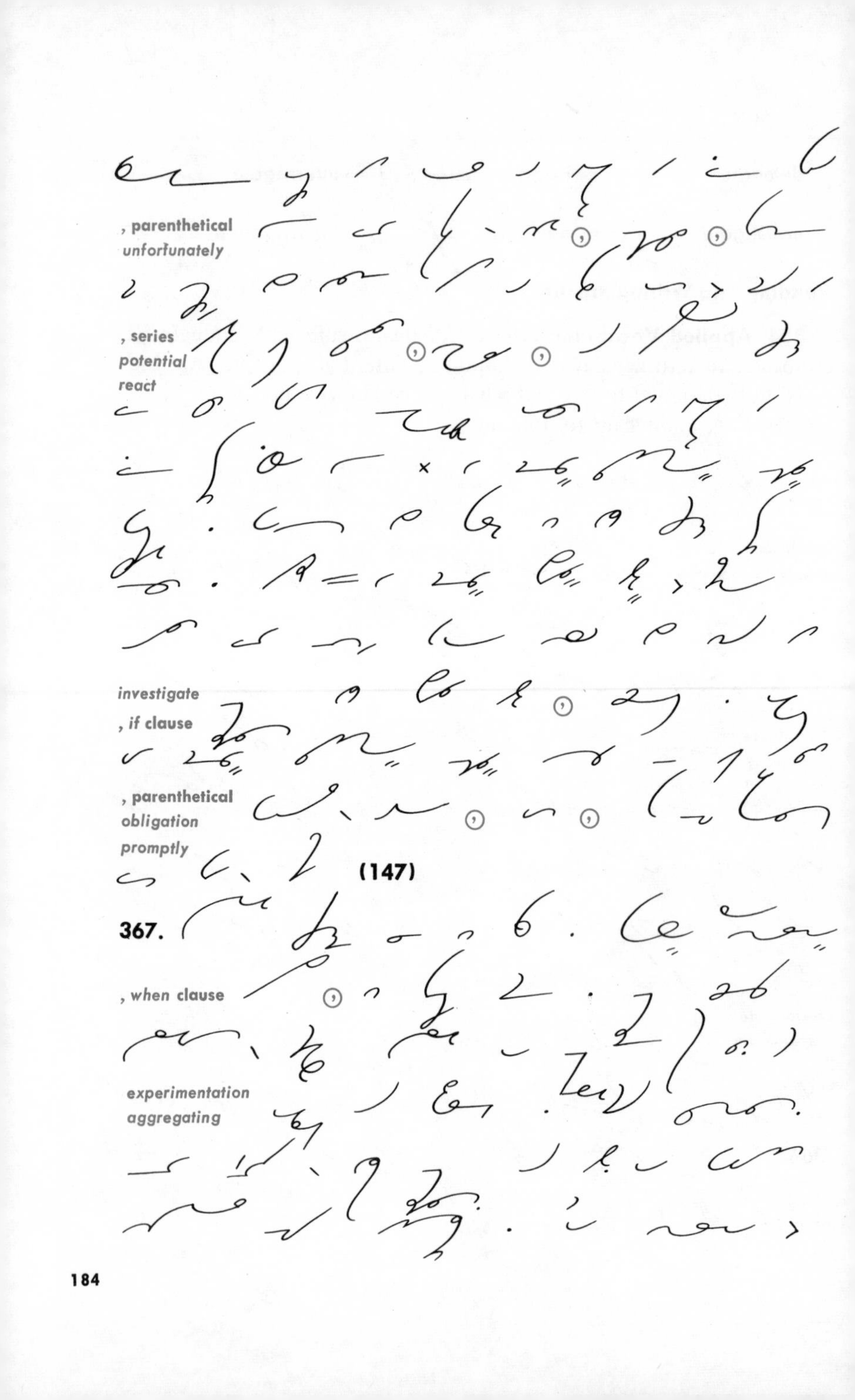

, parenthetical
unfortunately

, series
potential
react

investigate
, if clause

, parenthetical
obligation
promptly

(147)

367.

, when clause

experimentation
aggregating

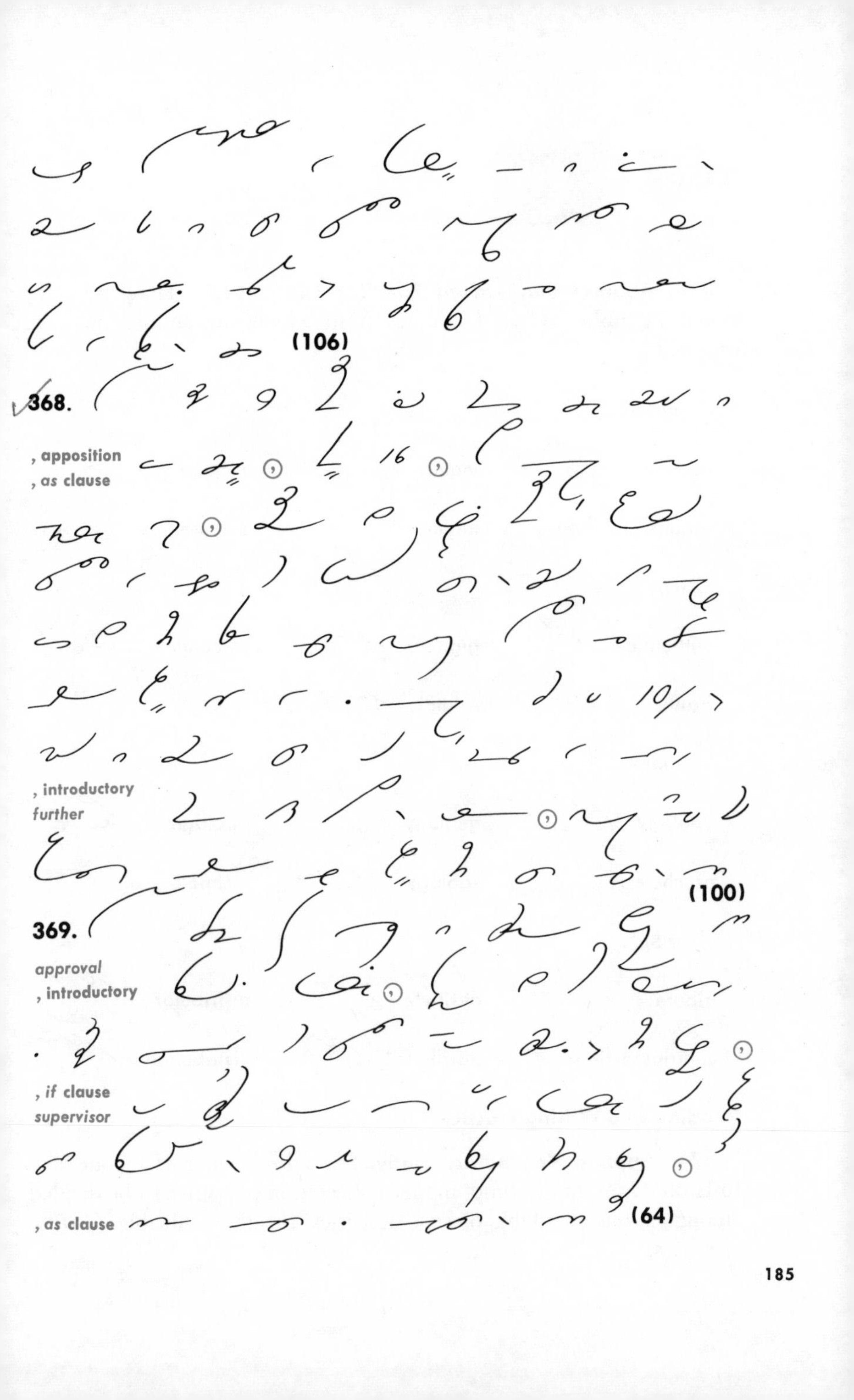

(106)

368.

, apposition
, as clause

, introductory
further

(100)

369.

approval
, introductory

, if clause
supervisor

, as clause

(64)

LESSON 40

370. Abbreviation — Word Families (Continued). Here are additional examples of word families from which the endings may be dropped.

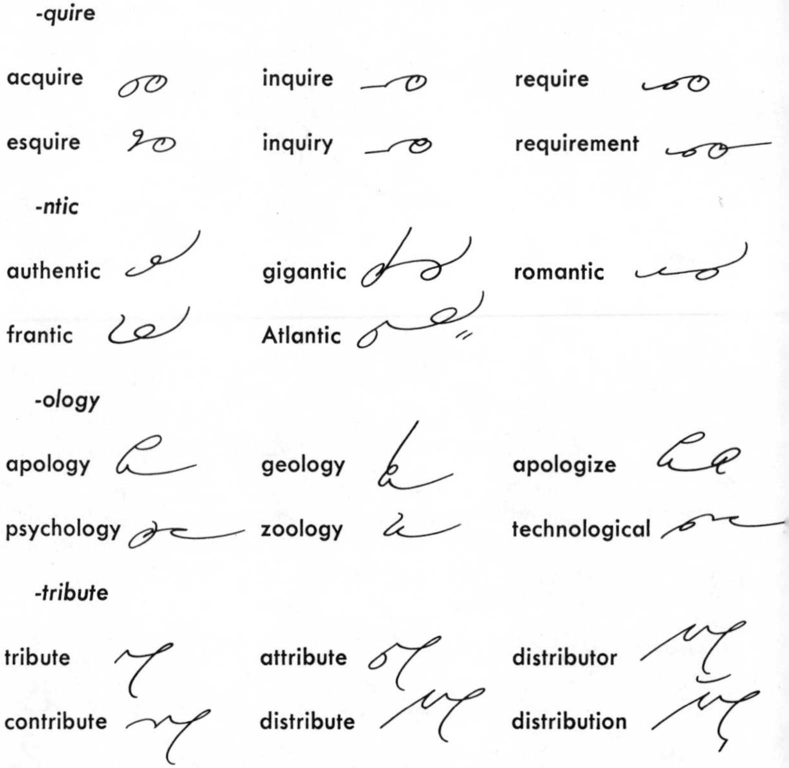

-quire

acquire, inquire, require, esquire, inquiry, requirement

-ntic

authentic, gigantic, romantic, frantic, Atlantic

-ology

apology, geology, apologize, psychology, zoology, technological

-tribute

tribute, attribute, distributor, contribute, distribute, distribution

Reading and Writing Practice

371. Applied Vocabulary Study. *Specialize,* concentrate one's efforts on. *Community fund,* money collected in one drive to be divided among various charitable or civic activities. *Precious,* valuable. *Clarity,* clearness.

372.

psychology
Association

, as clause

, if clause
specialize
described

, apposition
promptly

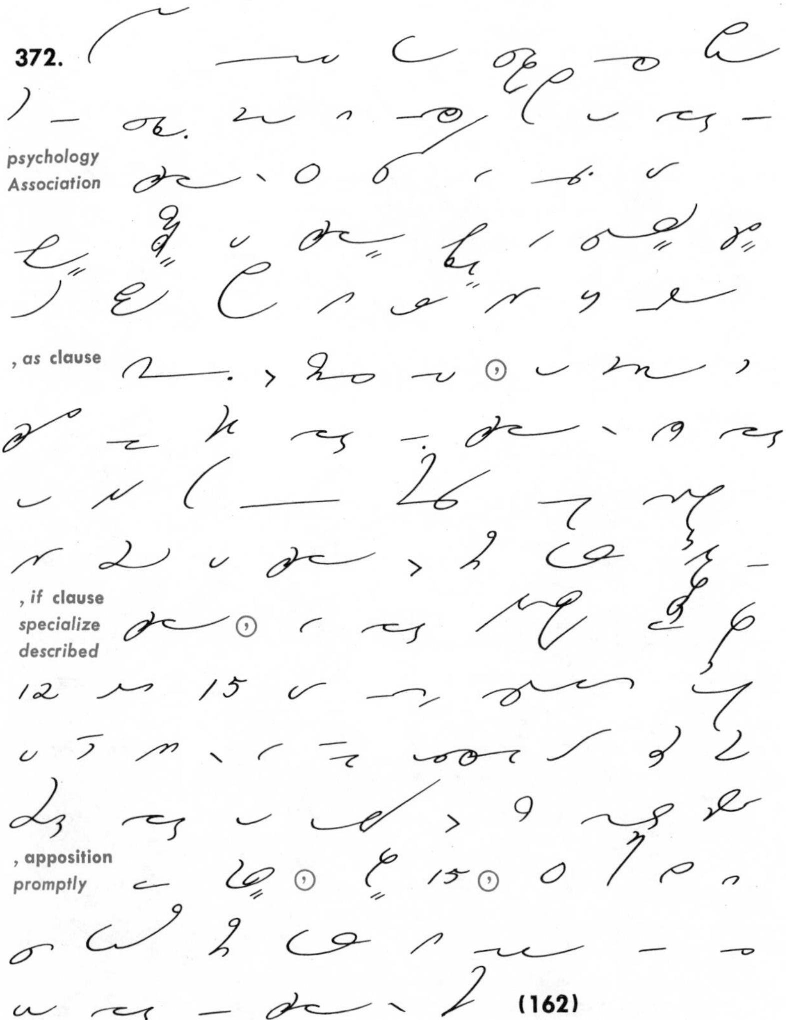

(162)

373.

acquire
, series

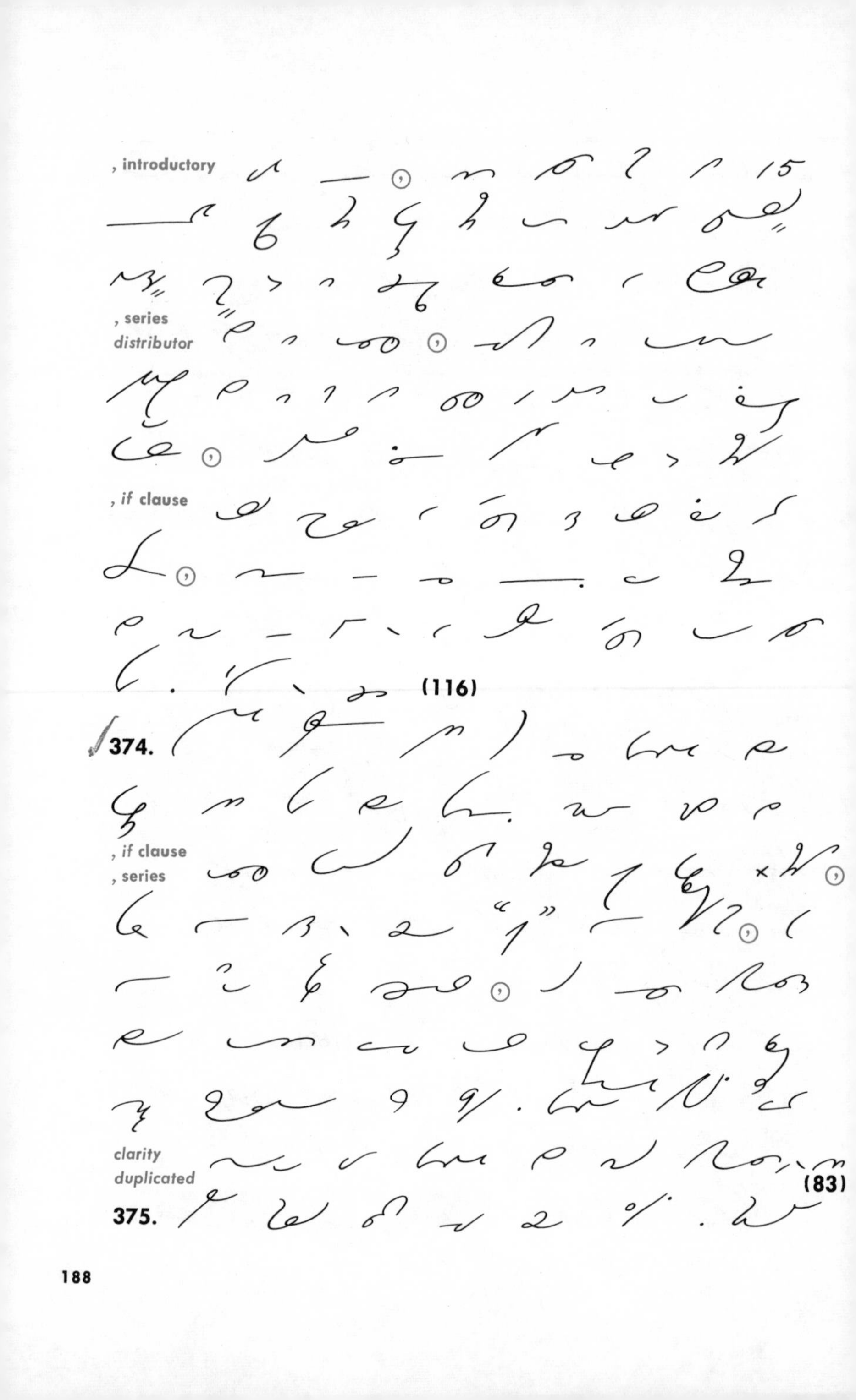

, introductory

, series
distributor

, if clause

(116)

374.

, if clause
, series

clarity
duplicated

(83)

375.

community
requirements
, as clause

, when clause
penny
ultimately

inquiries
communicate
, if clause

6-3470 (107)

376.

describing
mechanical

, if clause
postal card

(115)

LESSON 41

377. Abbreviation — Words Not in Families. Some words may be written without the ending, although they do not belong in groups of similar endings.

reluctant, reluctance | significant, significance | convenient, convenience
privilege | preliminary | alphabet
anniversary | arithmetic | atmosphere

378. Omission of Vowel Preceding -tion. When *t, d, n,* or *m* is followed by *-ition, -ation,* the circle is omitted.

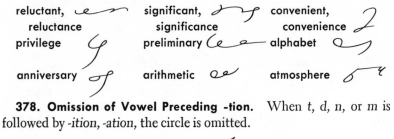

station | addition | transmission
importation | foundation | termination
quotation | permission | explanation

Reading and Writing Practice

379. Applied Vocabulary Study. *Significant,* important, full of meaning. *Motor vehicles,* automobiles, trucks, etc. *Reluctant,* unwilling.

380.

aware
, as clause

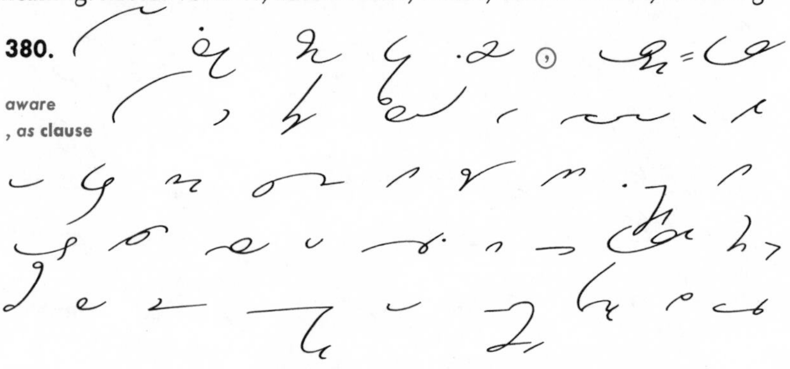

, introductory
convenient

Club's
significant
, introductory

Vehicles
permission

, parenthetical

(148)

381.

, as clause
, apposition
traffic

, introductory
reluctant
admission

, introductory
recommendations

, if clause

382. **(134)**

, as clause
patient

won't
, parenthetical
, introductory

, when clause
receive

(133)

383.
gratified
, parenthetical

, parenthetical **(66)**

LESSON 42 Recall

In Lesson 42 your task will be an easy one; you will have no new shorthand devices to learn. The Accuracy Practice will help you improve your writing of the diphthongs and the *nt*, *mt* blends. The Recall Chart will test your knowledge of the word beginnings and endings.

Be sure to pay close attention to the Reading and Writing Practice; it contains suggestions that will be of value to you in your social as well as in your business life.

Accuracy Practice

384. **My** **Lie** **Fight**

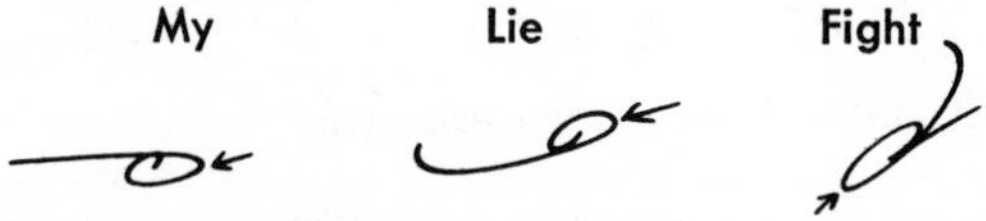

To write these combinations accurately:

a. Join the circle in the same way that you would join an *a* circle, but turn the end inside the circle.

b. Before turning the end of the circle inside, be sure that the stroke touches the stroke to which the *i* is joined.

c. Avoid making a point at the places indicated by arrows.

Practice Drill

My, night, sight, line, mile.

385. **Ow** **Oi**

To write these combinations accurately:

a. Keep the hooks deep and narrow.

b. Place the circles outside the hooks as indicated by the dotted lines.

Practice Drill

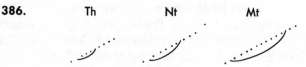

How-out, now, doubt, scout, toy, soil, annoy.

386. **Th** **Nt** **Mt**

To write these combinations accurately:

a. Slant the strokes as indicated by the dotted lines.
b. Start the *th*, *nt*, and *mt* to the right and upward.

Practice Drill

There are, and will, empty, health, lined, ashamed.

Compare:

Hint, heard; tamed, detailed.

387. Recall Chart. This chart contains a complete recall of all the disjoined word beginnings and disjoined word endings that you have studied thus far. There are 102 words.

Do you think you can read the entire chart in 6 minutes?

Disjoined Word Beginnings and Endings

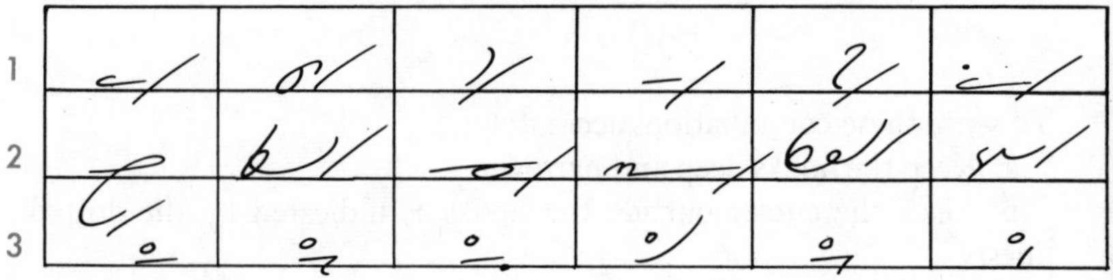

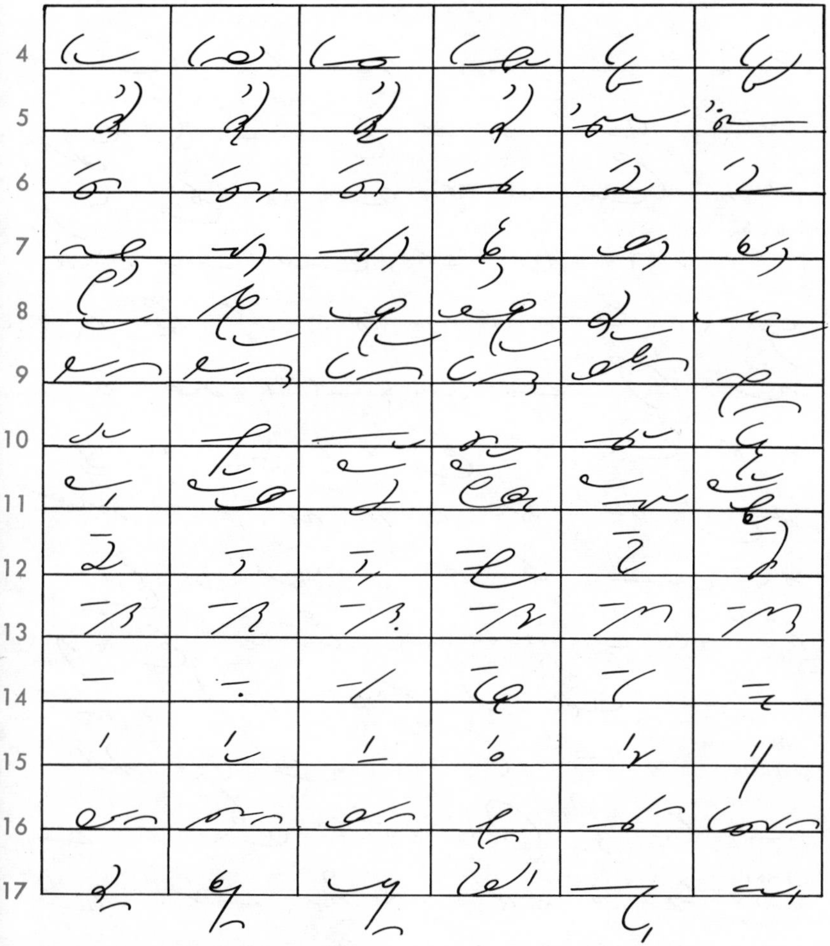

Reading and Writing Practice

388. Applied Vocabulary Study. *Possess,* have, own. *Indication,* sign. *Come in contact,* meet or work with. *Productive worker,* one who turns out a great deal of work.

√ **389. Do You Get Along with People?**

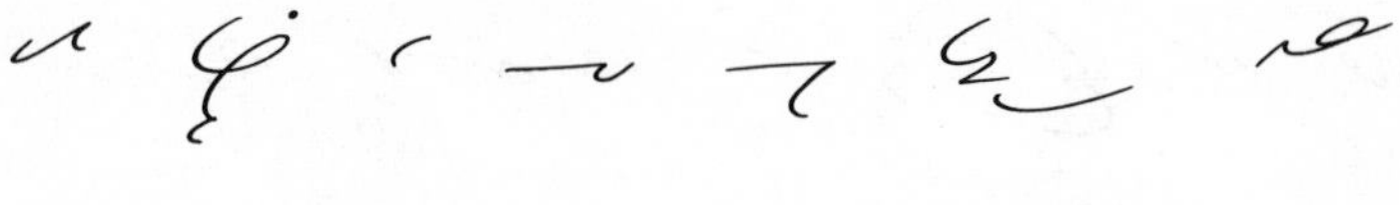

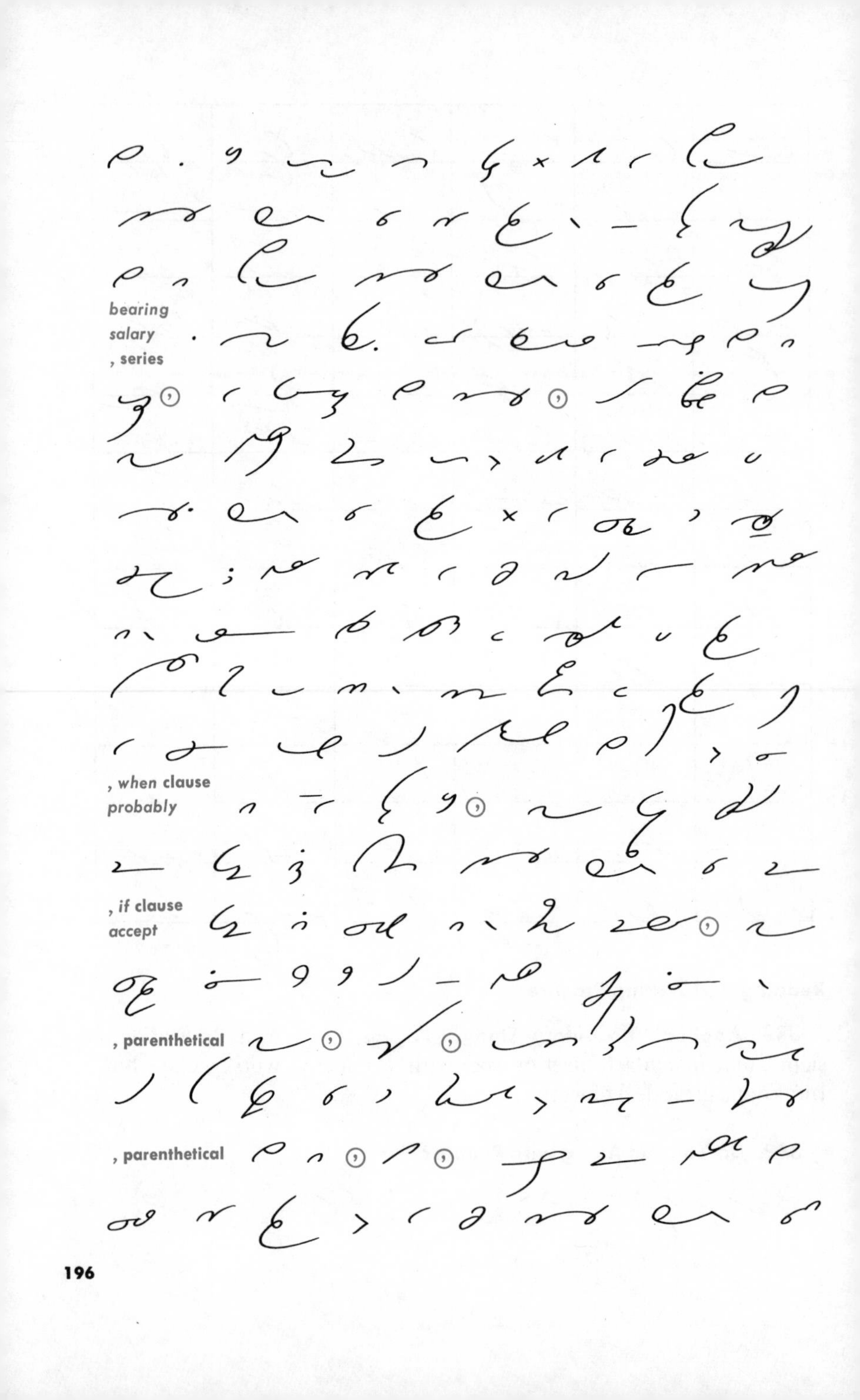

bearing
salary
, series

, *when* clause
probably

, *if* clause
accept

, parenthetical

, parenthetical

, series
family

associates
, if clause

, if clause
nerves

, when clause
pleasant

, as clause
productive
, when clause

(363)

CHAPTER 8

Pretranscription Quiz

In Chapter 8 you will take up the last use of the comma with which you will deal in this *Manual*—a comma used between independent clauses connected by a conjunction. You will also give special attention to hyphenated words.

Beginning with Lesson 43, you will have an opportunity to see how well you have mastered the seven uses of the comma that you studied in Chapters 6 and 7. From this point on, the last letter in each lesson (except Lesson 48, which contains article material) will be a pretranscription quiz letter. The letter will contain several illustrations of the uses of the comma that you have studied. These commas, however, will not be indicated in the printed shorthand. It will be your job, as you copy the letter in shorthand in your notebook, to insert the commas in the proper places and to give the reasons why the commas were used. To save time, you may abbreviate the reasons—*par* for *parenthetical, ap* for *apposition*, etc. The shorthand in your notebook should resemble the following example:

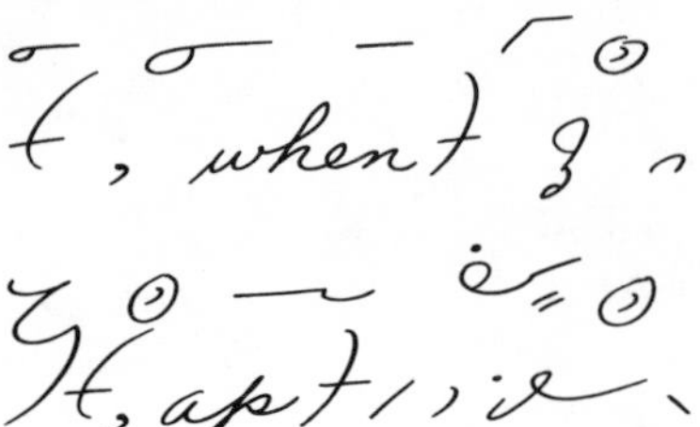
when
ap

Another feature of the pretranscription quiz that will be a challenge to you is the omission of an occasional word from the printed shorthand, a word that you will have to supply as you copy the letter in your shorthand notebook. Occasionally, a stenographer will

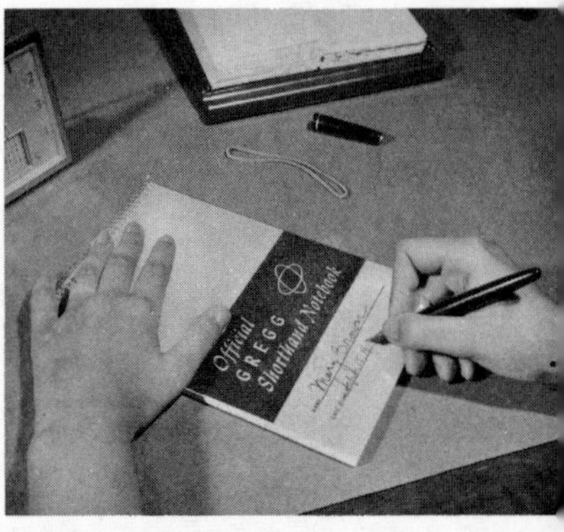
Official GREGG Shorthand Notebook

omit a word when he is taking dictation, either through oversight or because he did not hear it. Then, with the help of the meaning of the sentence, he will supply the missing word in transcribing.

Each pretranscription quiz will give you practice in handling this dictation and transcription problem. You will have no difficulty in supplying the missing word, as in each case only one possible word makes sense.

Caution: Please do not make any marks in your shorthand textbook. If you do, you will destroy the value of these pretranscription quizzes to anyone else who may use the book.

What's Ahead?

In the pretranscription quiz you will encounter a situation in which you will supply words missing from the shorthand. In the phrases in Lesson 43 you will deal with another omission – words omitted in phrases. This time, however, the words will have been omitted purposely!

In Chapter 8 you will find two groups of brief forms, four word beginnings and endings, in addition to shorthand devices to represent compound words, numbers, and special shorthand combinations.

By the way, wouldn't this be a good time to review all the brief forms you have studied thus far? Why not spend a few minutes on the chart of brief forms on pages 315 and 316?

The careful secretary or stenographer handles her notebook systematically by:

1. Indicating on the cover the first and last day that the notebook has been used.

2. Keeping a rubber band around the used portion of her book so that she will lose no time finding a blank sheet on which to write.

3. Drawing a line through all shorthand notes that have already been transcribed.

LESSON 43

Comma Separating Independent Clauses

, conjunction

A comma is used to separate two independent clauses that are joined by one of the conjunctions *and, but, or, for, neither, nor.*

> We have to meet all our bills, but we cannot do so until we collect all those due us from our customers.

The first independent or principal or main clause is

> We have to meet all our bills

because that clause could stand as a separate sentence. The second independent clause, which could stand as a separate sentence, is

> we cannot do so until we collect all those due us from our customers

These clauses could be written as two separate sentences with a period after each sentence. Because the thought of the two sentences is closely related, it seemed better to the writer of the letter to put them into one sentence. Because the two independent clauses are connected by the co-ordinating conjunction *but,* a comma is used between them.

Hyphenated before noun

No noun, no hyphen

Stenographers are often puzzled about the use of the hyphen in such expressions as *up to date, well planned, worth while,* and other similar expressions. The answer is quite simple. If a noun follows the expressions, the hyphen is inserted; if no noun follows the expression, no hyphen is used.

> The book is up to date. (No noun after the expression.)
> The up-to-date book. . . . (Noun follows the expression.)

390. Omission of Words in Phrases. It is often possible to omit one or more unimportant words in a shorthand phrase. In the phrase *one of the,* for example, the word *of* is omitted; and we write *one the.* When transcribing, the stenographer will insert the word *of,* as the phrase would make no sense without that word.

one of the		more or less	
one of our		in the world	
one of them		I should like to have	
some of them		will you please	
more and more		one of the most	
at a loss		one of the best	

391. *Understand, Understood.* When a short, common word or phrase comes before *understand* or *understood,* the *under* is omitted and the *stand* or *stood* is written under the short word or phrase.

I understand		I understood	
we understand		it is understood	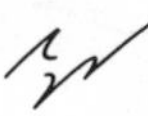
please understand		clearly understood	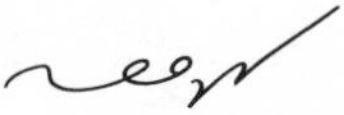
easily understand		thoroughly understood	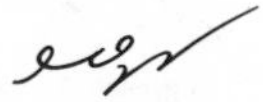

392. *Misunderstand, Misunderstood.* When *mis-* comes before *understand* or *understood,* the *under* is omitted and the *stand* or *stood* is written under the *mis-.*

misunderstand		misunderstanding	
misunderstands		misunderstood	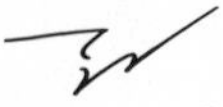

Reading and Writing Practice

393. Applied Vocabulary Study. *Misunderstood,* understood incorrectly. *Nicely groomed,* tidy. *Posthaste,* very fast, rapidly. *Stamp of approval,* a mark of approval or authorization; an O.K.

394.

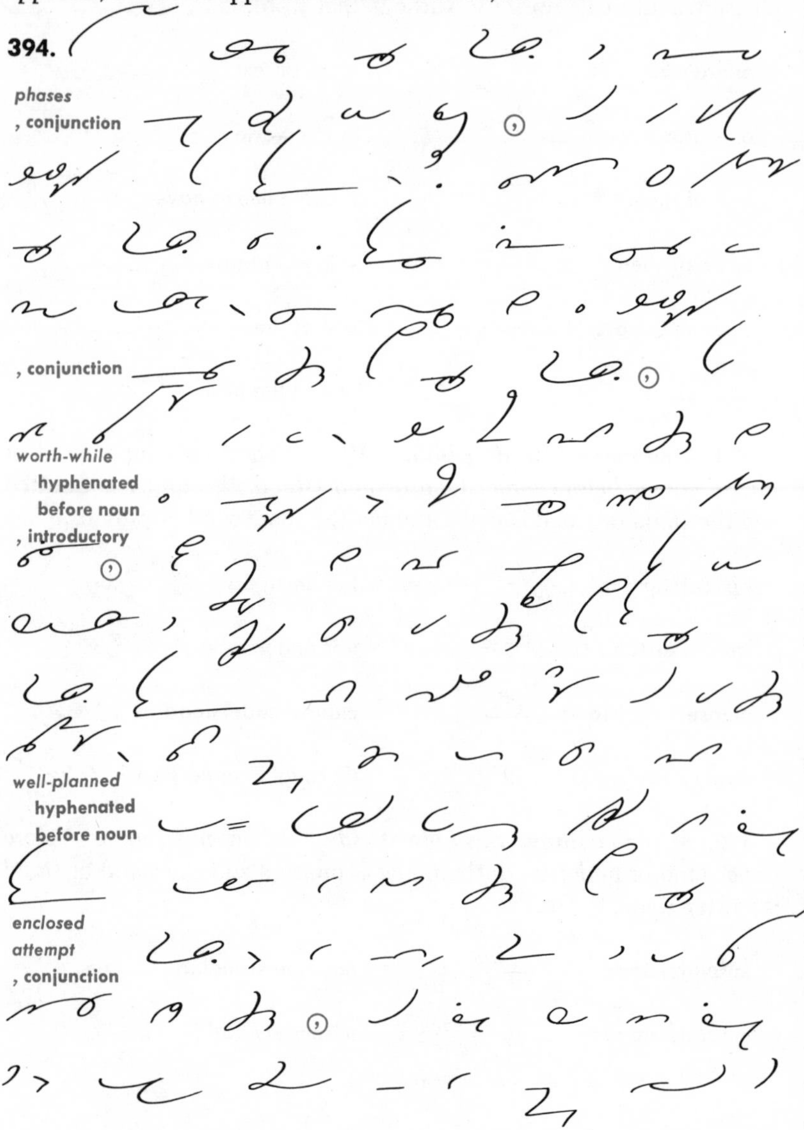
phases
, conjunction
, conjunction
worth-while hyphenated before noun
, introductory
well-planned hyphenated before noun
enclosed
attempt
, conjunction

, parenthetical

, introductory
necessary

(207)

395.

well-paying
hyphenated before noun

automatically
attitudes

qualifications
, *if clause*

, apposition

(123)

396.

already
, conjunction
, as clause
whether
, conjunction
, conjunction
transmitted
well-known
hyphenated
before noun

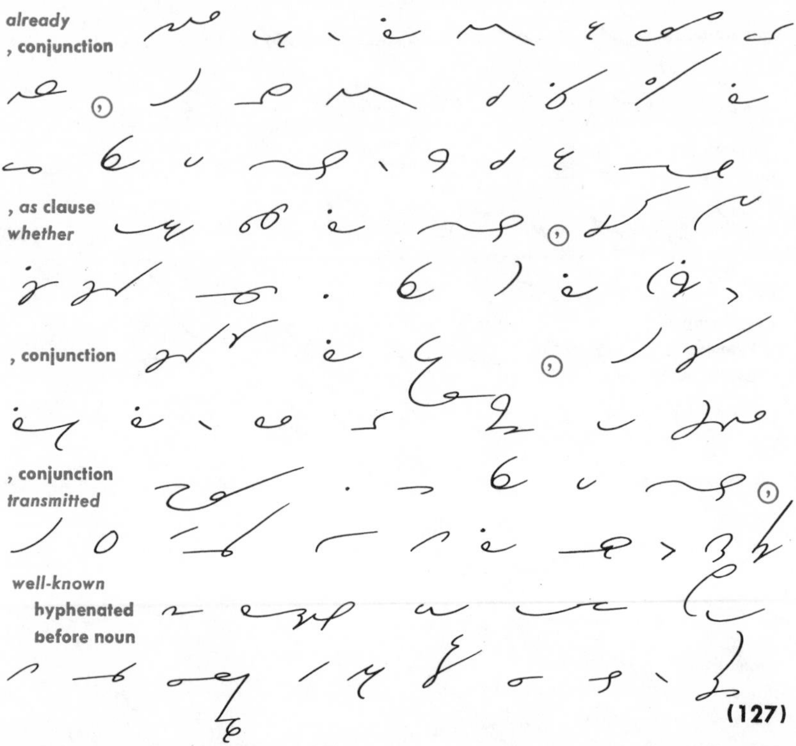

(127)

Pretranscription Quiz. The correct punctuation of the following letter calls for 5 commas – 1 comma *as* clause, 1 comma *if* clause, 2 commas parenthetical, and 1 comma *when* clause. As you copy the letter in your notebook, insert the necessary commas at the proper points and indicate the reason for the punctuation.

In addition, 2 words have been omitted from the shorthand. As you copy the letter, insert the correct words in your notes.

Remember, place no marks in your textbook.

397.

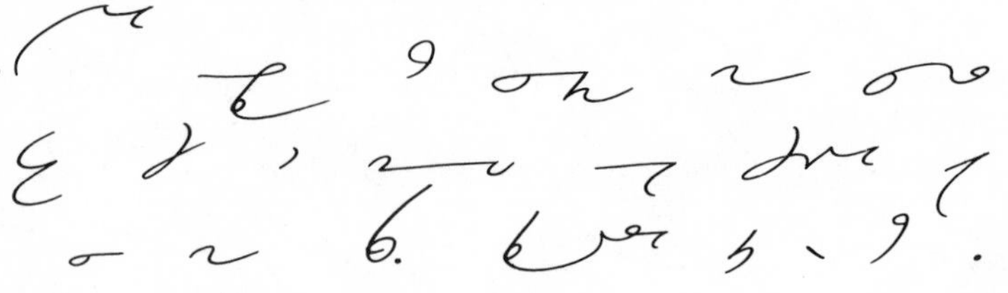

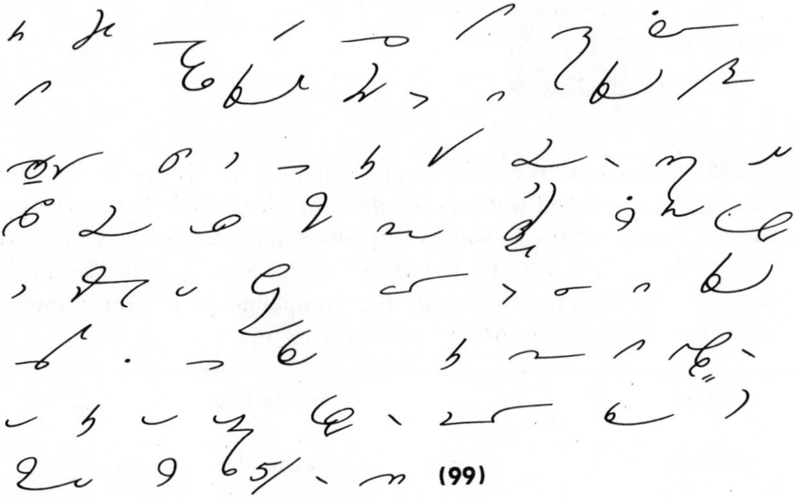

(99)

Spelling and Punctuation Check List

Are you careful to punctuate and spell correctly when

1. You write your compositions in English?
2. Prepare your reports for your social studies classes?
3. Correspond with friends to whom you must write in longhand?

In short, are you making correct spelling and punctuation a habit in all the longhand writing or typing that you do?

LESSON 44

398. Compound Words. Most compound words are formed by joining the shorthand outlines for the individual words that make up the compound words. In some compounds, however, it is desirable to modify the outline in order to obtain a better joining, as in the words *anyhow* and *however*. Many of the compound words form useful phrases by the addition of *else*, as shown below.

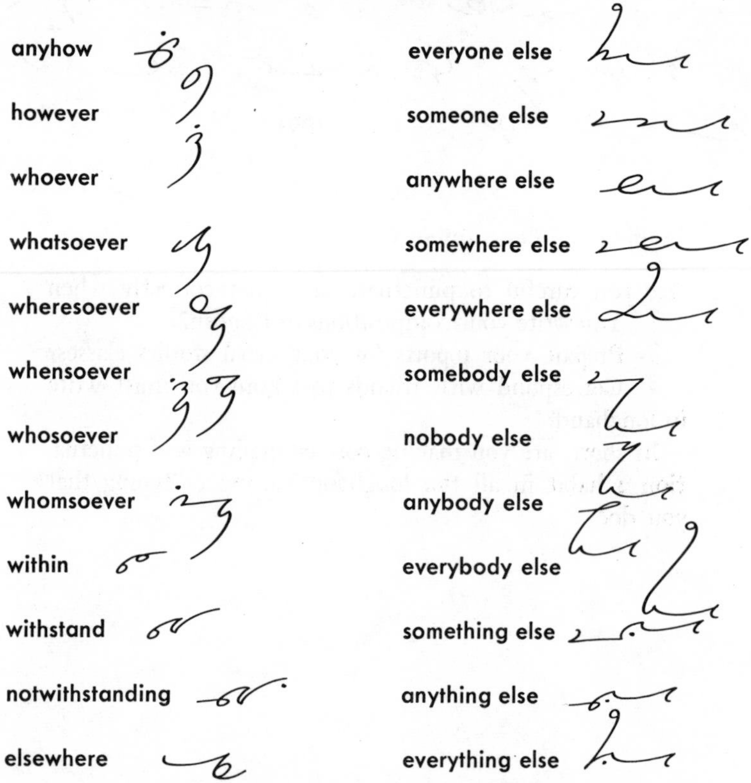
anyhow
however
whoever
whatsoever
wheresoever
whensoever
whosoever
whomsoever
within
withstand
notwithstanding
elsewhere
everyone else
someone else
anywhere else
somewhere else
everywhere else
somebody else
nobody else
anybody else
everybody else
something else
anything else
everything else

Did you notice that the dot is inserted in *anyhow* in order to distinguish it from *now*?

Reading and Writing Practice

399. Applied Vocabulary Study. *Relaxation,* recreation, rest. *Seasonal job,* a job that lasts only for some special season, such as the harvest season on the farm or the Christmas selling season in the city. *Liberal,* generous. *Expire,* to end. *Seldom,* not very often.

400.

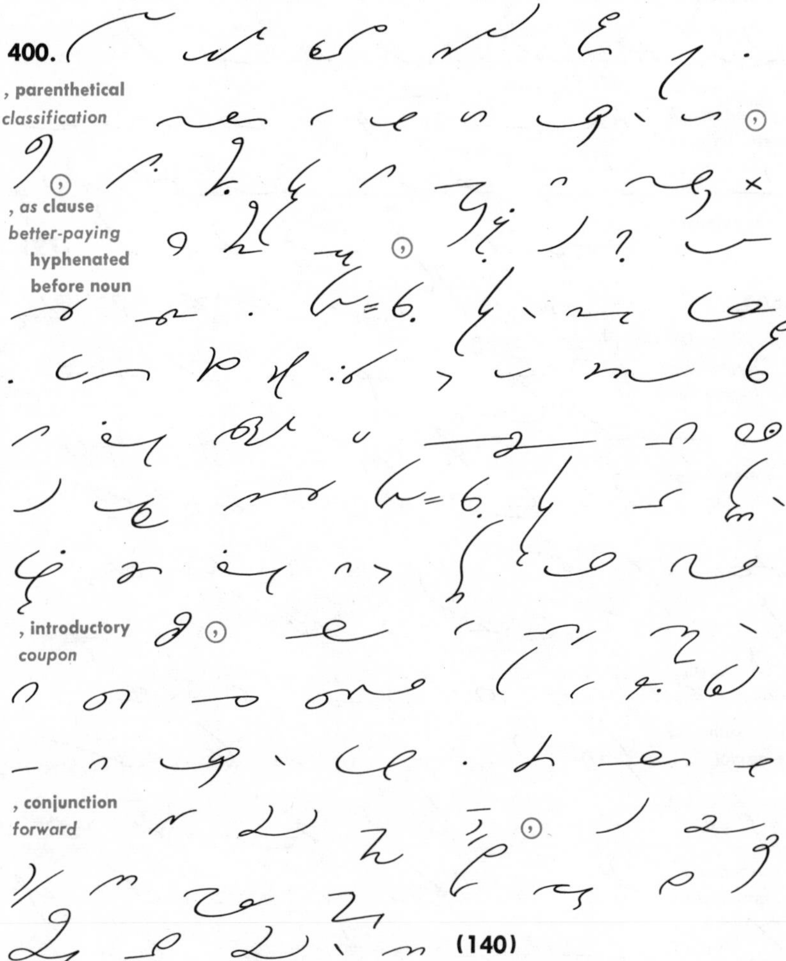

, parenthetical
classification
, as clause
better-paying hyphenated before noun
, introductory
coupon
, conjunction
forward

(140)

401.

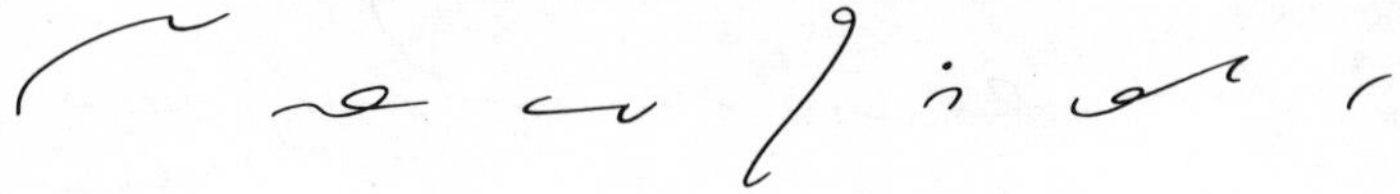

Somehow
, introductory
, parenthetical
enclosing
, when clause
(79)

402.

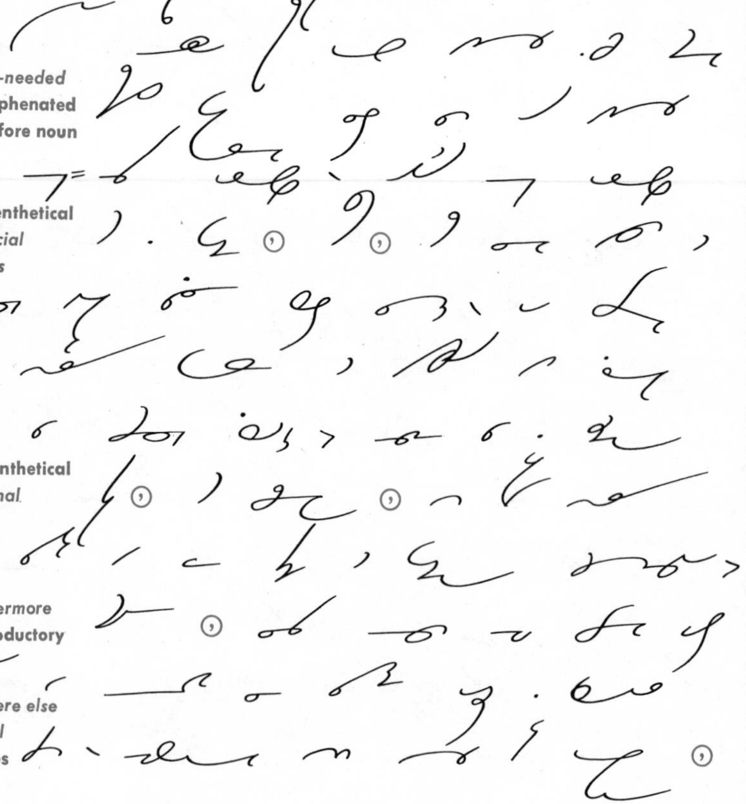

much-needed
hyphenated
before noun
, parenthetical
financial
bank's
, parenthetical
seasonal
Furthermore
, introductory
Nowhere else
liberal
, series

(132)

Pretranscription Quiz. In the following letter you must supply 10 commas – 1 comma as clause, 2 commas parenthetical, 3 commas apposition, 2 commas series, 1 comma *when* clause, and 1 comma introductory. You must also supply 2 words that have been omitted from the shorthand.

403. 

(120)

LESSON 45

404. Brief Forms

state		quantity		future	
never		public, publish		acknowledge	
situation		regular			

405. Quantities. Here are a few more helpful abbreviations for use after numerals and after such words as *few, several.*

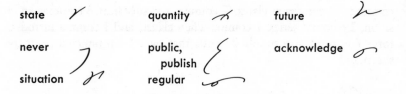

500		5 bushels	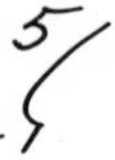
5,000,000		5 feet	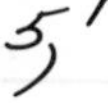
$500		a dollar	
$5,000,000		few hundred	
500,000,000		several hundred dollars	
5,000,000,000		a million	
5 pounds		a hundred	
5 gallons		5 per cent	
5 barrels		5 per cent per annum	

Did you notice that the *m* for *million* is written beside the figure as a positive distinction from *hundred* in which the *n* is written underneath the figure?

Reading and Writing Practice

406. Applied Vocabulary Study. *Proceed,* go ahead. *Acceptance,* approval, favorable reception. *Ultimately,* finally, eventually. *Publications,* books and magazines. *Legal formalities,* requirements of the law that must be met.

407.

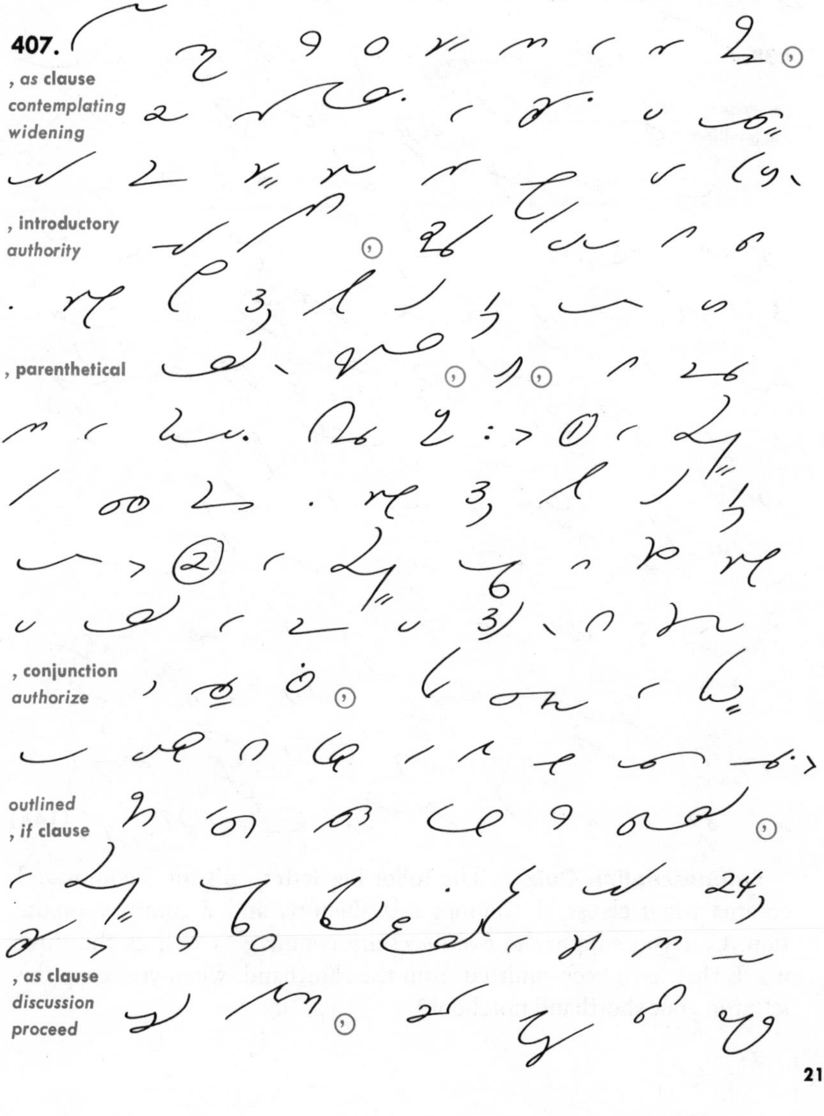

, as clause
contemplating
widening
, introductory
authority
, parenthetical
, conjunction
authorize
outlined
, if clause
, as clause
discussion
proceed

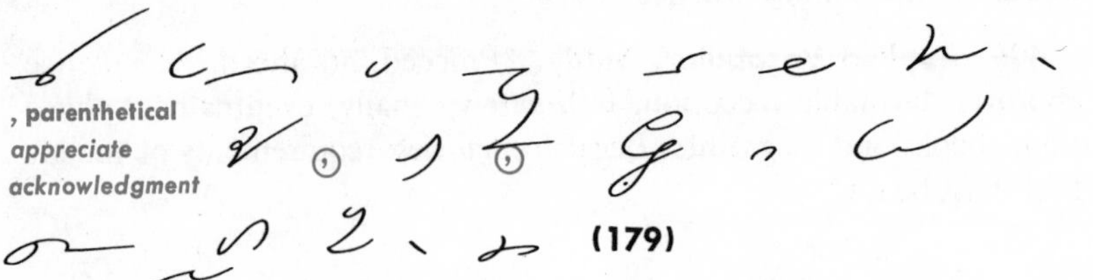

, parenthetical
appreciate
acknowledgment

(179)

408.

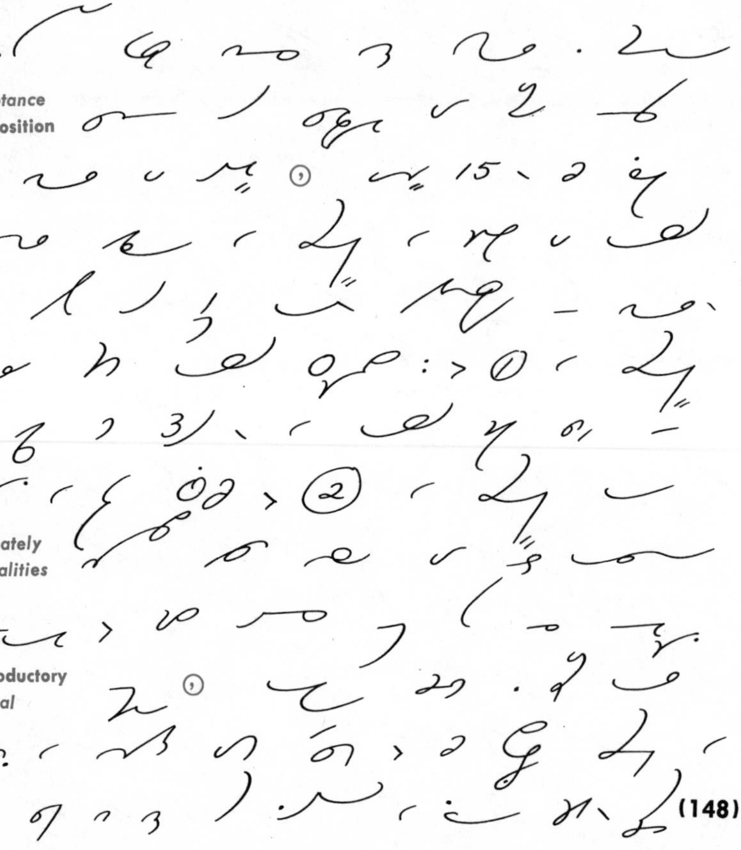

acceptance
, apposition

ultimately
formalities

, introductory
official

(148)

Pretranscription Quiz. The following letter calls for 5 commas: 1 comma *when* clause, 2 commas introductory, and 2 commas apposition. Can you supply the five necessary commas, as well as the three words that have been omitted from the shorthand, when you copy this letter in your shorthand notebook?

409.

(199)

LESSON 46

410. Brief Forms

newspaper		number		correct	
envelope, nevertheless		organize		allow	
idea		experience		request	

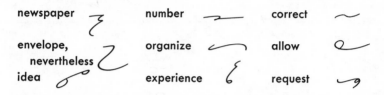

411. Intersection. Intersection, or the writing of one character through another, is sometimes useful for special phrases. You should not, however, attempt to memorize lists of such phrases; you should devise such phrases only when the constant repetition of certain phrases in your dictation makes it clearly worth while to form special outlines.

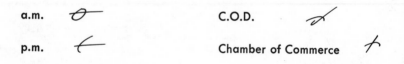

a.m.		C.O.D.	
p.m.		Chamber of Commerce	

Reading and Writing Practice

Reading Scoreboard. Thirteen lessons have gone by since you last measured your reading speed. You have, of course, continued to do each Reading and Writing Practice faithfully, and, consequently, your reading speed will reflect this faithfulness! The following table will help you measure your reading speed on the *first reading* of Lesson 46.

Lesson 46 contains 654 words.

If you read Lesson 46 in	your reading rate is
20 MINUTES	33 WORDS A MINUTE
22 MINUTES	30 WORDS A MINUTE
24 MINUTES	27 WORDS A MINUTE

26 MINUTES	25 WORDS A MINUTE
28 MINUTES	23 WORDS A MINUTE
30 MINUTES	21 WORDS A MINUTE

If you can read Lesson 46 through the first time in less than 20 minutes, you are doing well. If you take considerably longer than 30 minutes, perhaps you should

1. Pay closer attention in class while the shorthand devices are being presented to you.
2. Spend less time trying to decipher outlines that you cannot read.
3. Review, occasionally, all the brief forms you have studied through the charts on pages 315 and 316.

412. Applied Vocabulary Study. *Miniature* copy, a small copy. *Clerical jobs,* jobs in an office. *Forwarded,* sent. *Discontinuing,* stopping. *Luncheon,* a light meal, usually in the middle of the day.

413.

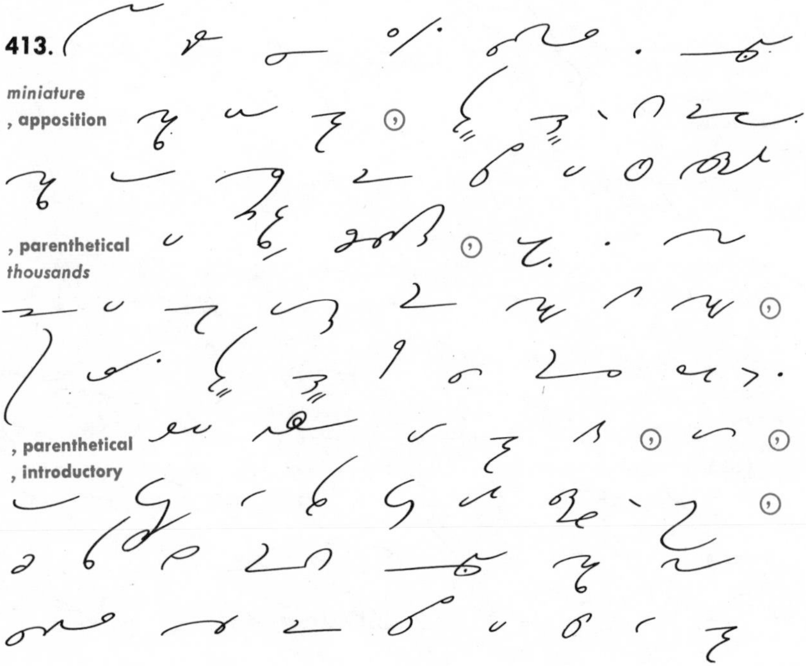
miniature
, apposition
, parenthetical
thousands
, parenthetical
, introductory

, series
correctness

(143)

414.

, conjunction
knowledge

, if clause
requested
already
accepted

, if clause

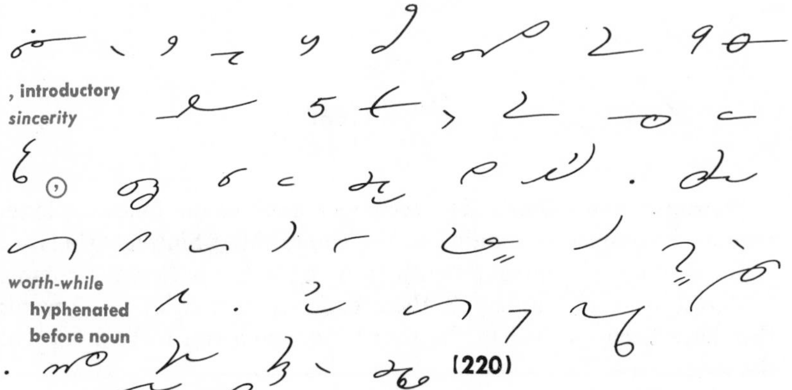

, introductory
sincerity

worth-while
hyphenated
before noun

(220)

415.

, parenthetical
balance

received
effect
, apposition

, parenthetical
business

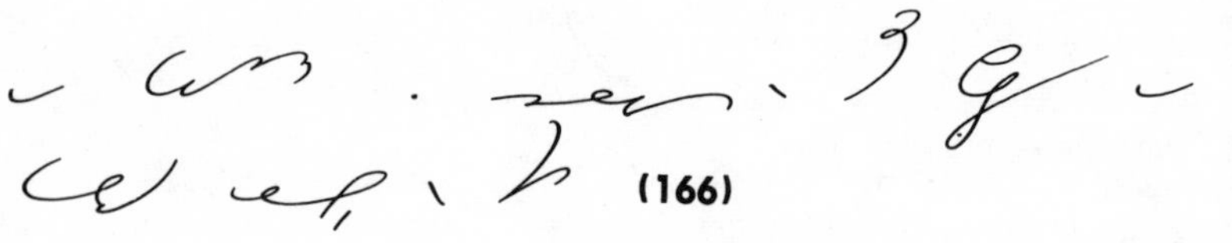

(166)

Pretranscription Quiz. Correct punctuation of the following letter requires 8 commas in addition to the comma after *Sincerely yours* – 2 commas series, 4 commas parenthetical, 1 comma *if* clause, 1 comma introductory. Can you supply these commas, as well as the 3 words that have been omitted in the shorthand, when you make a copy of the letter?

416.

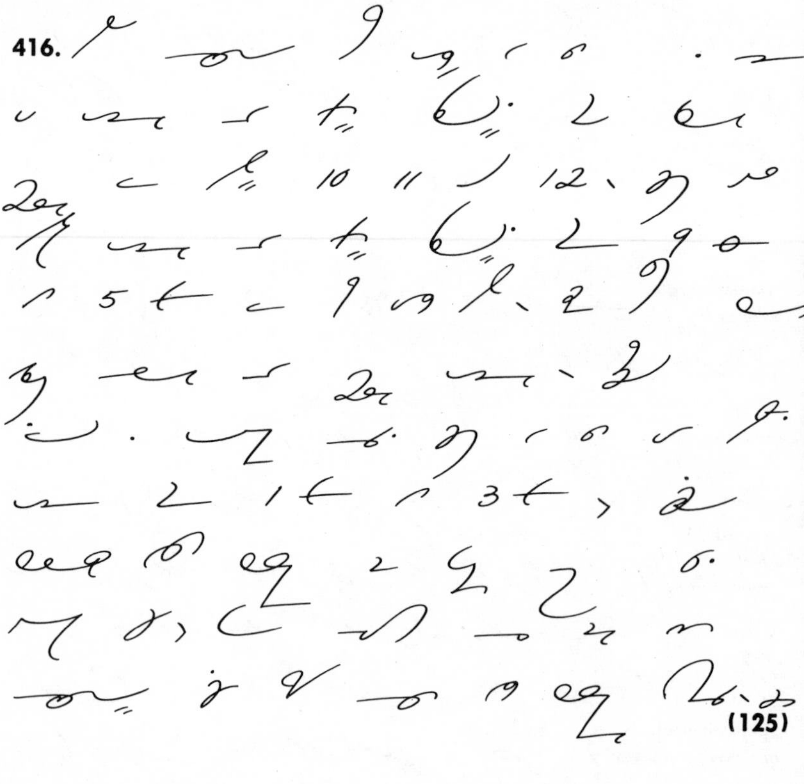

(125)

LESSON 47

417. Word Beginning Self-. The word beginning *self-* is represented by a disjoined left *s*.

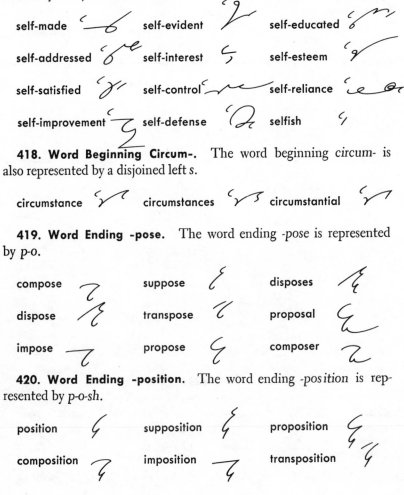

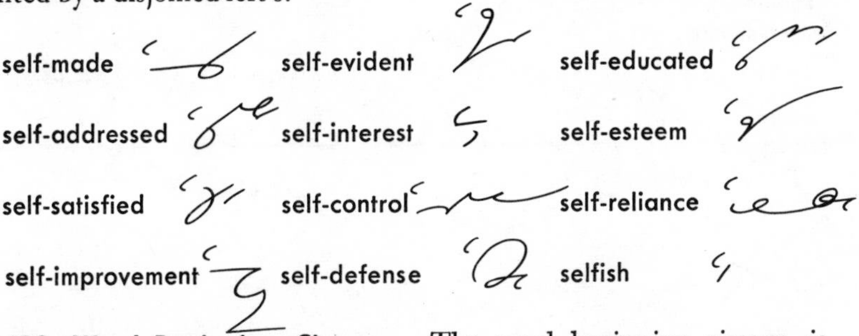
self-made
self-evident
self-educated
self-addressed
self-interest
self-esteem
self-satisfied
self-control
self-reliance
self-improvement
self-defense
selfish

418. Word Beginning Circum-. The word beginning *circum-* is also represented by a disjoined left *s*.

circumstance
circumstances
circumstantial

419. Word Ending -pose. The word ending *-pose* is represented by *p-o*.

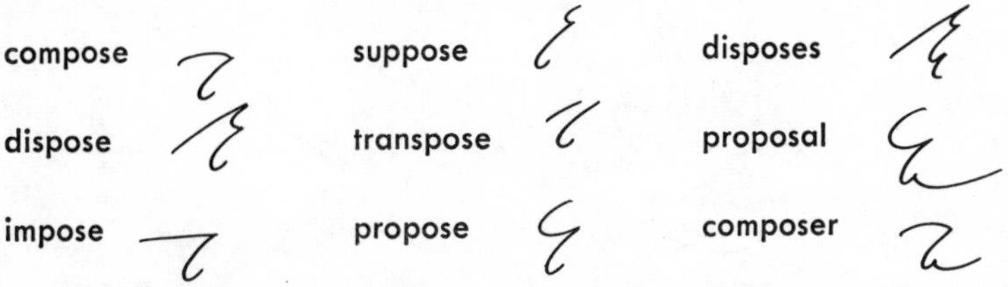
compose
suppose
disposes
dispose
transpose
proposal
impose
propose
composer

420. Word Ending -position. The word ending *-position* is represented by *p-o-sh*.

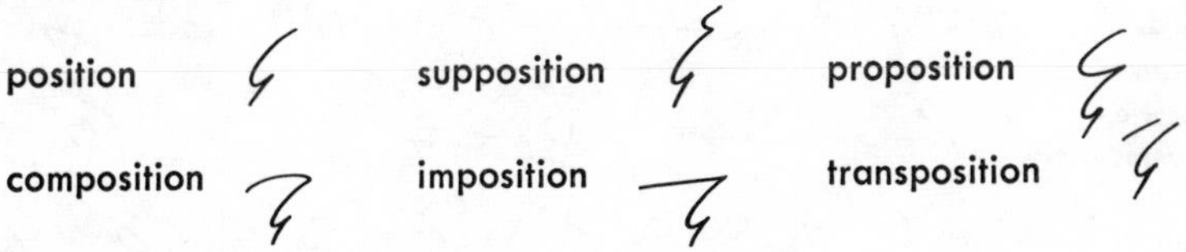
position
supposition
proposition
composition
imposition
transposition

Reading and Writing Practice

421. Applied Vocabulary Study. *Possibility,* chance. *Jet,* nozzle. *Self-supporting,* being able to earn one's own living. *Self-explanatory,* needing no explanation. *Imposition,* burden.

422.

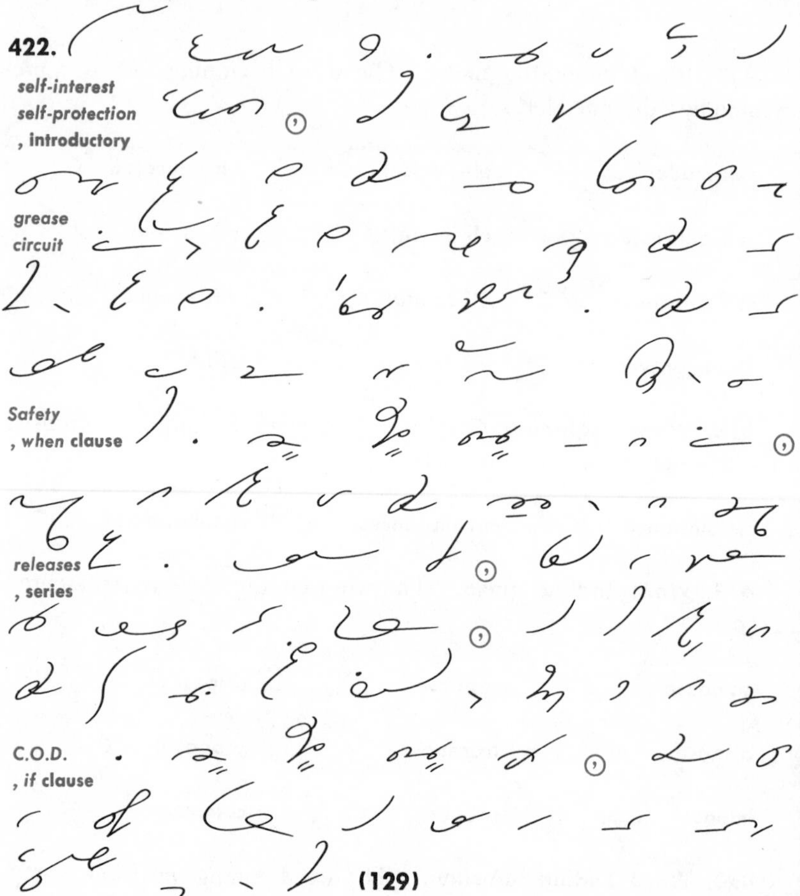

self-interest
self-protection
, introductory
grease
circuit
Safety
, when clause
releases
, series
C.O.D.
, if clause

(129)

423.

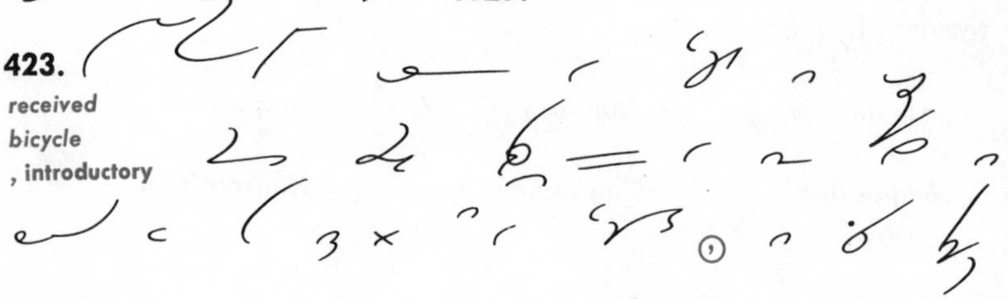

received
bicycle
, introductory

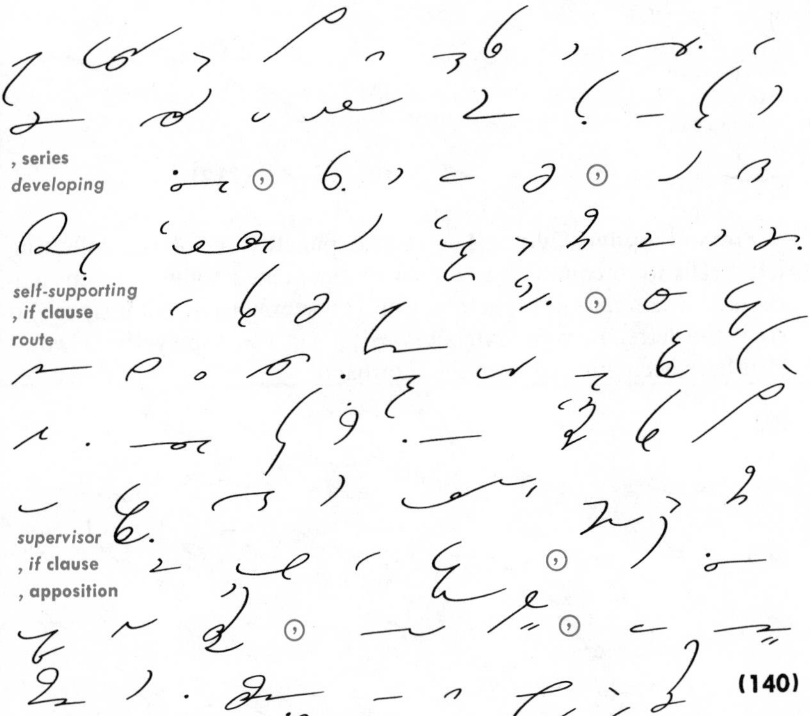

, series
developing

self-supporting
, if clause
route

supervisor
, if clause
, apposition

(140)

424.

, apposition
requested

, if clause
suggestions

self-addressed
envelope
, conjunction

(112)

Pretranscription Quiz. The correct punctuation of the following letter calls for 6 commas: 1 comma conjunction, 2 commas parenthetical, and 3 commas introductory. Can you supply those commas as you copy the letter in your notebook? Also, can you supply the 3 words that have been omitted from the shorthand?

425. 

(136)

LESSON 48 Recall

Lesson 48 is another "breather," with no new shorthand devices for you to learn. In this lesson you will brush up on your writing of some important blends. You will also review the joined word beginnings and endings, as well as the brief forms and phrases of Chapter 8.

Accuracy Practice

426. **Dev, Tive** **Gent**

To write these strokes accurately:

a. Make them large, almost the full height of your notebook line.

b. Make them narrow.

c. Start and finish the strokes on the same level of writing, as indicated by the dotted lines.

Practice Drill

Divide, definite, defeat, native, gentle, spent, happened.

427. **Th** **Ten** **Tem**

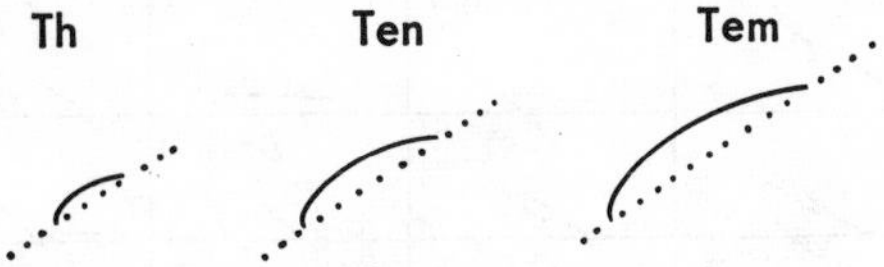

To write these strokes accurately:

a. Slant the strokes as indicated by the dotted lines.

b. Make the beginning of the curves deep.

c. Make the *tem* large, about the full height of the line; the *th*, small; the *ten* about half the size of the *tem*.

Practice Drill

In the, in time, tender, teeth, detain, medium.

428. Recall Chart. This chart contains all the brief forms in Chapter 8 and a complete recall of all the joined word beginnings and endings that you have studied thus far. There are 96 words and phrases in the chart.

Can you read the entire chart in 5 minutes or less?

Words

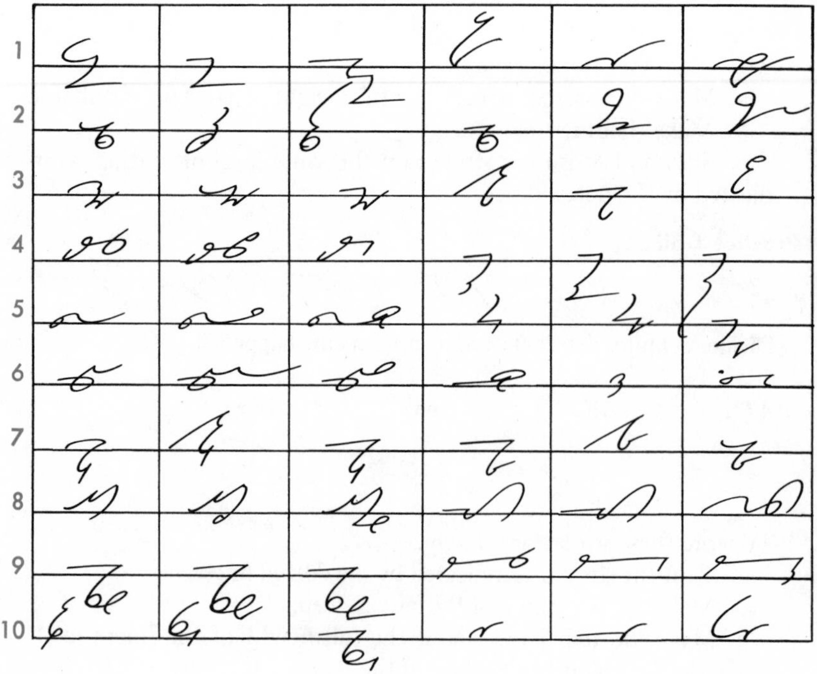

1
2
3
4
5
6
7
8
9
10

Brief Forms

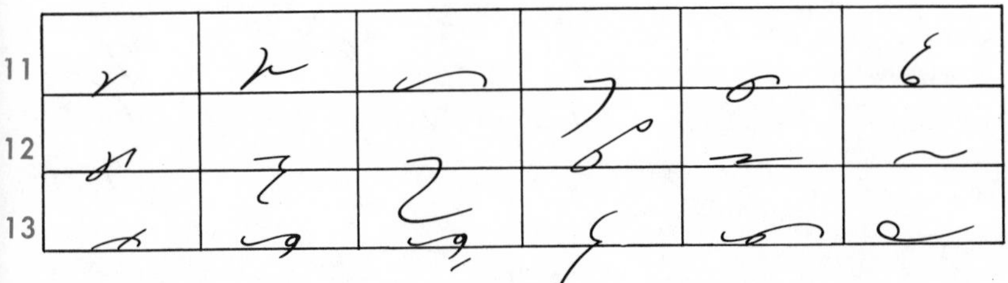
11
12
13

Phrases

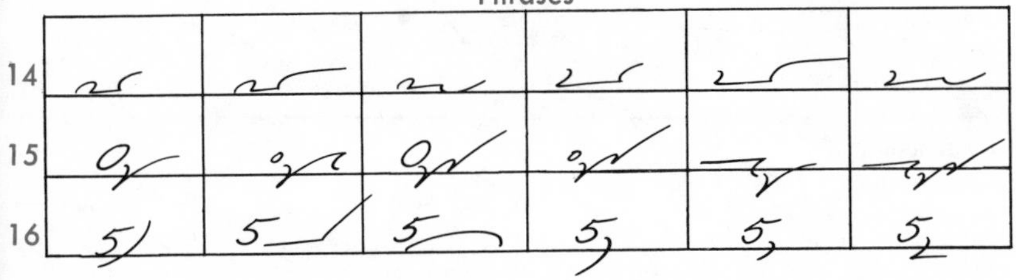
14
15
16

Reading and Writing Practice

429. Applied Vocabulary Study. *Etiquette*, rules of good conduct. *Prescribes*, directs. *Oust*, fire. *Revealed*, showed, displayed. *Fret and fume*, worry and complain.

430. Composure

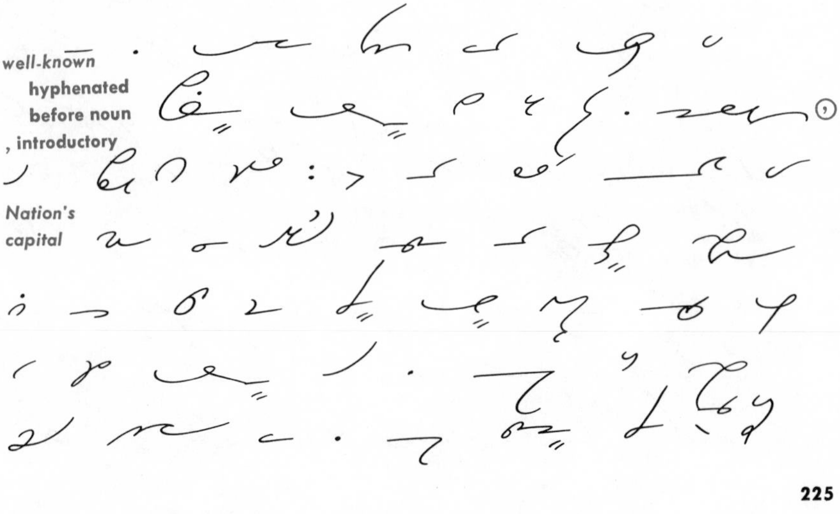
well-known
hyphenated
before noun
, introductory
Nation's
capital

etiquette
, conjunction
, as clause
parlor
, introductory
, parenthetical
supposed
, parenthetical
, introductory
, introductory
embarrassment
, introductory
already
, when clause
anger
oust

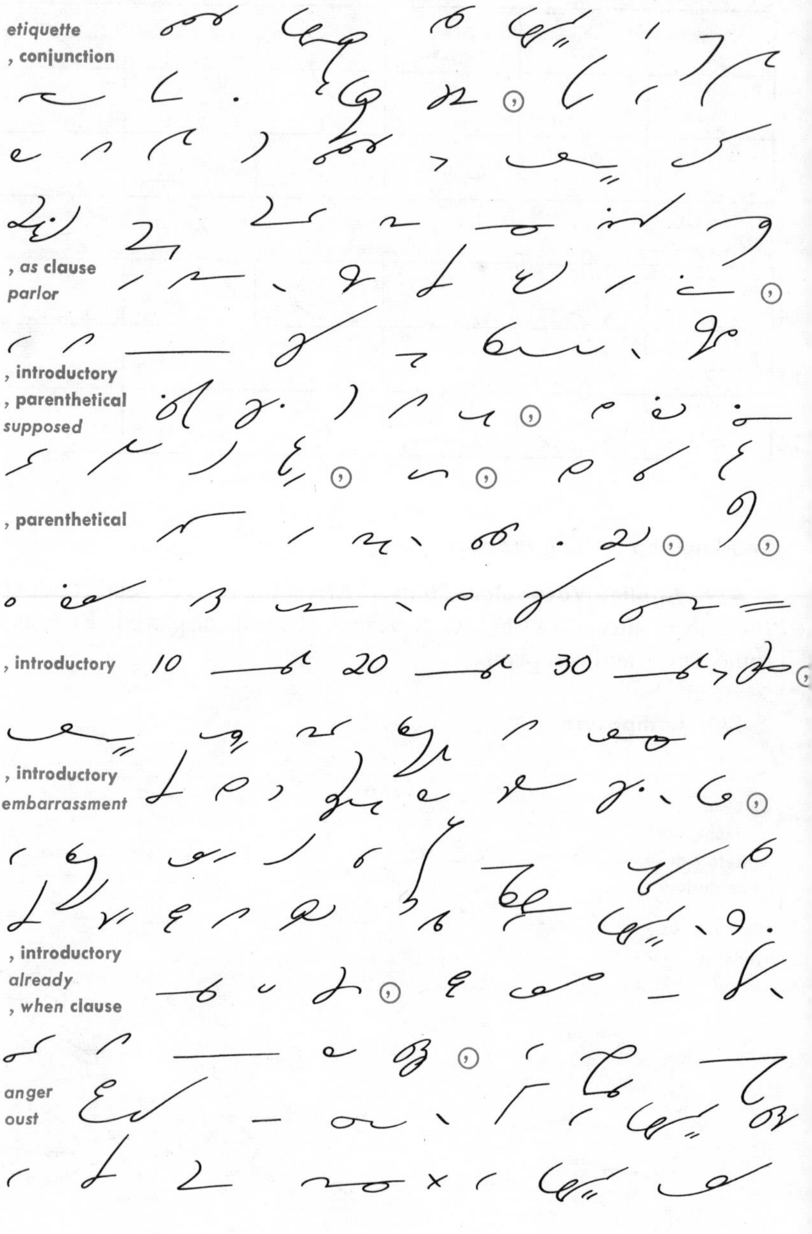

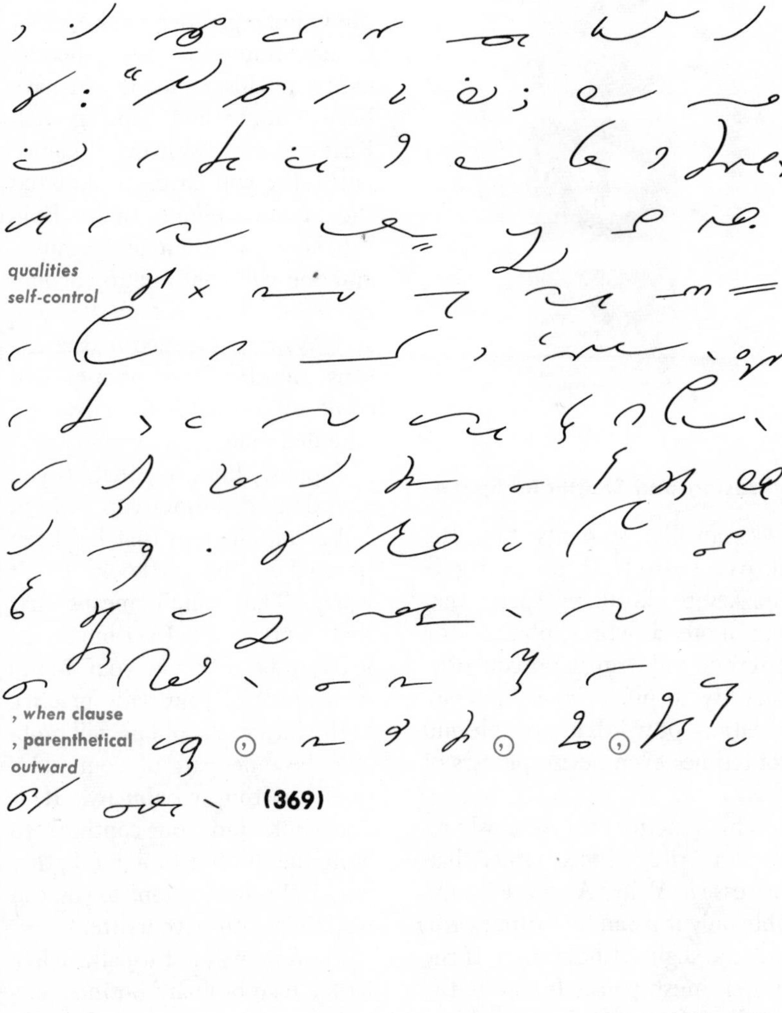

qualities

self-control

, when clause

, parenthetical

outward

(369)

CHAPTER 9

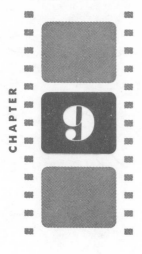

Phrasing and Shorthand Speed

Occasionally, students gain the impression that phrasing is the key to shorthand speed, that the more a writer phrases the faster he will write. Consequently, they try to phrase as many combinations of words as possible and sometimes even devise phrases of their own.

This practice may seriously reduce a writer's speed rather than increase it. Why? A phrase is valuable only if it can be written without the slightest hesitation. If the writer must pause for even the smallest fraction of a second in composing or thinking of a phrase, that phrase becomes a speed handicap.

The phrase that can be written without hesitation is the one that has occurred again and again in the writer's practice work so that it has impressed itself permanently on his mind. If you have been reading and copying each Reading and Writing Practice faithfully, you have encountered the common phrases of the English language again and again—and you will continue to encounter them often in each Reading and Writing Practice in the lessons ahead. These phrases will come to you naturally when you take dictation.

Suppose, however, that, as you are taking dictation, you write in full a combination that has been phrased in the textbook. Don't worry! That simply means that that phrase has not yet impressed itself sufficiently on your mind. As a result of your daily practice in the future, the phrase will probably become part of your automatic writing vocabulary. If it does not, and you continue to write the combination in full, that is all right, too—as long as you can read what you have written!

Phrasing will not usually help a writer take ordinary business dictation more rapidly; it will simply enable him to take it with less effort. If he does not phrase enough, he will write at about the same speed but he will become tired sooner.

If you have the feeling that you should be phrasing more, dismiss the matter from your mind. Simply continue to read and copy faithfully each Reading and Writing Practice, and your ability to phrase will take care of itself.

What's Ahead?

Chapter 9 contains the last of the new shorthand devices that you will have to learn. You will find it to be the easiest chapter in the book! It contains four sets of brief forms, seven simple word endings, and a number of abbreviating devices for expressing frequently used endings that occur in proper names and geographical expressions.

When you have completed Lesson 53, you will have all the shorthand devices of Gregg Shorthand at your disposal for the construction of a readable outline for any word in the English language.

Executives as well as secretaries and stenographers often use shorthand in making memoranda, in composing reports, in making notes of telephone conversations. It saves time!

LESSON 49

431. Brief Forms

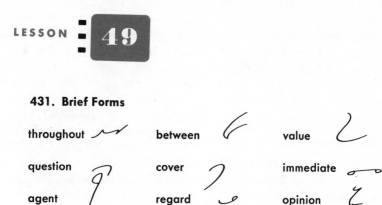

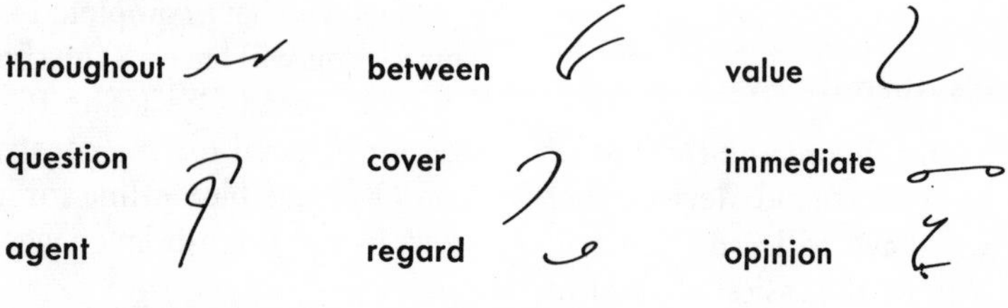
throughout
between
value
question
cover
immediate
agent
regard
opinion

432. Word Ending -ings. The word ending *-ings* is represented by left *s* placed in the position of the *-ing* dot.

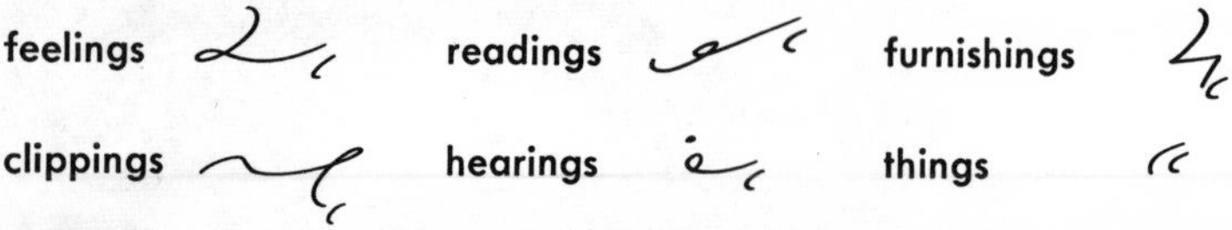
feelings
readings
furnishings
clippings
hearings
things

433. Word Ending -ingly. The word ending *-ingly* is represented by a disjoined e circle placed in the position of the *-ing* dot.

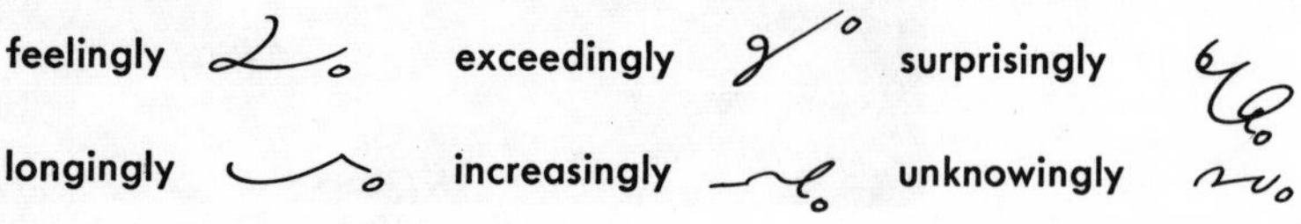
feelingly
exceedingly
surprisingly
longingly
increasingly
unknowingly

Reading and Writing Practice

434. Applied Vocabulary Study. *Coverage,* the extent and kind of protection provided by an insurance policy. *Utilize,* use. *Men's furnishings,* men's clothing, especially the smaller articles like *neckties, gloves,* and the like.

435.

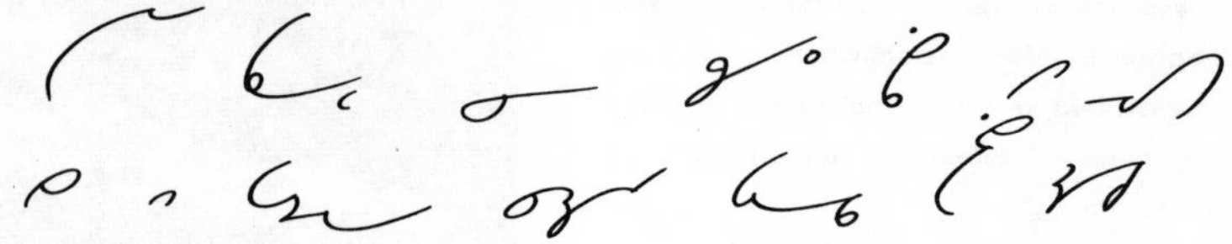

altered
commercial
coverage
, if clause
, apposition

(92)

436.

, as clause
becoming
increasingly
, introductory
advisable
, parenthetical
sufficient
surprisingly
forward-looking
hyphenated
before noun

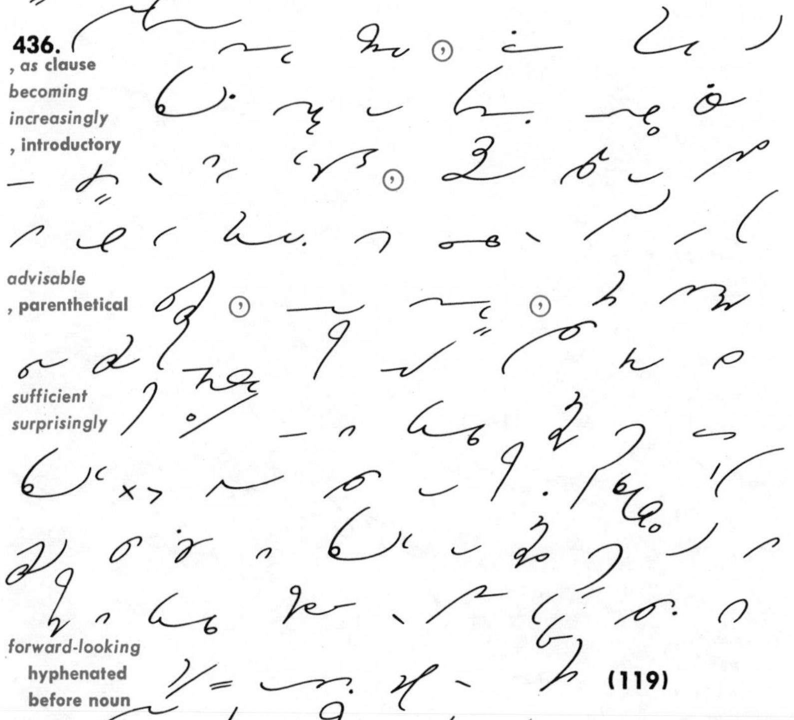

(119)

437.

promotion
, series

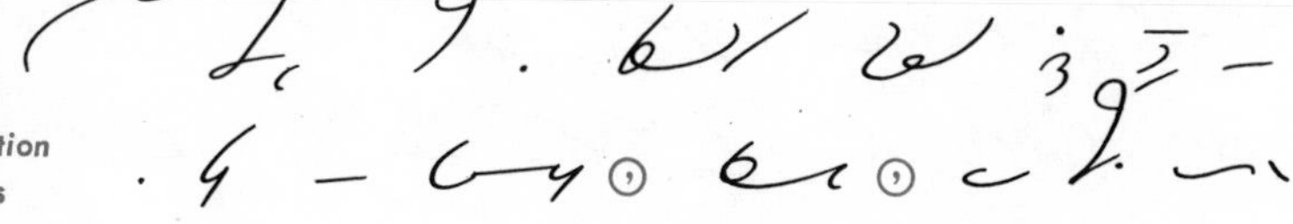

, conjunction

men's furnishings

best-known hyphenated before noun

, if clause

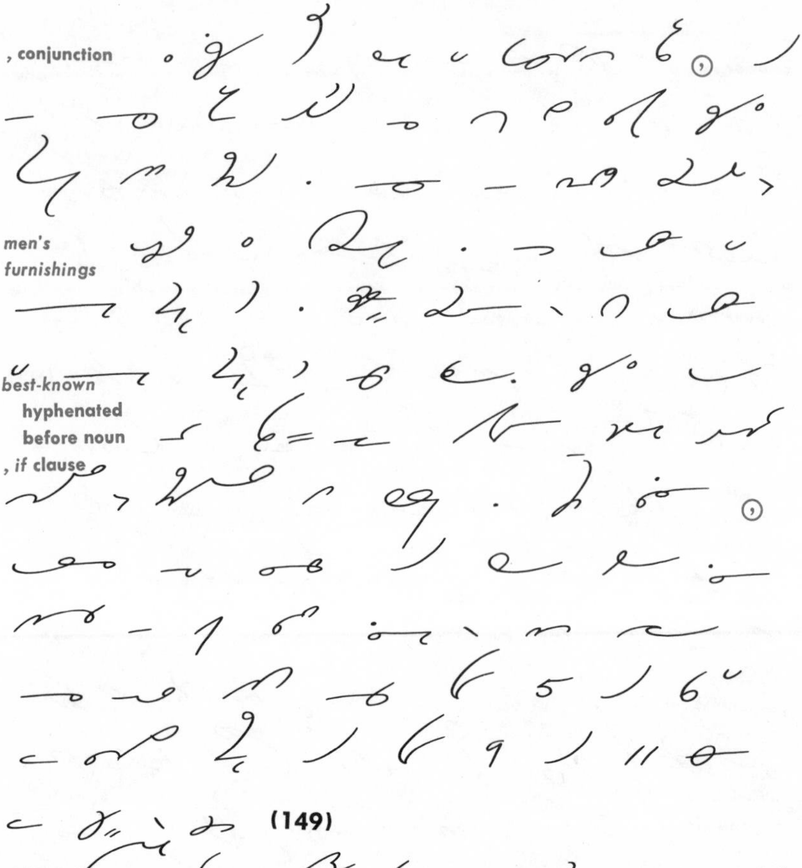

(149)

438.

five-year hyphenated before noun

, introductory

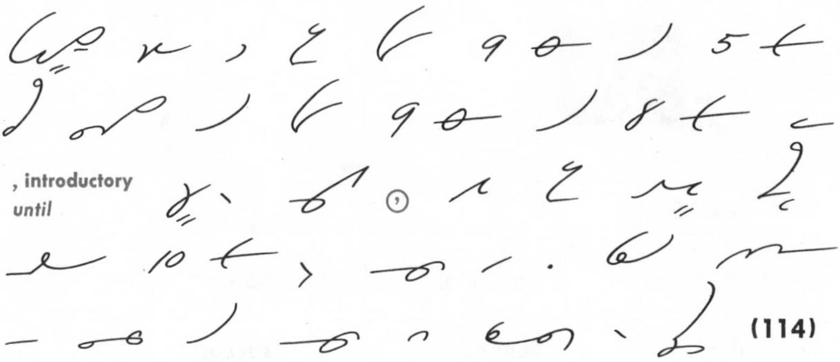

, introductory
until

(114)

Pretranscription Quiz. For you to supply: 6 commas – 1 comma introductory, 1 comma as clause, and 4 commas parenthetical; 3 missing words.

439.

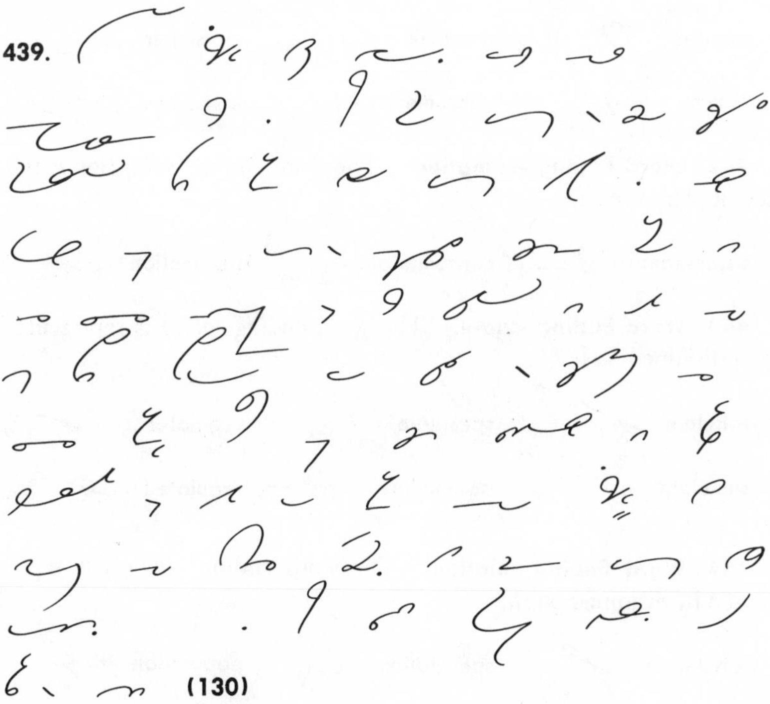

(130)

LESSON 50

440. Brief Forms

conclude	particular	house
conclusion	confident, confidence	success
object	subject	

441. Word Ending -sume. The word ending *-sume* is represented by *s-m.*

assume	presume	consumer
resume	consume	consumed

442. Word Ending -sumption. The word ending *-sumption* is represented by *s-m-sh.*

assumption	consumption	resumption

443. Word Ending -ulate. The word ending *-ulate* is represented by a disjoined oo hook.

tabulate	speculate	regulates
stimulate	accumulate	regulated

444. Word Ending -ulation. The word ending *-ulation* is represented by disjoined *oo-sh.*

tabulation	speculation	population

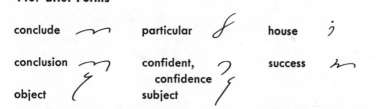

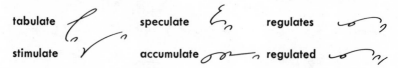

Reading and Writing Practice

445. Applied Vocabulary Study. *Accumulated,* collected. *Calculator,* machine that does mathematical operations such as adding, multiplying, etc. *Objective,* impersonal, not prejudiced. *Expenditures,* amounts of money spent. *Stimulating,* exciting. *Consumer education,* teaching a person to spend time and money wisely.

446.

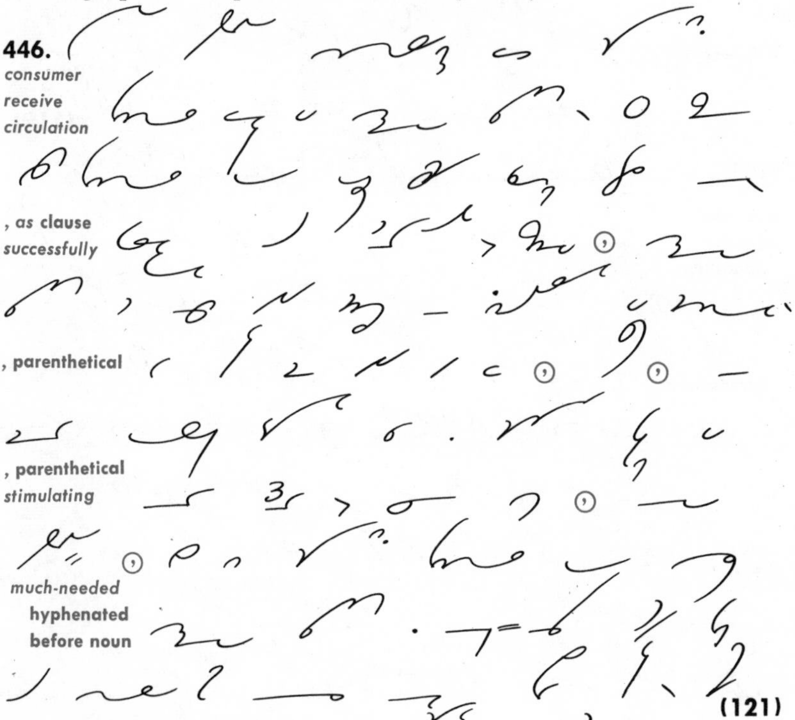

consumer
receive
circulation

, as clause
successfully

, parenthetical

, parenthetical
stimulating

much-needed
hyphenated
before noun

(121)

447.

, if clause
confusing
installation

objective
survey

(119)

448.

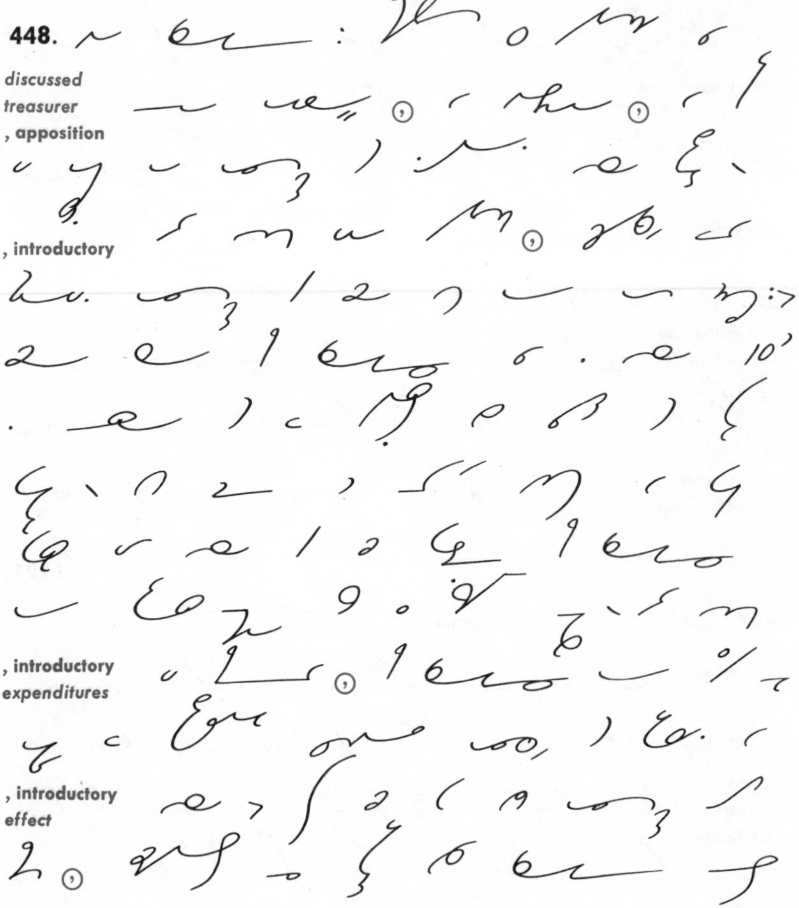

discussed
treasurer
, apposition
, introductory
, introductory
expenditures
, introductory
effect

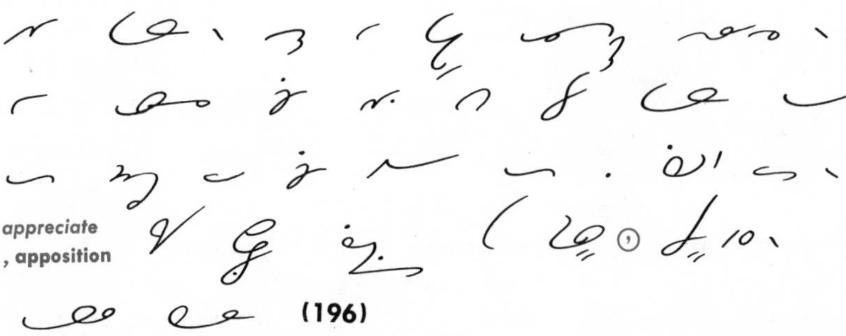

appreciate
, apposition

(196)

Pretranscription Quiz. For you to supply: 7 commas — 1 comma *if* clause, 1 comma introductory, 4 commas parenthetical, 1 comma conjunction; 3 missing words.

449.

(132)

LESSON 51

450. Brief Forms

advantage

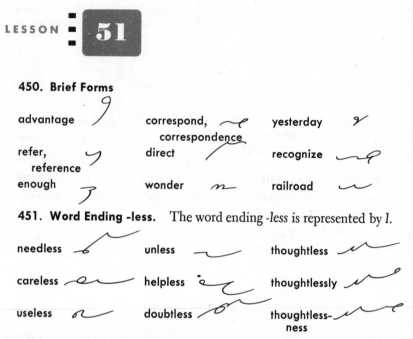

correspond, correspondence

yesterday

refer, reference

direct

recognize

enough

wonder

railroad

451. Word Ending -less. The word ending *-less* is represented by *l*.

needless

unless

thoughtless

careless

helpless

thoughtlessly

useless

doubtless

thoughtlessness

Reading and Writing Practice

452. Applied Vocabulary Study. *Beautifying,* making beautiful or attractive. *Maintenance,* upkeep of property, especially making repairs. *Directory,* a book containing names and addresses. *Questionnaire,* a set of questions to be answered, usually for the purpose of research. (Notice the double *n*.)

453.

Directors

, introductory

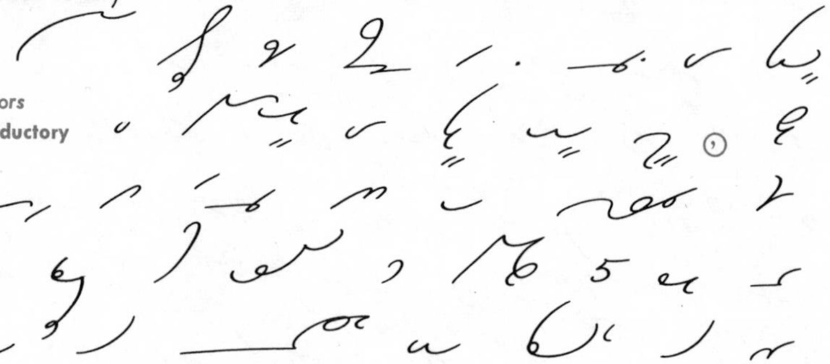

, introductory
reference

clients
, if clause

(131)

454.

shiny
Peerless
endless

enjoyment
, parenthetical

carefree
, introductory

(73)

455.

, series
authentic
dependable

questionnaire

, when clause

up-to-date hyphenated before noun

, parenthetical

(86)

456.

received

ever-increasing hyphenated before noun

, series

Unless

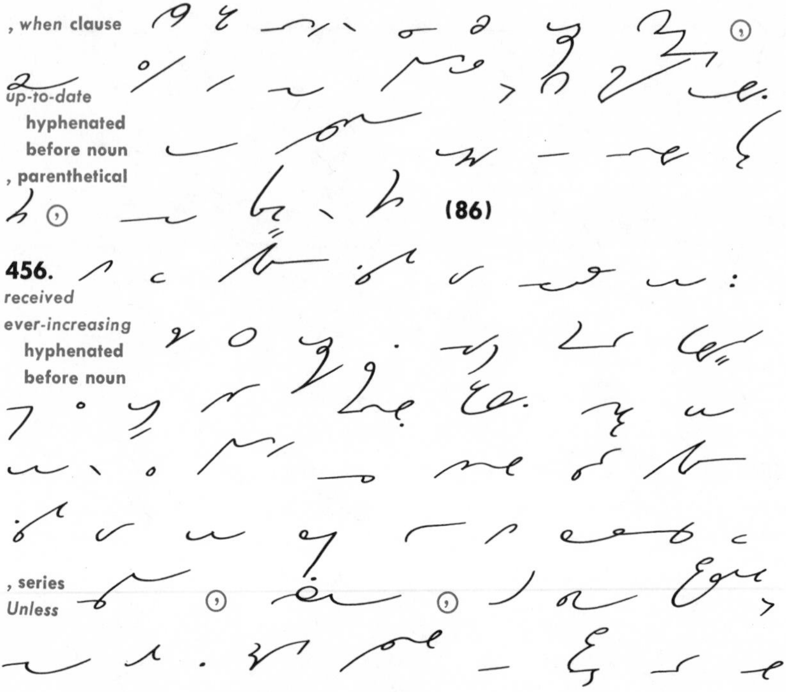

Shorthand Notebook Check List

So that you can use your notebook efficiently, do you

1. Write your name on the cover of your notebook?
2. Indicate on the cover the first and last days on which you used the notebook?
3. Place the date *at the bottom* of the first page of each day's dictation?
4. Place a rubber band around the completed pages of your notebook so that you lose no time finding the first blank page on which to start the day's dictation?
5. Draw a line through the shorthand notes that you have transcribed or read back so that you will know you are through with them?

, introductory
hopelessly

necessity
economy
, conjunction

(131)

Pretranscription Quiz. For you to supply: 5 commas – 1 comma as clause, 2 commas introductory, and 2 commas parenthetical; 3 missing words.

457.

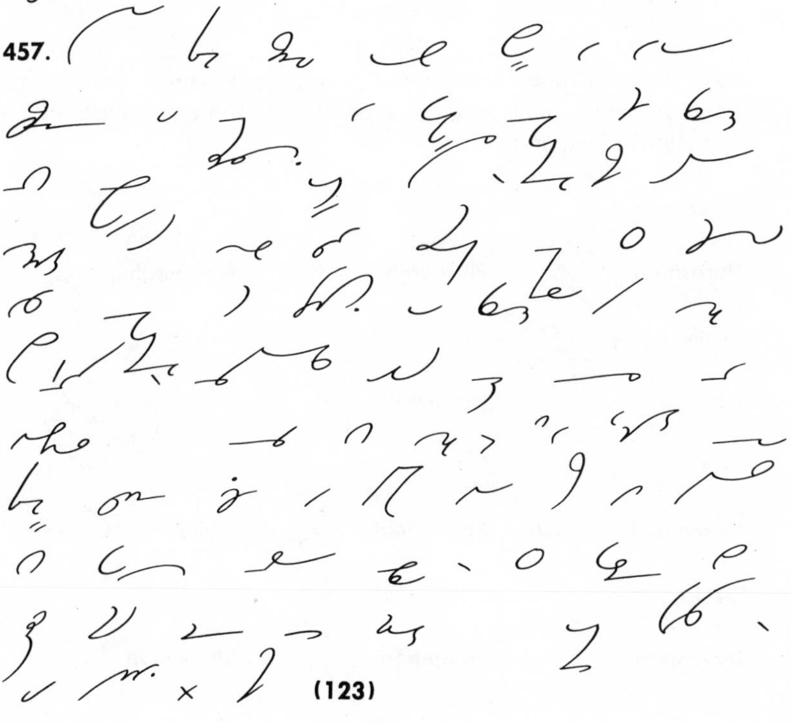

(123)

LESSON 52

458. Brief Forms. This is the last set of brief forms that you will have to learn.

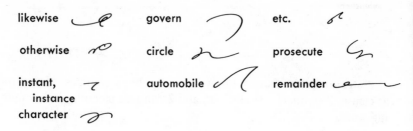

likewise		govern		etc.	
otherwise		circle		prosecute	
instant, instance		automobile		remainder	
character					

459. Proper-Name Terminations. In proper names, the terminations *-burg, -ville, -field, -port* are represented by the first letter of the termination, joined or disjoined.

-burg

Harrisburg		Pittsburgh		Newburgh	

-ville

Danville		Nashville		Jacksonville	

-field

Greenfield		Springfield		Plainfield	

-port

Davenport		Bridgeport		Shreveport	

Reading and Writing Practice

460. Applied Vocabulary Study. *Inflict*, cause to suffer. *Prosecute*, to sue, in a court, for the righting of a wrong or the punishment of a crime. (But *persecute* means to harm or annoy with urgent attacks.) *Emphasize*, stress. *Remainder*, what is left. *Etc.*, and so forth. (The full spelling is "et cetera" in two words.)

461.

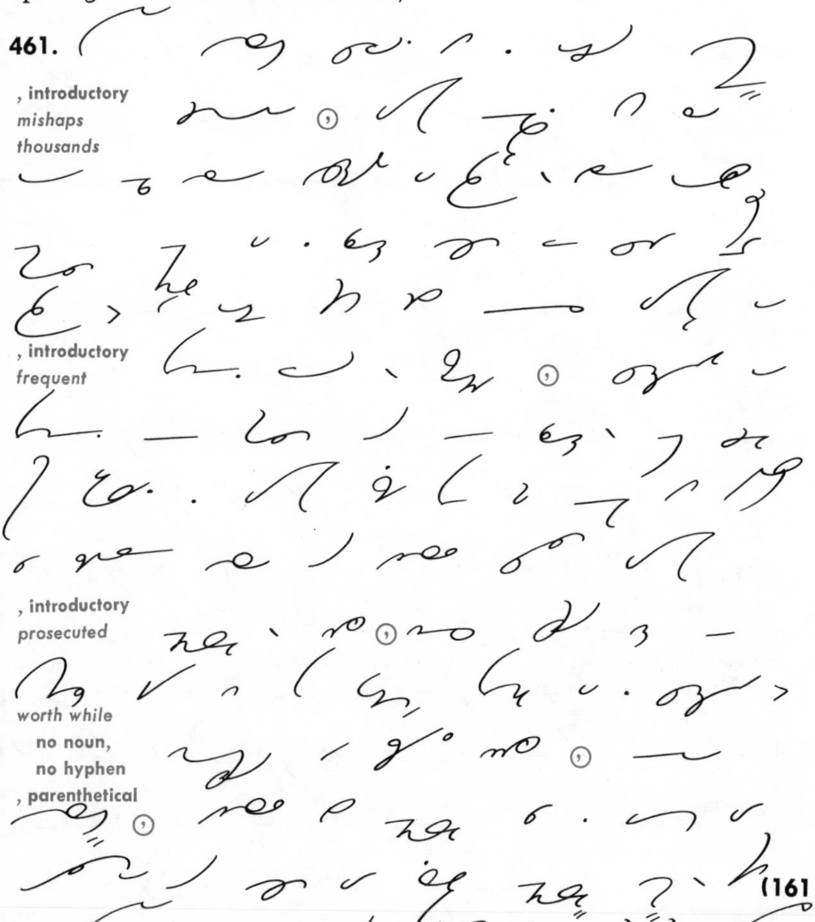

, introductory
mishaps
thousands
, introductory
frequent
, introductory
prosecuted
worth while
no noun,
no hyphen
, parenthetical

(161)

462.

circulars
, series

witnessed
superior

(97

463.

emphasize
effect
, parenthetical

, as clause
, apposition
resigned
previous

(8

464.

, apposition
men's

high-quality
hyphenated
before noun
, series

15/

15

, when clause

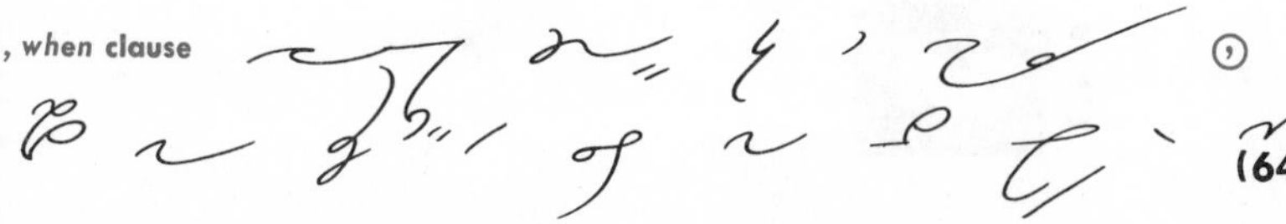

(64)

Pretranscription Quiz. For you to supply: 7 commas – 1 comma introductory, 2 commas series, 1 comma conjunction, 2 commas parenthetical, 1 comma *if* clause; 4 missing words.

465.

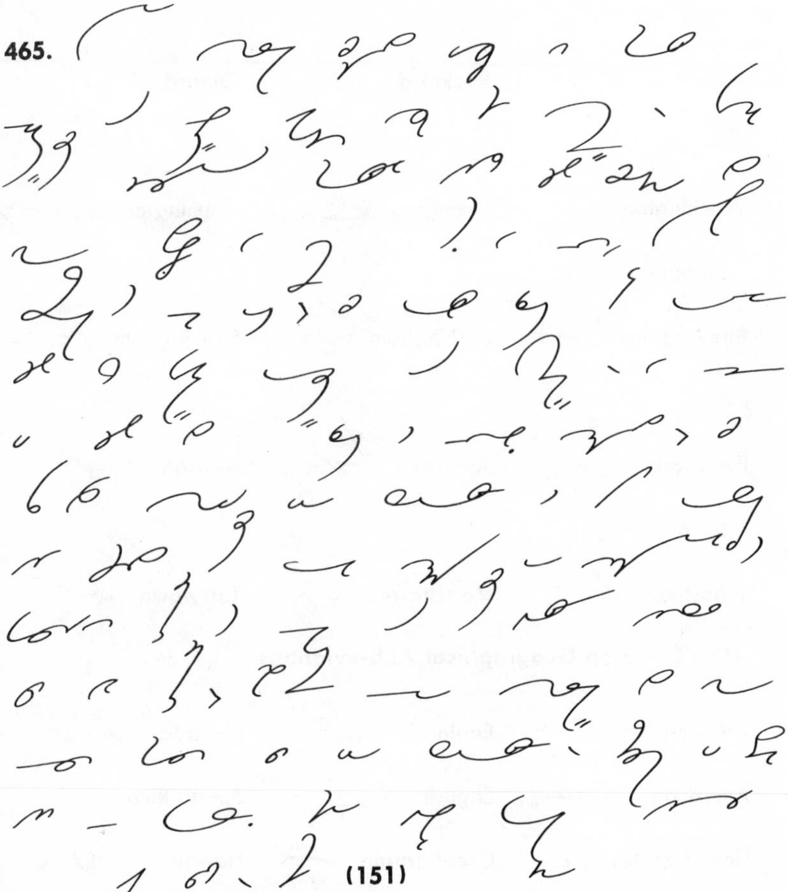

(151)

LESSON 53

466. Proper-Name Terminations (Concluded). In proper names, *-ford* is represented by *f-d*; *-ington*, by disjoined *ten*; *-ingham*, by disjoined *m*; *-ton*, by *ten*; *-town*, by *t-n*.

-ford

Stamford		Rockford		Oxford	

-ington

Washington		Lexington		Wilmington	

-ingham

Birmingham		Buckingham		Framingham	

-ton

Evanston		Johnston		Newton	

-town

Johnstown		Morristown		Tarrytown	

467. Common Geographical Abbreviations

America		England		Canada	
American		English		Puerto Rico	
United States		Great Britain		Hawaii	

Reading and Writing Practice

Reading Scoreboard. Now that you are on the last lesson that contains new shorthand devices, how fast can you read shorthand? How much has your reading speed increased over your first score in Lesson 18? The following table will help you determine your reading speed on Lesson 53.

Lesson 53 contains 625 words.

If you read Lesson 53 in	your reading rate is
18 MINUTES	35 WORDS A MINUTE
20 MINUTES	31 WORDS A MINUTE
22 MINUTES	28 WORDS A MINUTE
24 MINUTES	26 WORDS A MINUTE
26 MINUTES	24 WORDS A MINUTE
28 MINUTES	22 WORDS A MINUTE
30 MINUTES	20 WORDS A MINUTE

468. Applied Vocabulary Study. *Air-conditioned rooms,* rooms in which the temperature is comfortable no matter what the weather outside. *Overseas branches,* offices in foreign countries. *Termed,* called. *Distinguished,* notable, famous. *Assignment,* job.

469.

, apposition
, when clause
Association

Wilmington's
well-known
hyphenated before noun

, conjunction
air-conditioned

(122)

470.

whether
, series
, introductory
overseas
, series
Foreign
, as clause
unusual
substantial

(144)

471.

America's
distinguished
, introductory

refurnishing
beauty

guest
Its
steadily
pace

travelers
preference

neighborhood
, parenthetical

(167)

472.

, apposition
accepted
secretary
submitted
assignment
, when clause

(70)

Pretranscription Quiz. For you to supply: 4 commas – 1 comma *if* clause, 2 commas apposition, and 1 comma parenthetical; 2 missing words.

473.

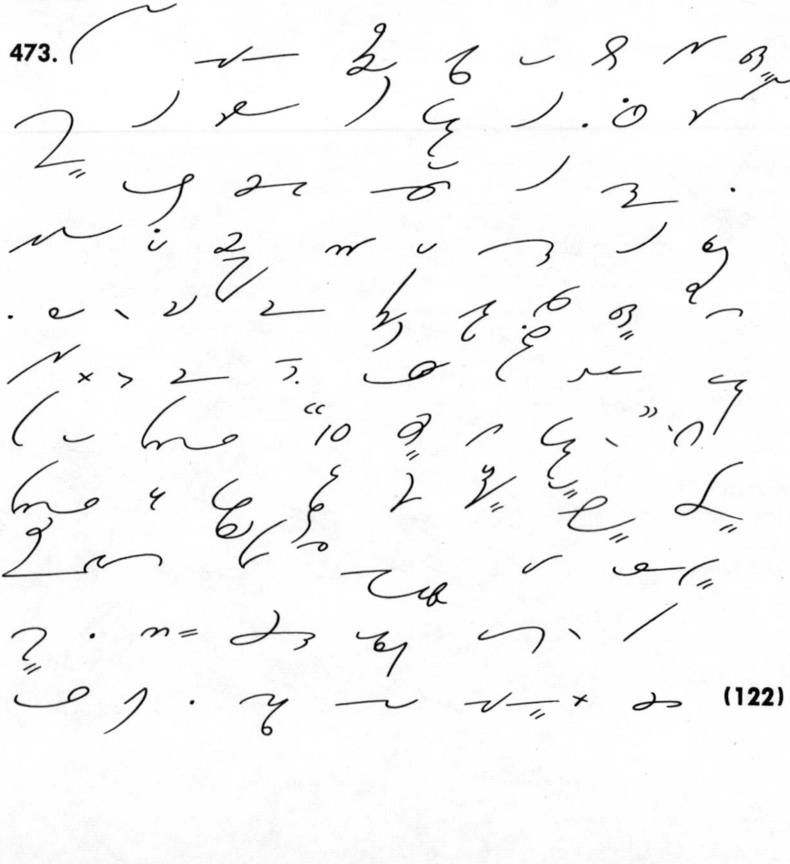

(122)

LESSON 54 Recall

In Lesson 54—and all following lessons—there will be no more new shorthand devices for you to learn. In this lesson, you will practice the *-ous* ending so that you can write it fluently; you will review through the Recall Chart all the shorthand devices of Gregg Shorthand; and you will get some sound advice in the Reading and Writing Practice on how to build good will.

Accuracy Practice

474. Word Ending -ous. In most of the shorthand outlines for words ending in *-ous,* the *-ous* combination is written with an angle between the hook and the *s.* Because of the frequency of this combination, you should practice it until it comes unhesitatingly to your mind.

The combination standing alone also represents *yourself.* Practice the outline for *yourself* until you can write the combination without a pause between the hook and the *s.* The writing motion is very much like that used in writing the figure 3 in longhand.

Practice the following words containing the *-ous* combination after *t, d, n, m.* In each case the straight line and the *-ous* should be written with one movement of the hand, at the same time keeping the straight line straight.

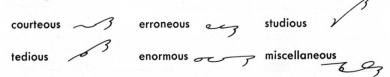

courteous  erroneous  studious 

tedious  enormous  miscellaneous 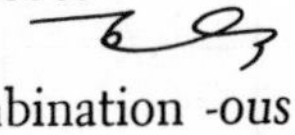

Now practice the following words, in which the combination *-ous* comes after *r* and *l.* Write the *r* or *l* and the hook with one sweep of the pen, adding the *s* without a pause.

generous  victorious  zealous 

In some words, the *-ous* ending follows *u*. The shorthand combination resembles the small letter *n* in longhand and should be written with the same speed and fluency, without a pause between the two hooks.

conspicuous  **strenuous**  **continuous** 

475. Recall Chart. This chart contains all the brief forms in Chapter 9. It also contains one or more illustrations of all the major word-building principles of Gregg Shorthand. There are 108 words in the chart. Do you think that you can read the entire chart in 5 minutes or less?

Words

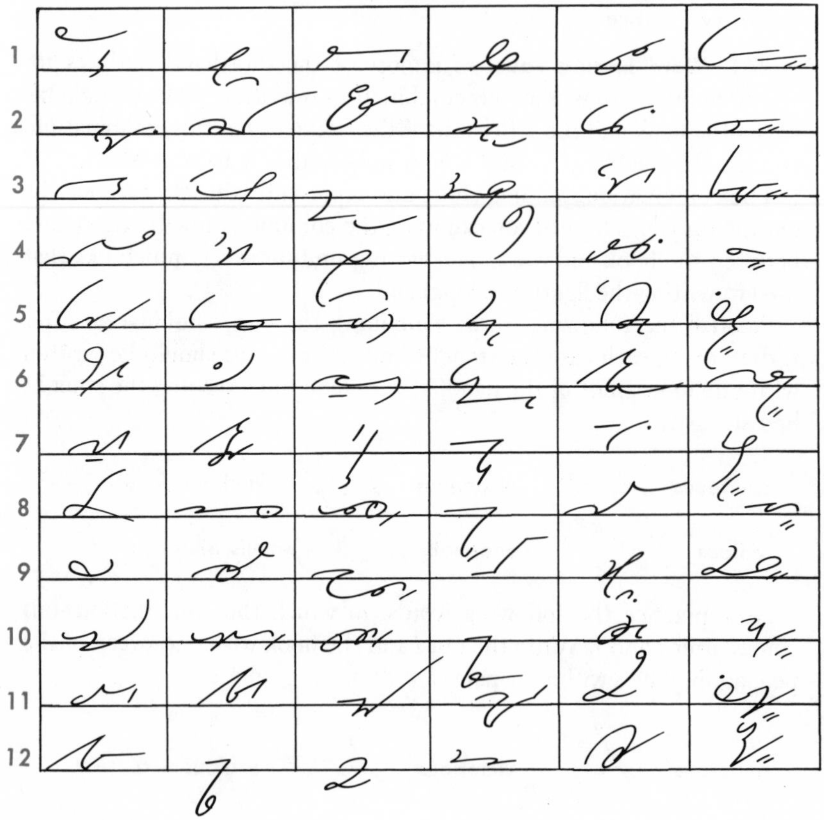
1
2
3
4
5
6
7
8
9
10
11
12

Brief Forms

13
14
15
16
17
18

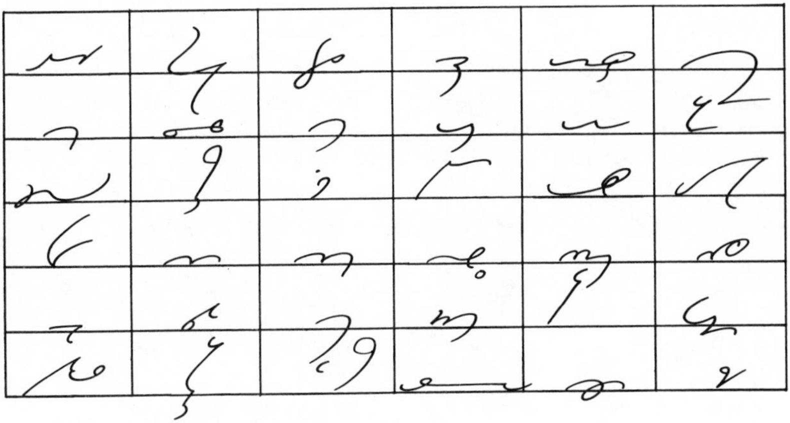

Reading and Writing Practice

476. Applied Vocabulary Study. *Formula,* an established method or form. *Principles,* rules of conduct or action. (But *principal* means main or chief.) *Chip on his shoulder,* looking for a fight or an argument. *Retaliation,* returning like for like, usually evil for evil.

477. Building Good Will

junior executives

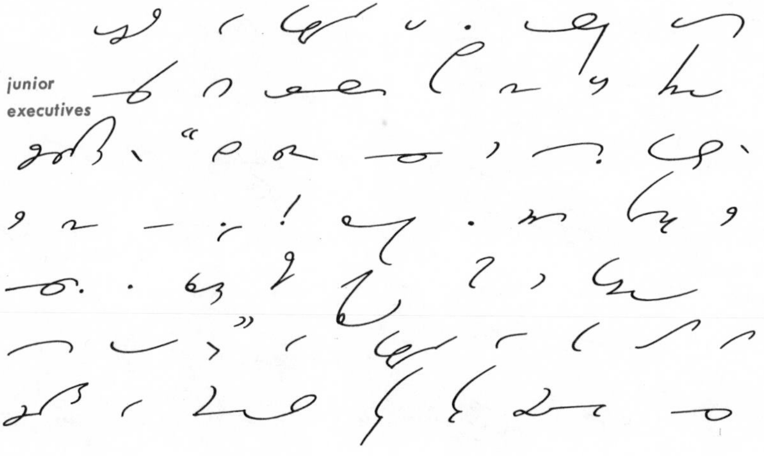

, introductory

, introductory
individuals

favorable
attitudes
toward

, conjunction
multiplying

, parenthetical
principles

, as clause
honesty

, series
weight
retaliation

, when clause
creating

excelling
well known
no noun,
no hyphen

, introductory
, if clause

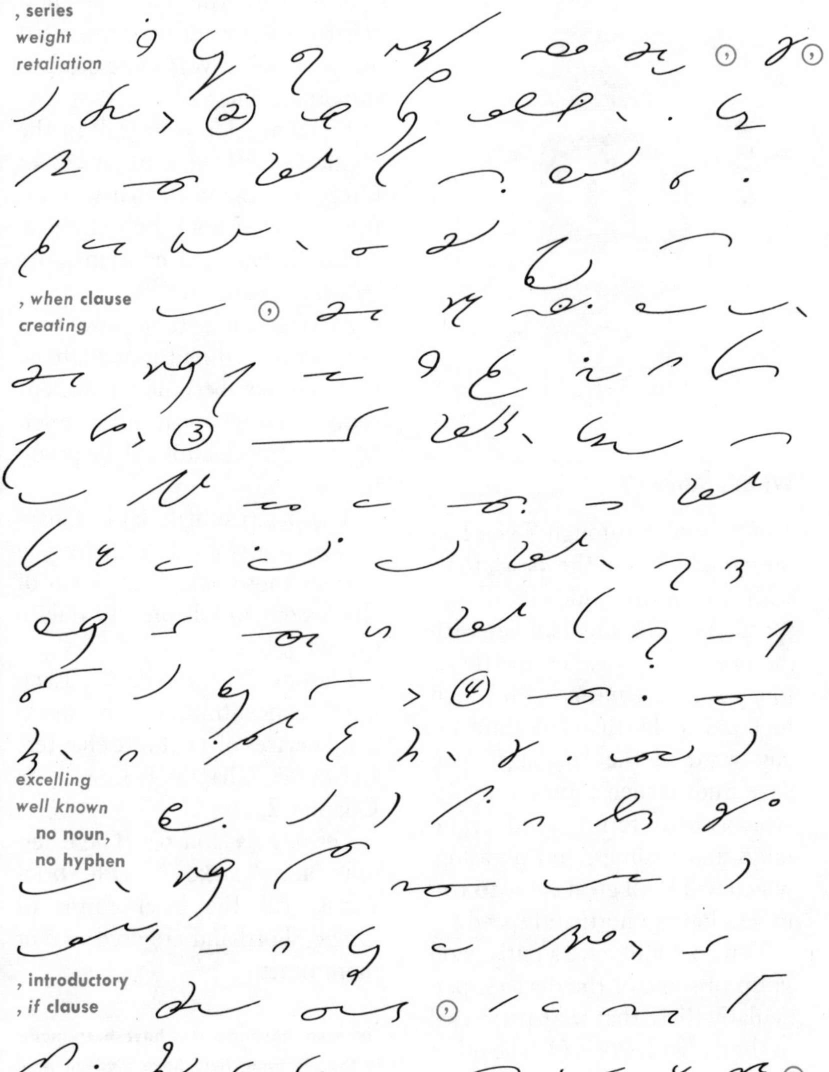

(390)

CHAPTER 10

What's Ahead?

In Chapters 1 through 9 you had presented to you the basic tools with which to build shorthand speed. You are now familiar with the shorthand alphabet, and therefore possess the means with which to build a shorthand outline for any word of the language. You have studied such abbreviating devices as brief forms, word beginnings and endings, and phrasing, which will be of great value to you in developing shorthand speed.

You no doubt have a fairly good grasp of some of the devices, particularly those that were presented in the earlier lessons. On the other hand, there are some devices that are not yet old friends, particularly those that you have studied quite recently.

Now that you have no new shorthand devices to learn, what are your objectives? Here are two important ones:

1. To develop your skill in the application of all the devices of Gregg Shorthand so that you can use them without hesitation in taking dictation at constantly increasing speeds.

2. To continue to improve your ability to spell and punctuate so that you may become an efficient transcriber, who can produce letters that the dictator will be proud to sign.

The practice material in Chapter 10 is designed to help you achieve those objectives. Each of the lessons in Chapter 10 does a specific job.

Lessons 55 through 63. Each lesson concentrates on the shorthand devices of a definite chapter: Lesson 55, Chapter 1; Lesson 56, Chapter 2; etc.

Lessons 64 and 65. These lessons are "packed" with brief forms. All the brief forms of Gregg Shorthand are used one or more times.

The great advances that have been made in the recording field have made it possible to get extra dictation outside of class by the use of phonograph records and tape recordings that supply large quantities of carefully timed dictation at proper speeds.

Lessons 66 and 67. These lessons give special attention to word beginnings and endings.

Lessons 68 and 69. These lessons provide intensive practice on useful and frequently used business phrases.

Lesson 70. This lesson provides a general review.

From this point on, there are three activities that will help you build your shorthand speed:

1. *Plenty of reading and copying of well-written shorthand.* Read all the well-written shorthand on which you can lay your hands. The more shorthand you read and copy, the more rapidly will your dictation speed rise.

2. *Plenty of dictation at the proper speeds.* Your teacher, no doubt, will see to it that you get all the dictation you need. If you are ambitious, you can supplement your teacher's dictation with dictation from phonograph records and tapes, provided that you have the necessary equipment.

3. *Personal use of shorthand.* The student who substitutes his shorthand for longhand wherever possible gains dictation speed more rapidly than does the student who confines his shorthand writing to the few minutes he spends in his shorthand class and the time in which he does his shorthand homework.

Haven't you found shorthand to be a fascinating study thus far? Haven't you been pleased to see your ability to read and write shorthand develop from day to day? You will derive even greater pleasure and satisfaction from your shorthand study in the days ahead, as you come closer and closer to your goal of being a competent and efficient stenographer!

LESSON 55

The letters in this lesson concentrate on the shorthand devices in Chapter 1.

Reading and Writing Practice

478. 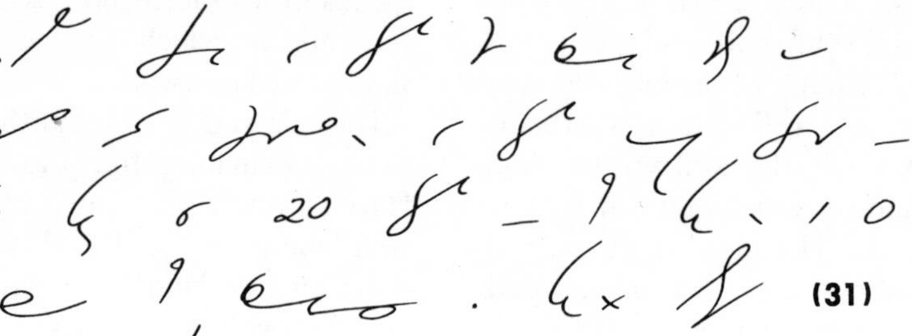 (31)

479. 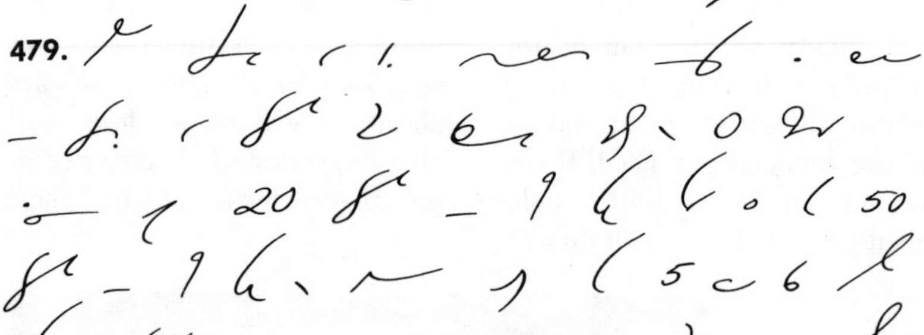 (47)

480. 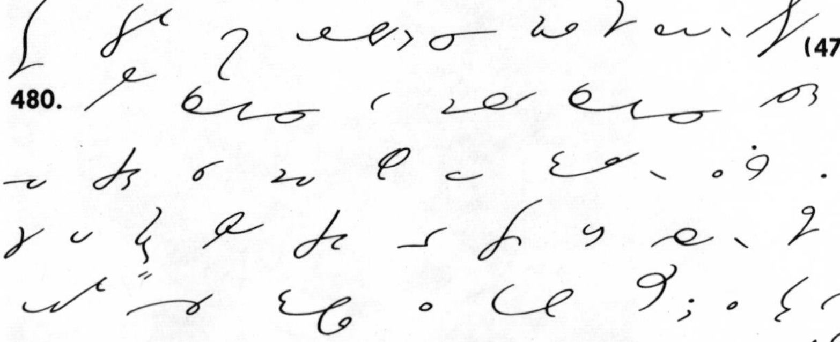

(73)

481.

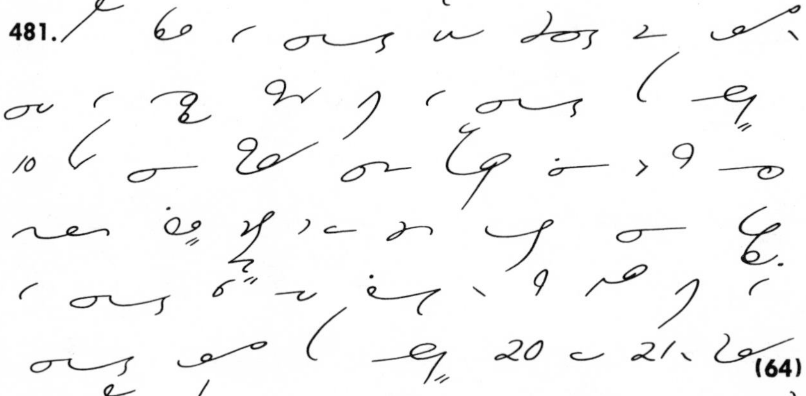

(64)

482.

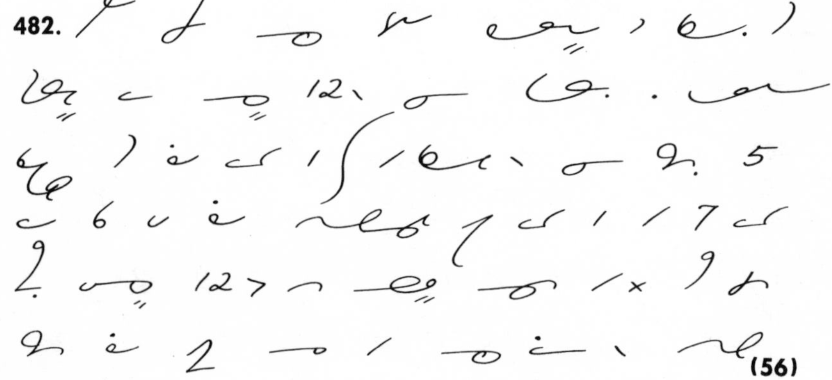

(56)

483.

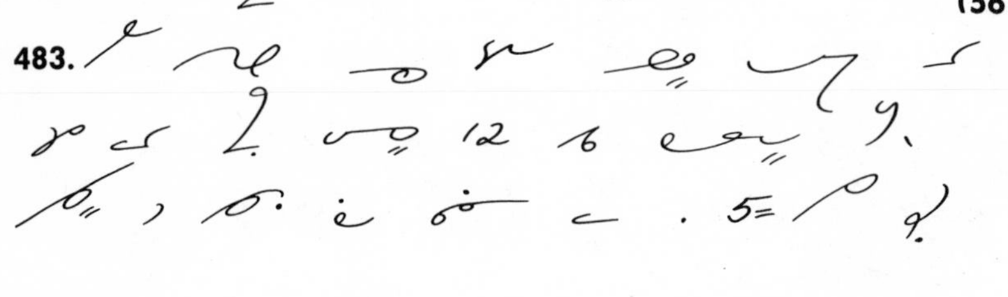

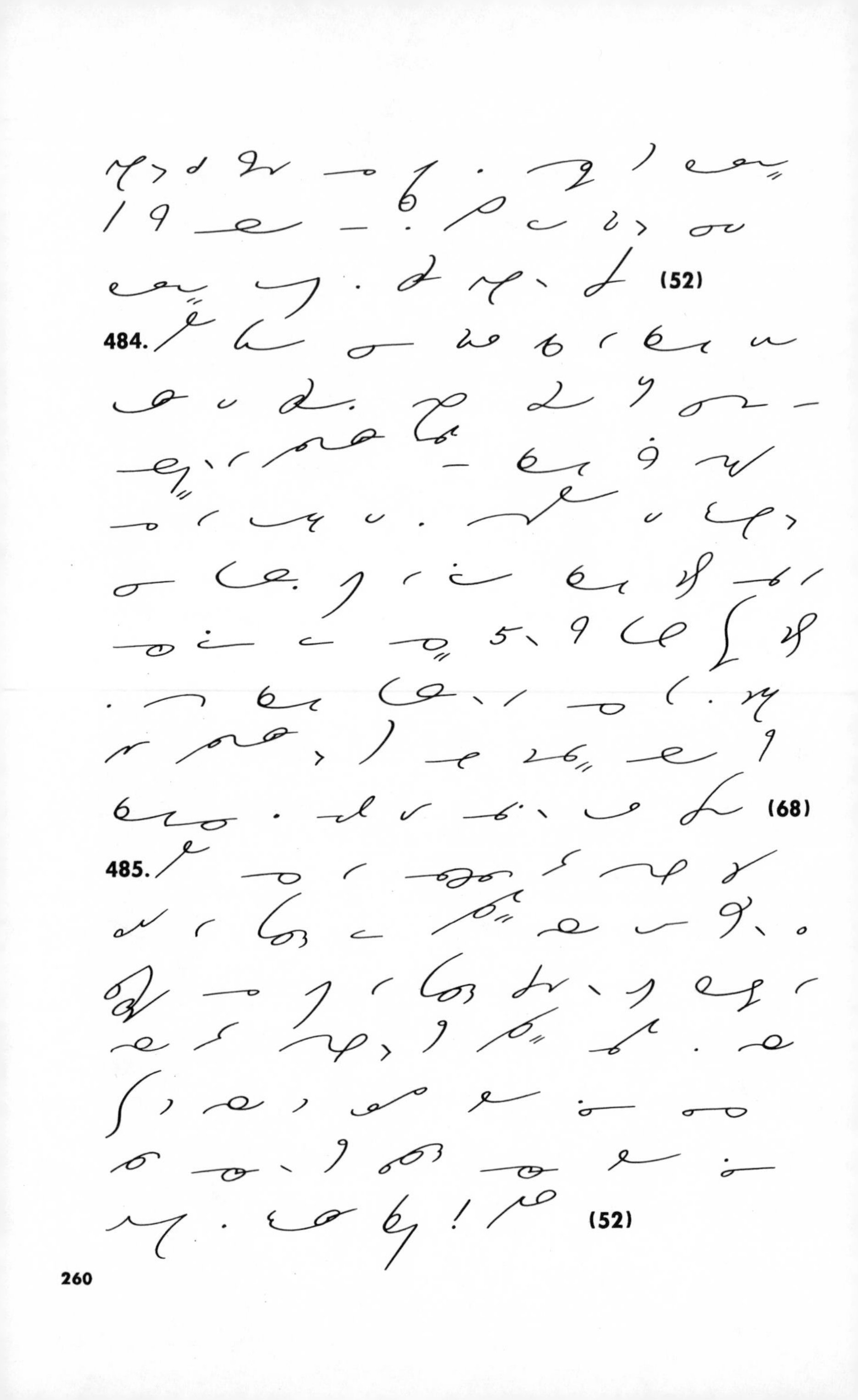

(52)

484.

(68)

485.

(52)

LESSON 56

The letters in this lesson concentrate on the shorthand devices in Chapter 2.

Reading and Writing Practice

486. Applied Vocabulary Study. *Crate,* a box used for packing fruit. *Via,* by way of. *On an even keel,* running smoothly.

487.

(78)

488.

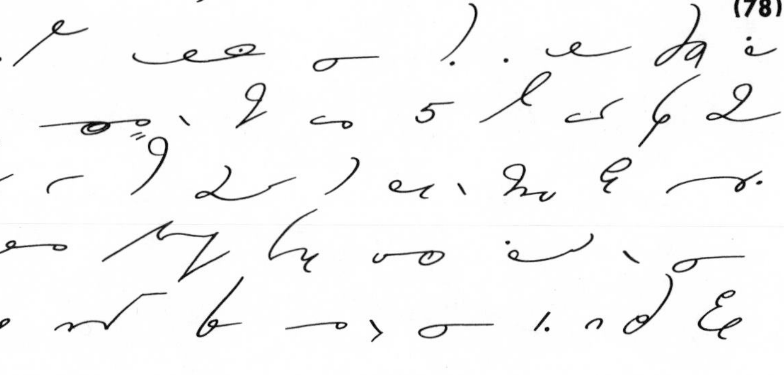

(70)

489.

(56)

490.

(116)

491.

(84)

492.

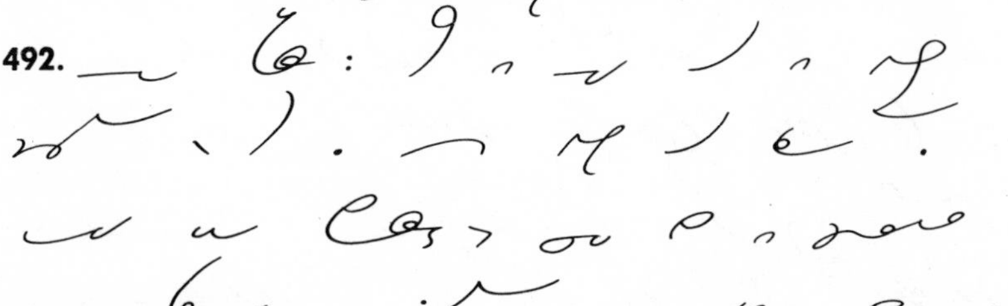

(41)

493.

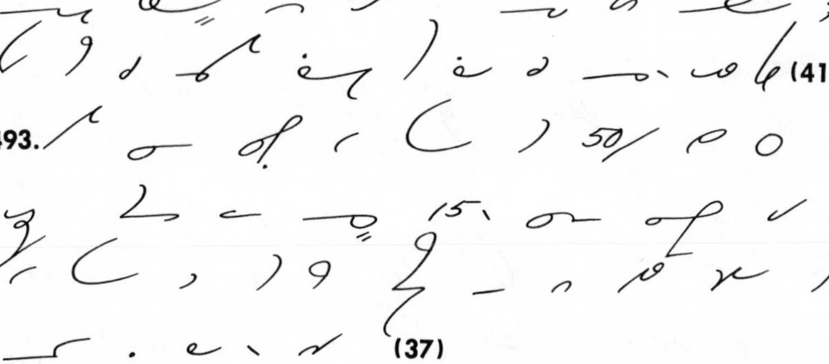

(37)

LESSON 57

The letters in this lesson concentrate on the shorthand devices in Chapter 3.

Reading and Writing Practice

494. Applied Vocabulary Study. *Hesitate,* pause. *Handling charges,* charges for wrapping, addressing, shipping, etc. *Overhead,* costs of running a business, such as rent, heat, taxes, etc.

495.

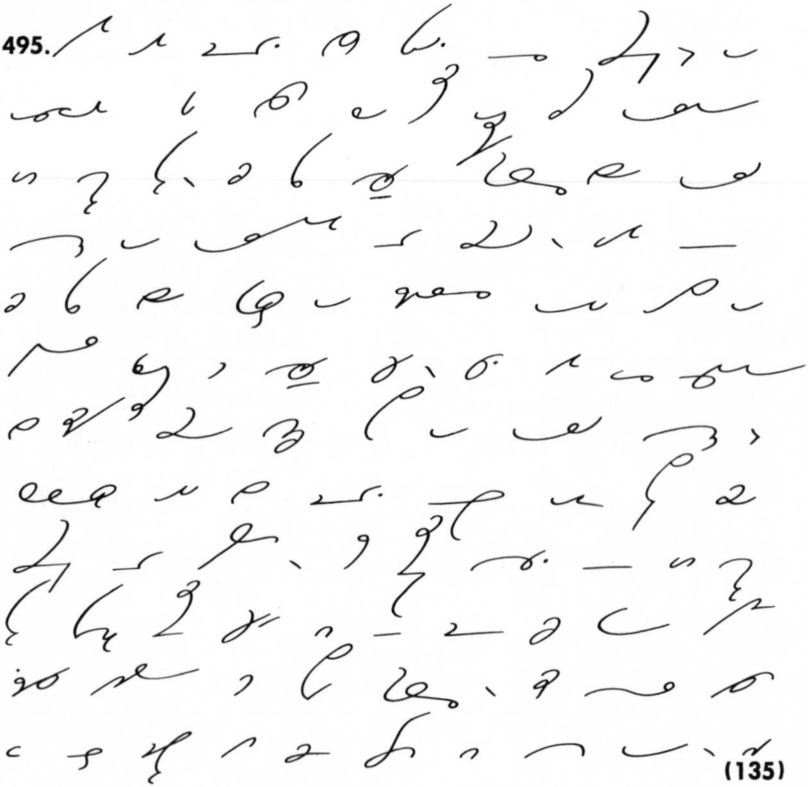

(135)

496. ... 50' ... (153)

497. ... 20 ...

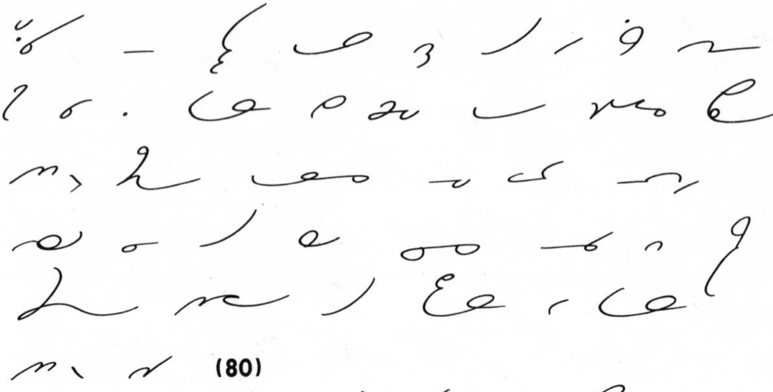

(80)

498.

(109)

LESSON 58

The material in this lesson concentrates on the shorthand devices in Chapter 4.

Reading and Writing Practice

499. Applied Vocabulary Study. *Fulfill,* carry out. *Reasoned,* thought. *Sacrifice,* giving up. *Pursue,* follow.

500. Study

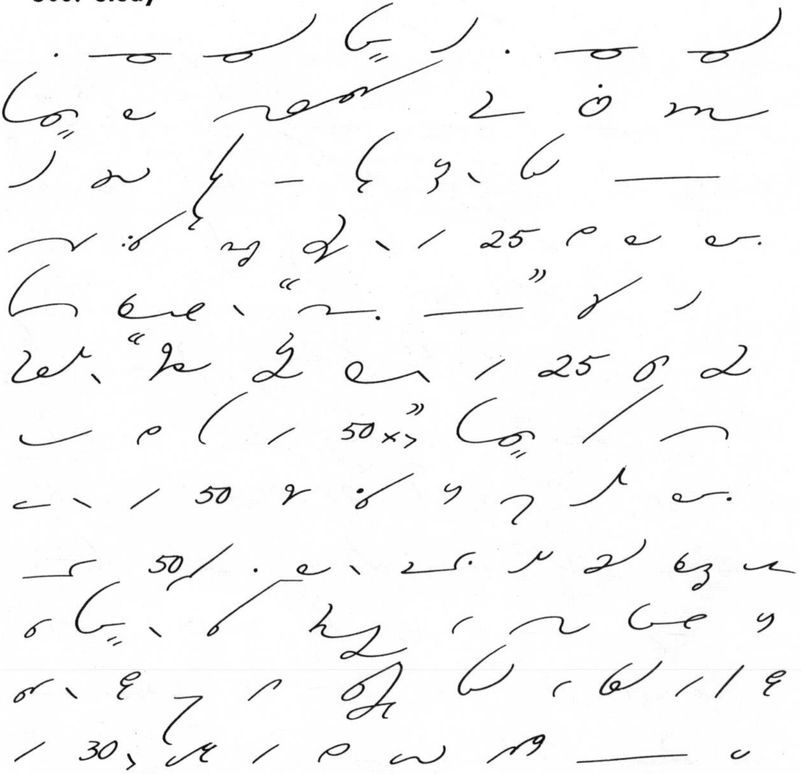

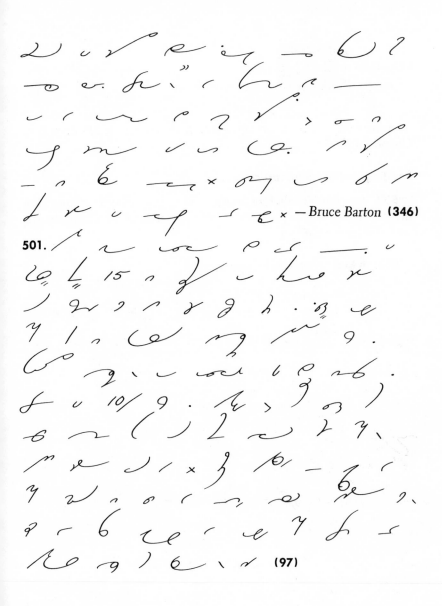

—Bruce Barton (346)

501.

(97)

LESSON 59

The material in this lesson concentrates on the shorthand devices in Chapter 5.

Reading and Writing Practice

502. Applied Vocabulary Study. *Role,* part. *Shipshape,* neat, orderly. *Pending,* not yet decided. *Hobby,* an interest to which one devotes his spare time.

503. A Businessman's Secretary

– A Businessman (273)

504. 

(117)

505.

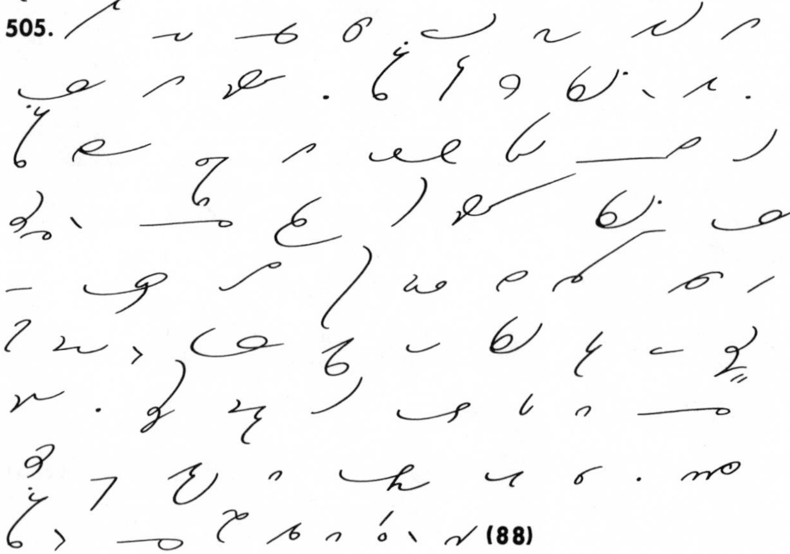

(88)

LESSON 60

The letters in this lesson concentrate on the shorthand devices in Chapter 6 .

Reading and Writing Practice

Reading Scoreboard. Time to measure your reading speed again! At this stage you are probably reading shorthand quite fluently and are hesitating over only an occasional outline. Use the following table in determining your present reading rate.

Lesson 60 contains 567 words.

If you read Lesson 60 in	your reading rate is
14 MINUTES	40 WORDS A MINUTE
16 MINUTES	35 WORDS A MINUTE
18 MINUTES	31 WORDS A MINUTE
20 MINUTES	28 WORDS A MINUTE
22 MINUTES	26 WORDS A MINUTE

506. Applied Vocabulary Study. *Portable,* capable of being carried. *Quarterly,* appearing four times a year. *Exhausted,* gone. *Air Transport,* shipping by air.

507.

customer

, parenthetical

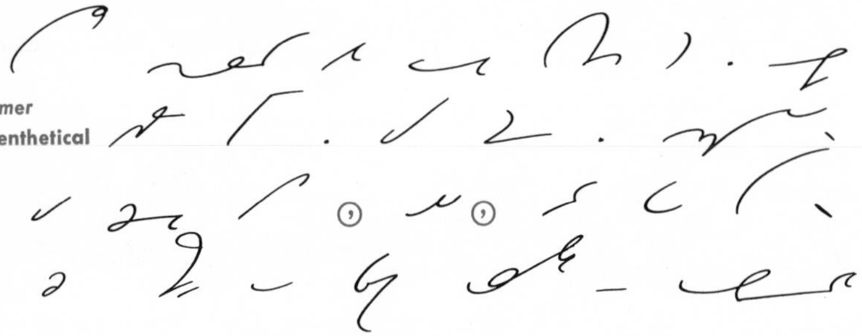

Quarterly

exhausted

, parenthetical
opportunity
some time

(120)

508.

, series
crowded
hurry

inclined
, parenthetical

Christmas
tomorrow

, parenthetical
superior
choose

(134)

509.

eyes
, parenthetical

enclosed
post card

(115)

510.

elsewhere
ordinarily
, parenthetical
, series

(116)

511.

recommending
typist
, apposition
interviewed
, series
, parenthetical
outstanding

(82)

LESSON 61

The material in this lesson concentrates on the shorthand devices in Chapter 7.

Reading and Writing Practice

512. Applied Vocabulary Study. *Simplify*, make easy. *Untiring*, never growing weary. *Adults*, grownups.

513. This Thing Called Success

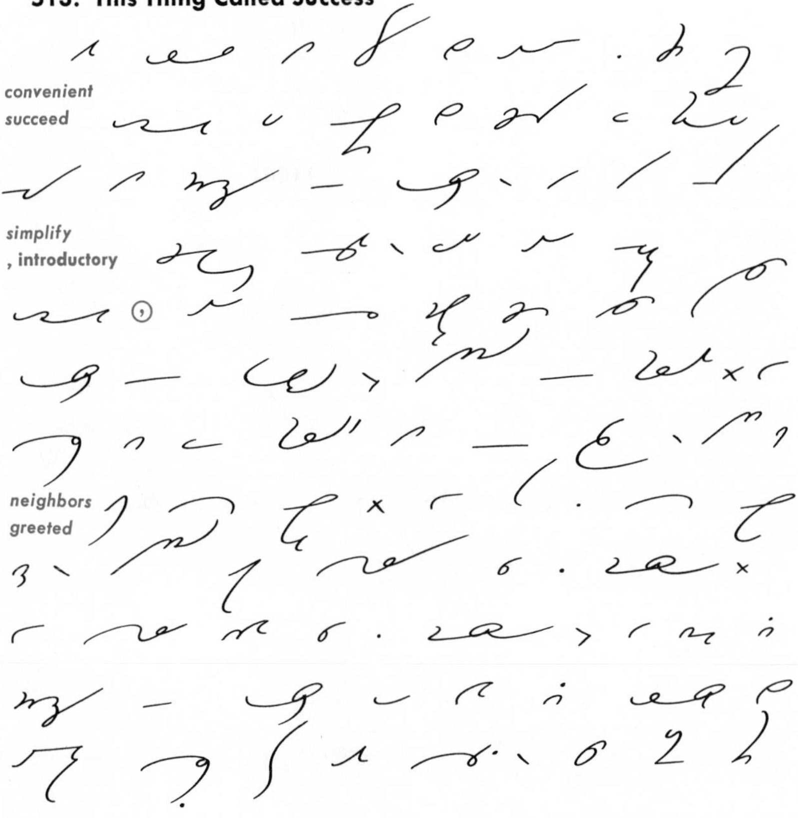

convenient
succeed
simplify
, introductory
neighbors
greeted

, when clause
failure
, if clause

, series
energy

(184)

514.

recently

, if clause
hesitate
competent

description
, introductory

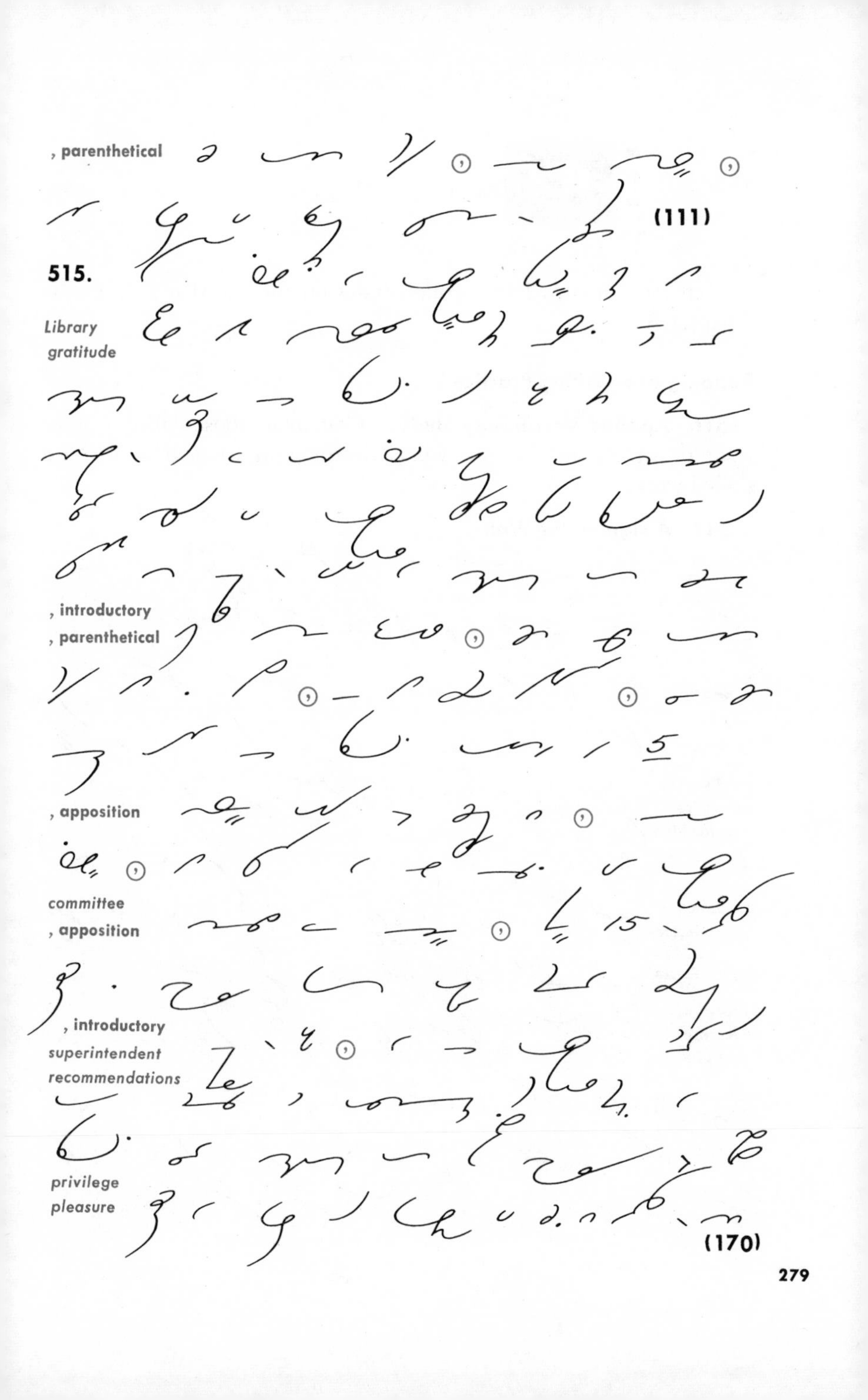

, parenthetical (,) (,)

(111)

515.

Library
gratitude

, introductory
, parenthetical (,) (,) (,)

5

, apposition (,)

(,)

committee
, apposition (,) 15

, introductory
superintendent
recommendations (,)

privilege
pleasure

(170)

LESSON **62**

The material in this lesson concentrates on the shorthand devices in Chapter 8.

Reading and Writing Practice

516. Applied Vocabulary Study. *Craftsmen,* those skilled in some trade or art. *Apprentice,* one who is learning an art or trade under a skilled worker.

517. A Sign on the Wall

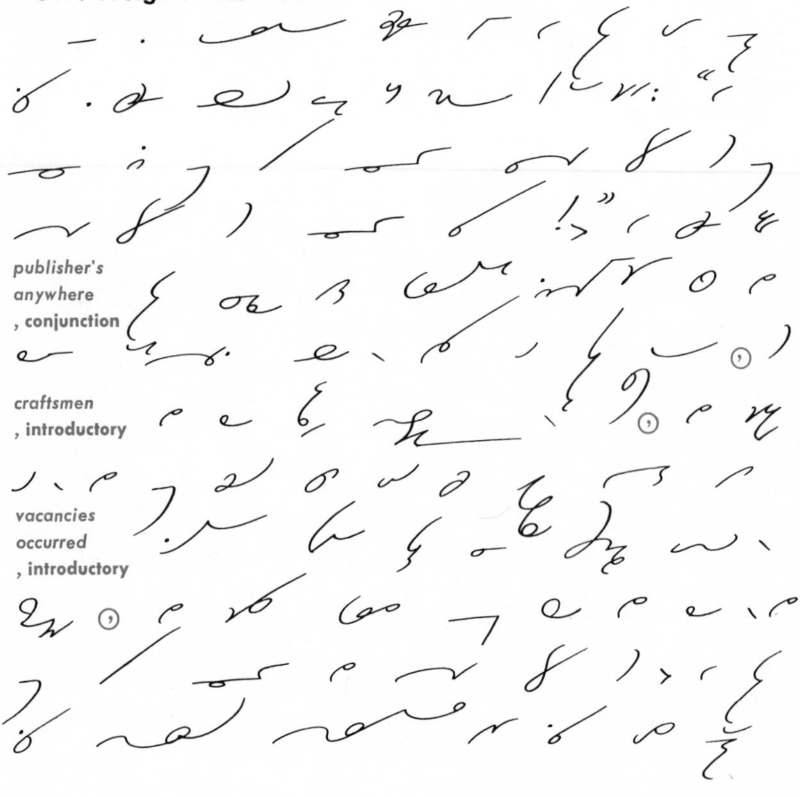

publisher's
anywhere
, conjunction

craftsmen
, introductory

vacancies
occurred
, introductory

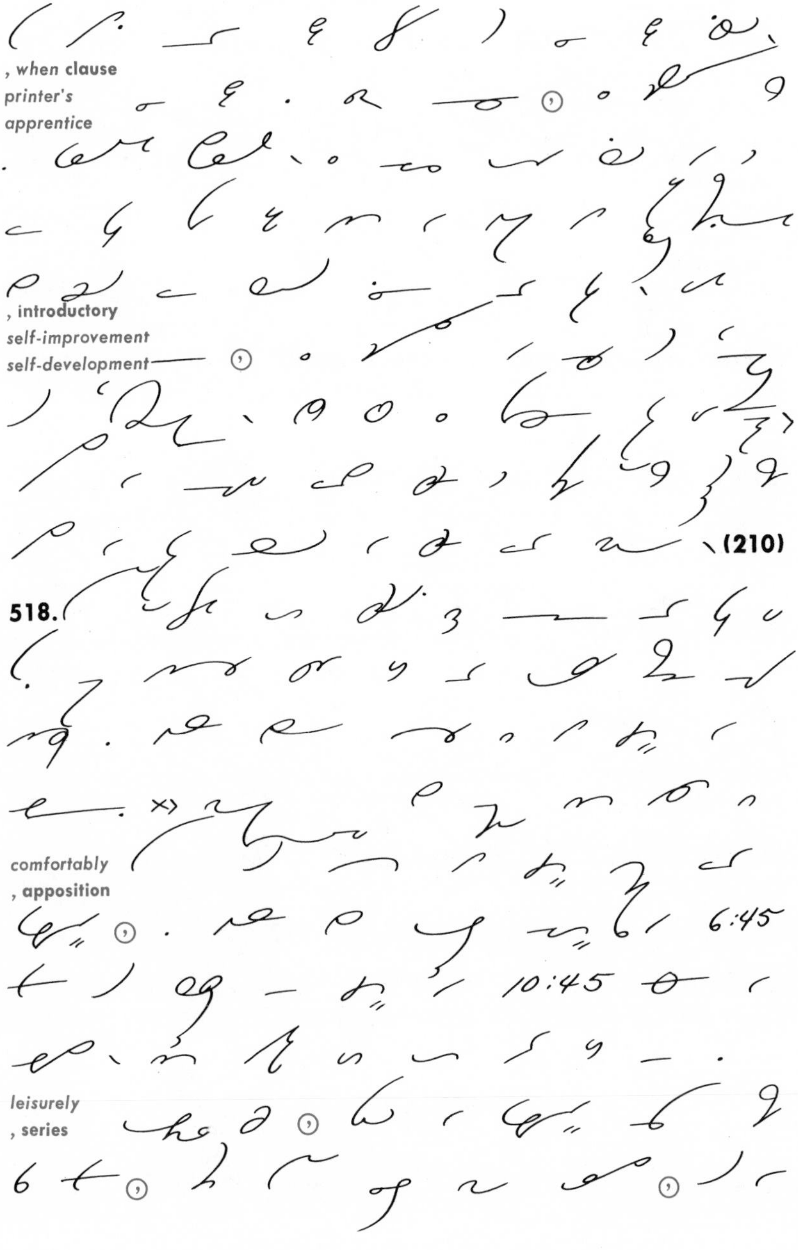
, when clause
printer's
apprentice
, introductory
self-improvement
self-development
(210)
518.
comfortably
, apposition
6:45
10:45
leisurely
, series

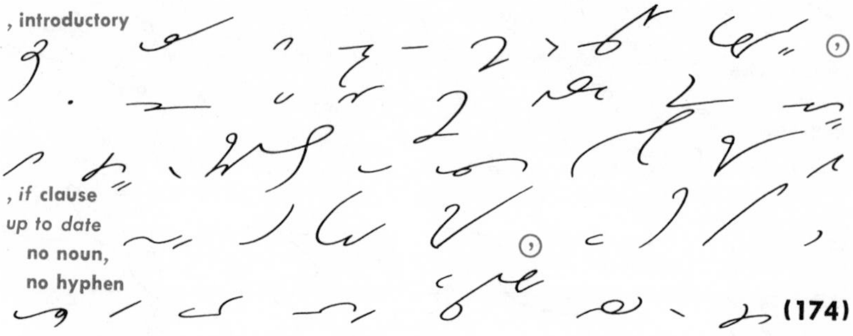
, introductory
, if clause
up to date
no noun,
no hyphen

(174)

Pretranscription Quiz. For you to supply: 5 commas – 4 commas series, 1 comma as clause; 3 words missing from the shorthand.

519.

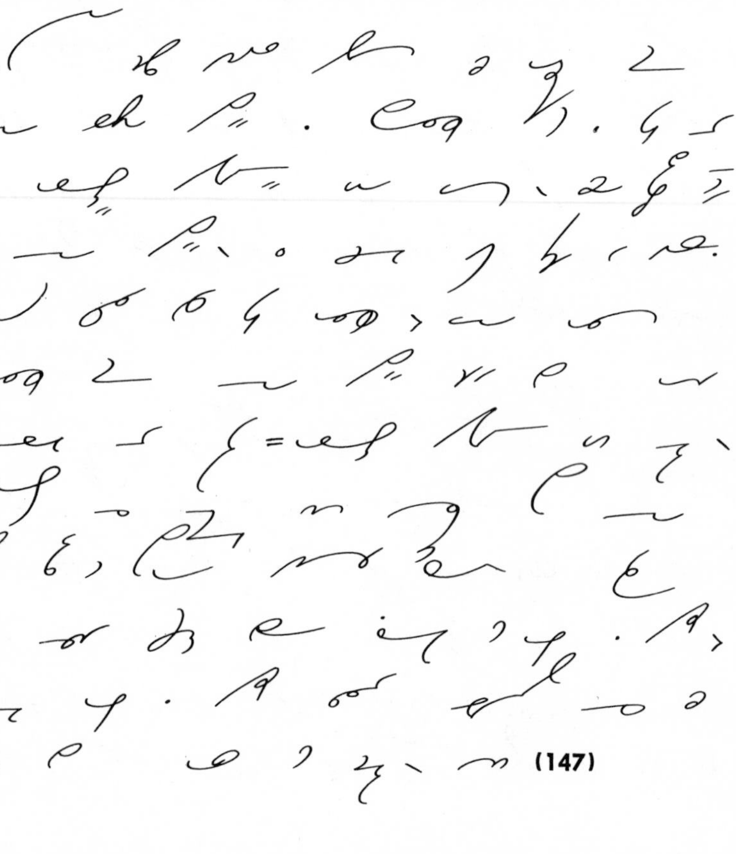

(147)

LESSON 63

The material in this lesson concentrates on the shorthand devices in Chapter 9.

Reading and Writing Practice

520. Applied Vocabulary Study. *Epitaph,* an inscription on a gravestone. *Memorial,* a monument intended to preserve the memory of a person. *Humorist,* one who displays humor or wit in his speaking or writing.

521. He Liked Everybody

epitaph
, parenthetical
prominent
, conjunction
, when clause
probably
memorial
, when clause

, when clause

, introductory

twinkle

, conjunction

search

astonishingly

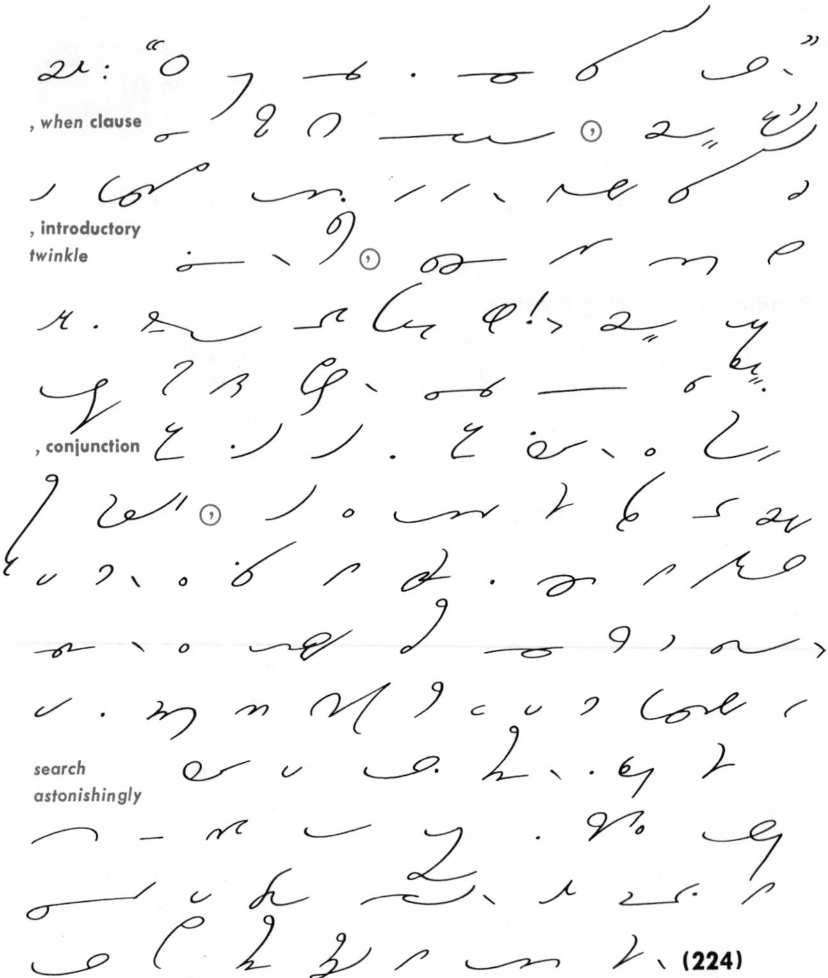

(224)

522.

birth

, *as* clause

, introductory

, series

, introductory

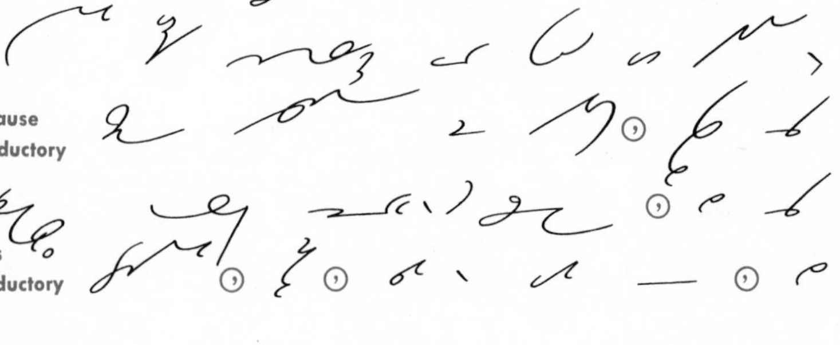

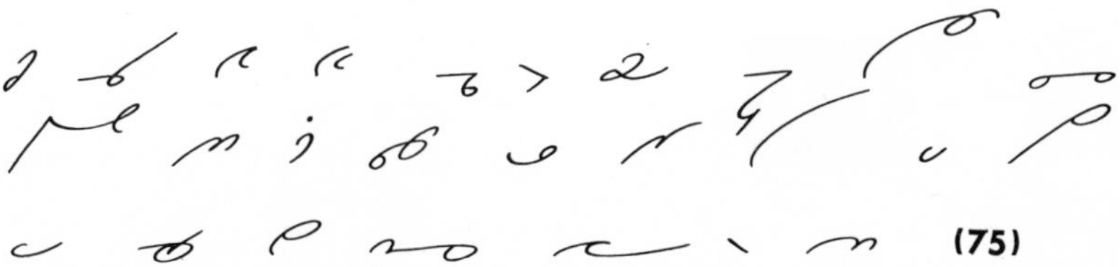

(75)

Pretranscription Quiz. For you to supply: 5 commas—3 commas introductory, 2 commas *if* clause; 3 words missing from the shorthand.

523.

(187)

LESSON 64

The following letters concentrate on brief forms. The letters contain 173 different brief forms; 469, counting repetitions.

Reading and Writing Practice

524. Applied Vocabulary Study. *Advantageously,* profitably. *Objective,* aim. *Turnover,* old employees leaving and being replaced by new ones. *Extraordinary,* remarkable.

525.

, conjunction
hundreds

, series
magazines

, parenthetical
advantageously

, parenthetical
regardless

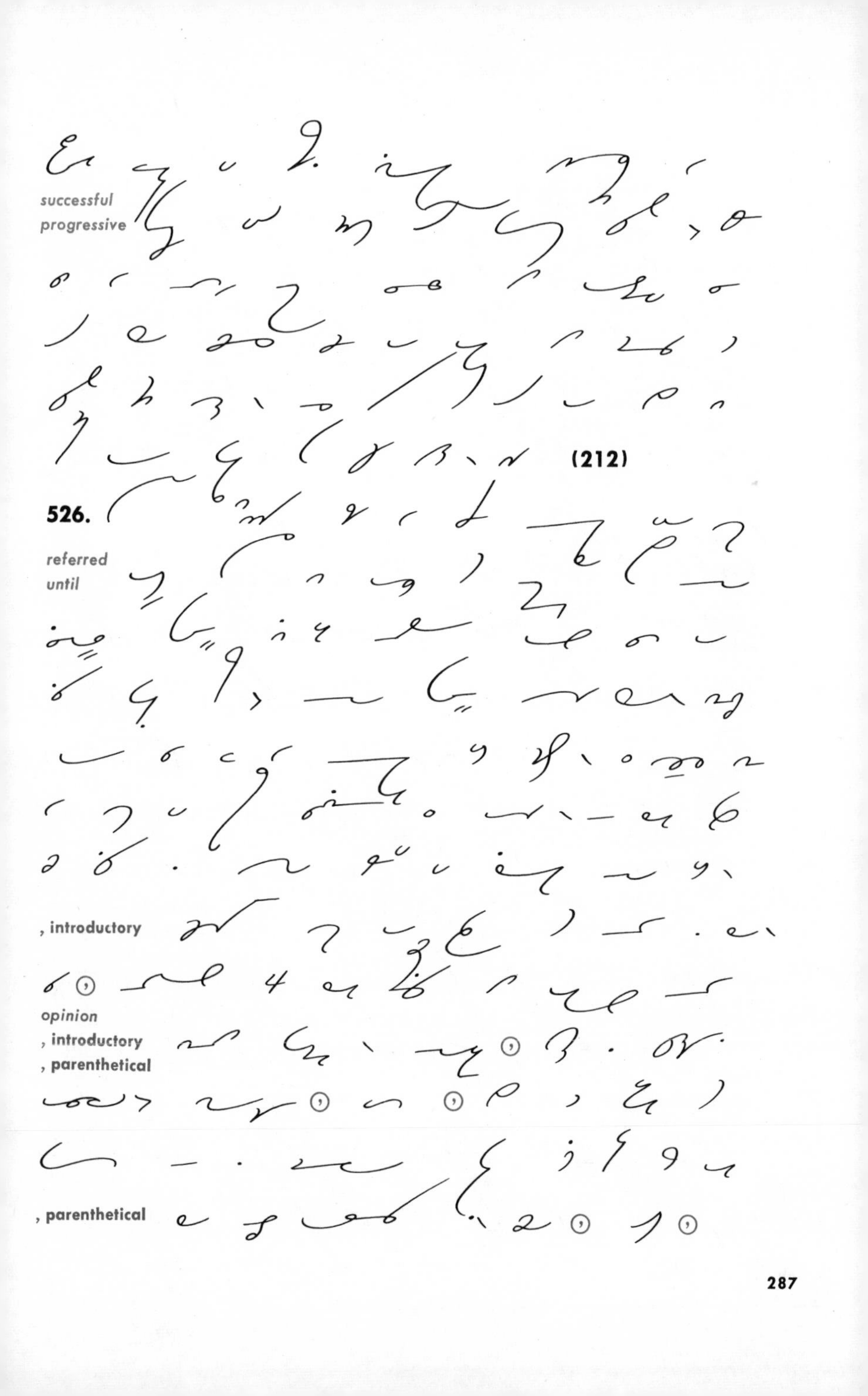

successful
progressive

(212)

526.

referred
until

, introductory

opinion
, introductory
, parenthetical

, parenthetical

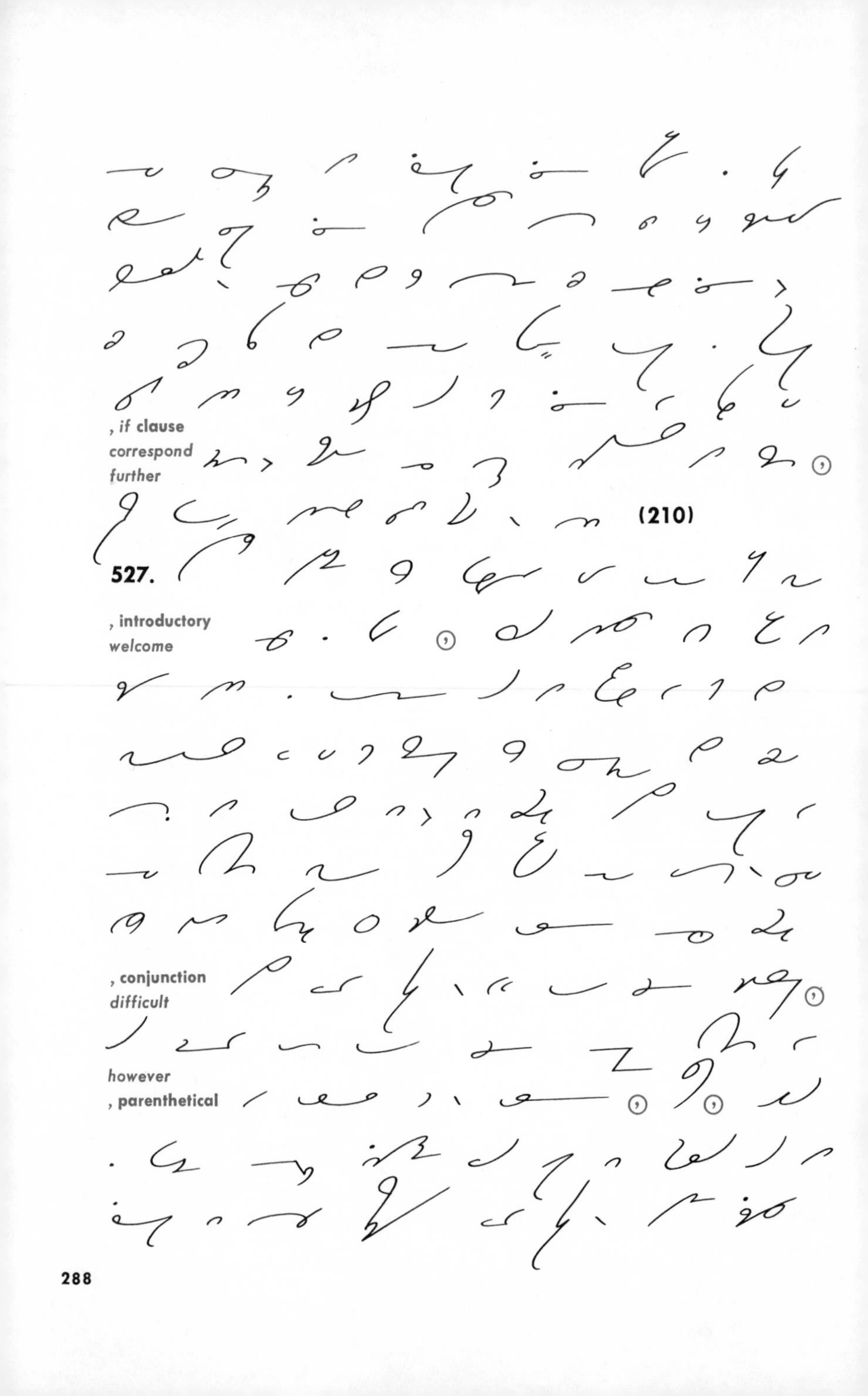

, *if clause*
correspond
further

(210)

527.

, *introductory*
welcome

, *conjunction*
difficult

however
, *parenthetical*

, parenthetical
, conjunction

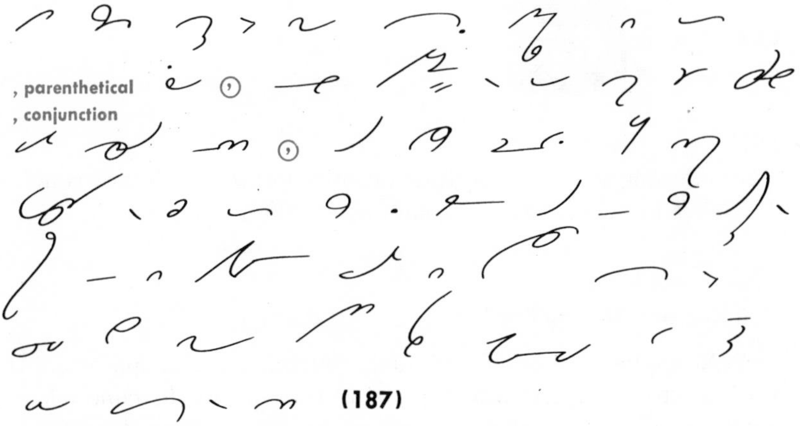

(187)

Pretranscription Quiz. For you to supply: 5 commas – 2 commas introductory, 2 commas parenthetical, 1 comma *if* clause; 2 words missing from the shorthand.

528.

(111)

LESSON 65

The following letters concentrate on brief forms. The letters contain 142 different brief forms; 427, counting repetitions.

Reading and Writing Practice

529. Applied Vocabulary Study. *Intentionally*, on purpose. *Assurance*, guarantee, certainty. *Inferior*, of poor quality. *Pertains*, relates, applies.

530.

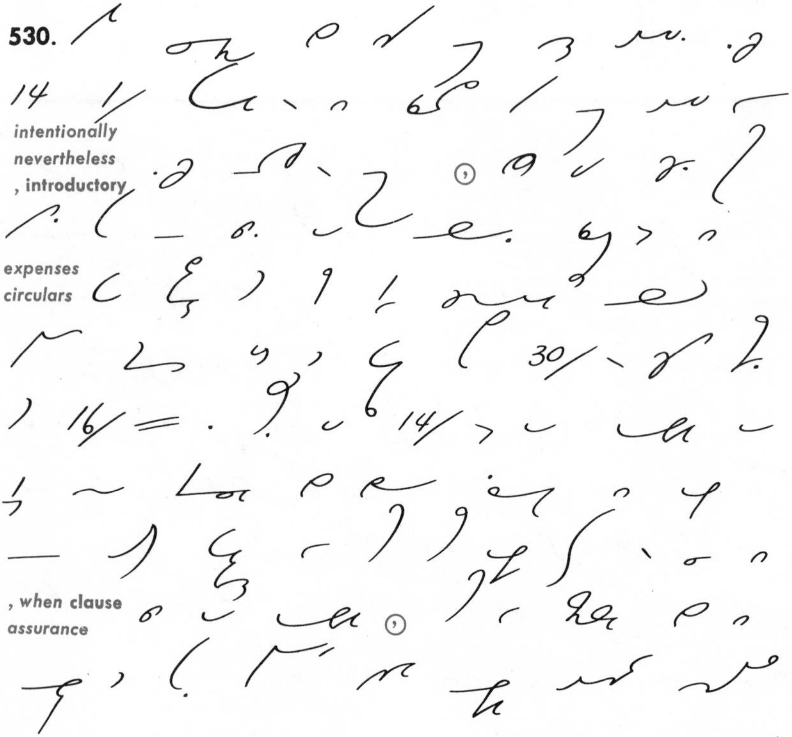

14
intentionally
nevertheless
, introductory
expenses
circulars
30/
16/
14/
, when clause
assurance

, if clause

, when clause
worth while
no noun,
no hyphen

(198)

531.

pertains
engagement
likewise

, introductory
character

, introductory
, apposition
, introductory

(114)

532.

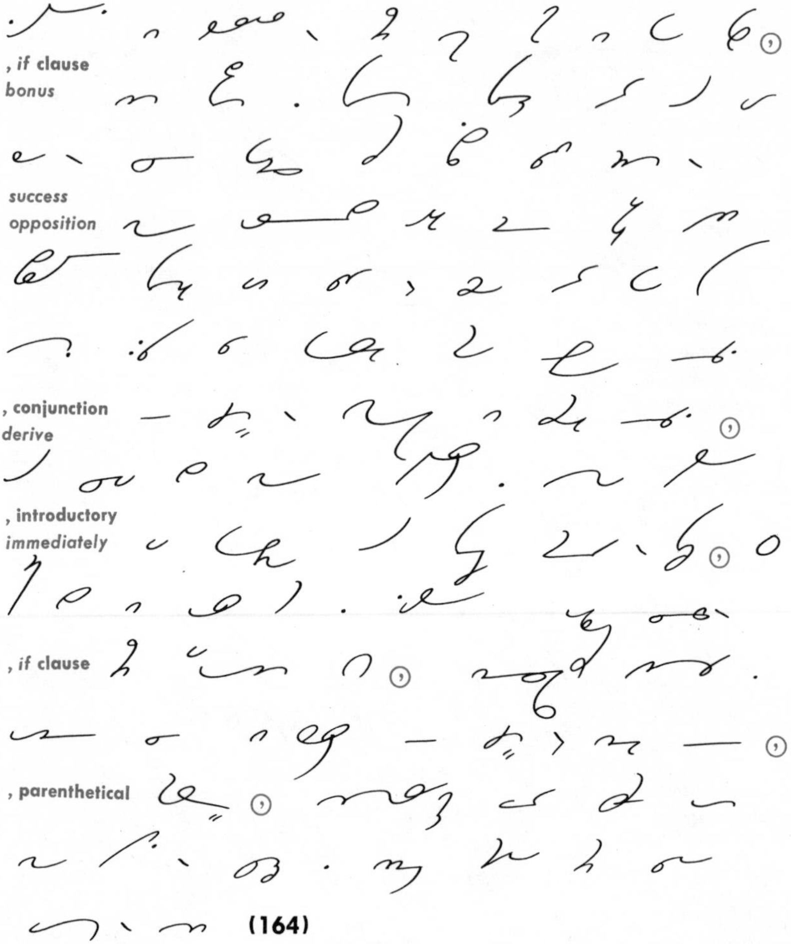
, if clause
bonus
success
opposition
, conjunction
derive
, introductory
immediately
, if clause
, parenthetical
(164)

Pretranscription Quiz. For you to supply: 6 commas – 2 commas *when* clause, 2 commas conjunction, 1 comma introductory, 1 comma parenthetical; 3 words missing from the shorthand.

533.

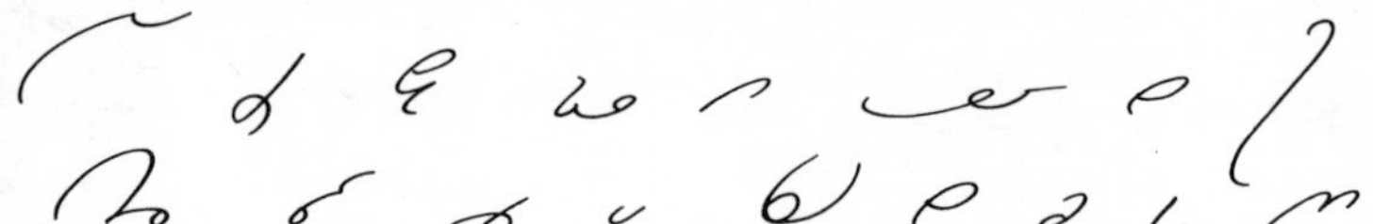

(195)

LESSON 66

The letters in this lesson concentrate on word beginnings. There are 72 words illustrating word beginnings. Each word beginning of Gregg Shorthand is illustrated one or more times.

Reading and Writing Practice

534. Applied Vocabulary Study. *Documents,* official papers. *Postpone,* put off, delay. *Competent,* able. *Impressive,* favorable, very good.

535.

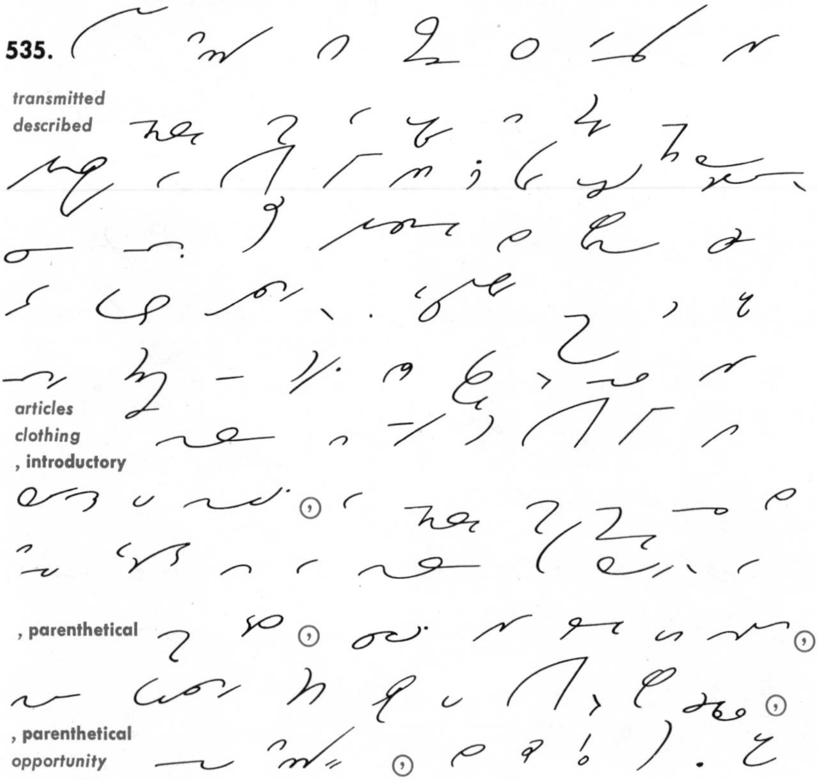

transmitted
described
articles
clothing
, introductory
, parenthetical
, parenthetical
opportunity

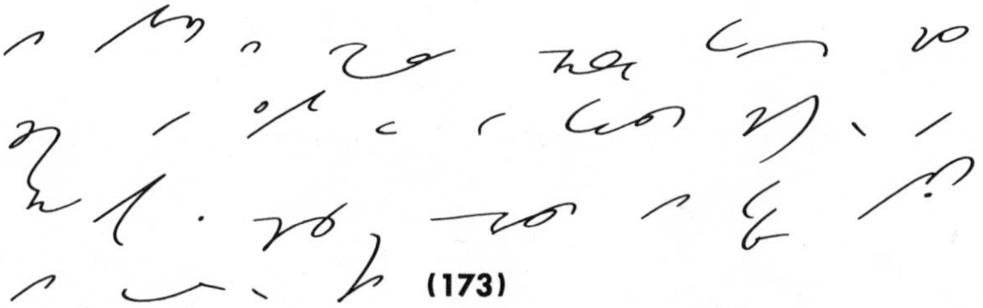

(173)

536. 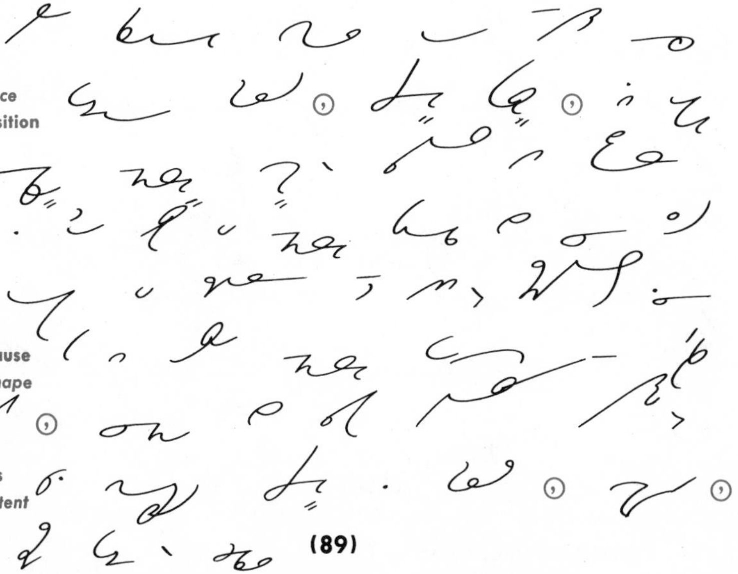

introduce
, apposition
, if clause
shipshape
, series
competent

(89)

Pretranscription Quiz. For you to supply: 7 commas – 3 commas introductory, 2 commas parenthetical, 2 commas apposition; 3 words missing from the shorthand.

537. 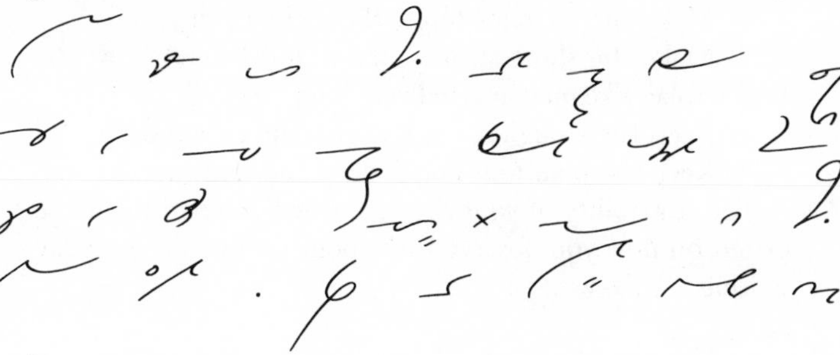

(164)

Proportion Check List

As a result of the shorthand writing that you have already done, no doubt you have come to realize how important it is to

1. Make the *a* circles huge; the *e* circles tiny.
2. Make the short strokes like *n* and *t* very short; the long strokes like *men* and *ted* very long.
3. Keep the straight lines straight; the curves deep.
4. Keep the *o* and *oo* hooks deep and narrow.

The readability of your shorthand will depend to a large extent on how you observe these pointers in your everyday writing.

The letters in this lesson concentrate on word endings. There are 76 words illustrating word endings. Each word ending of Gregg Shorthand is illustrated one or more times.

Reading and Writing Practice

538. Applied Vocabulary Study. *Forward-looking,* looking to the future. *Prudent,* cautious, sensible. *Specifications,* detailed descriptions. *Tentatively,* not finally.

539.

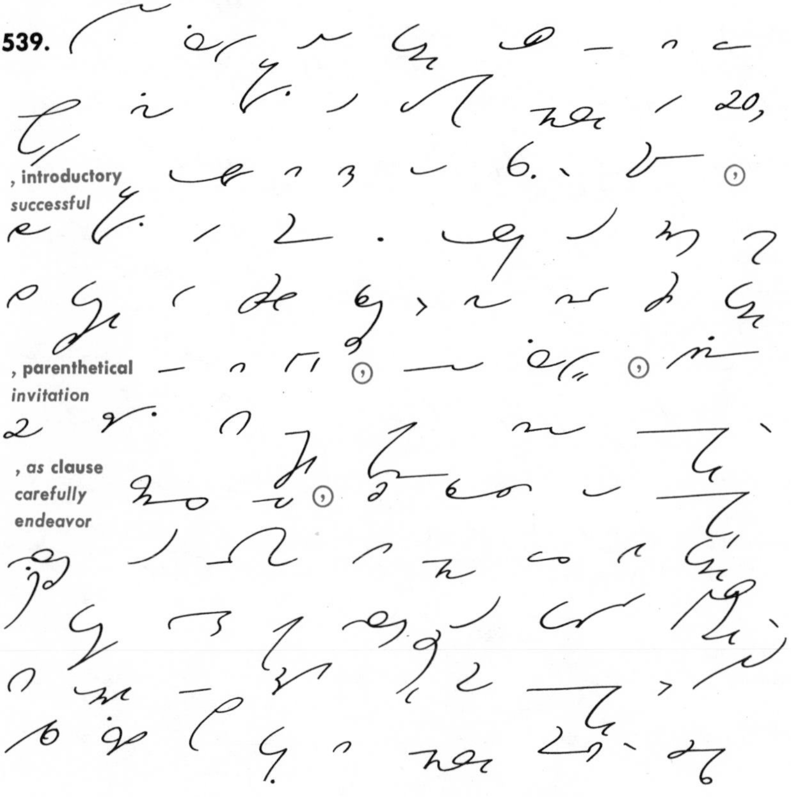
, introductory
successful
, parenthetical
invitation
, as clause
carefully
endeavor

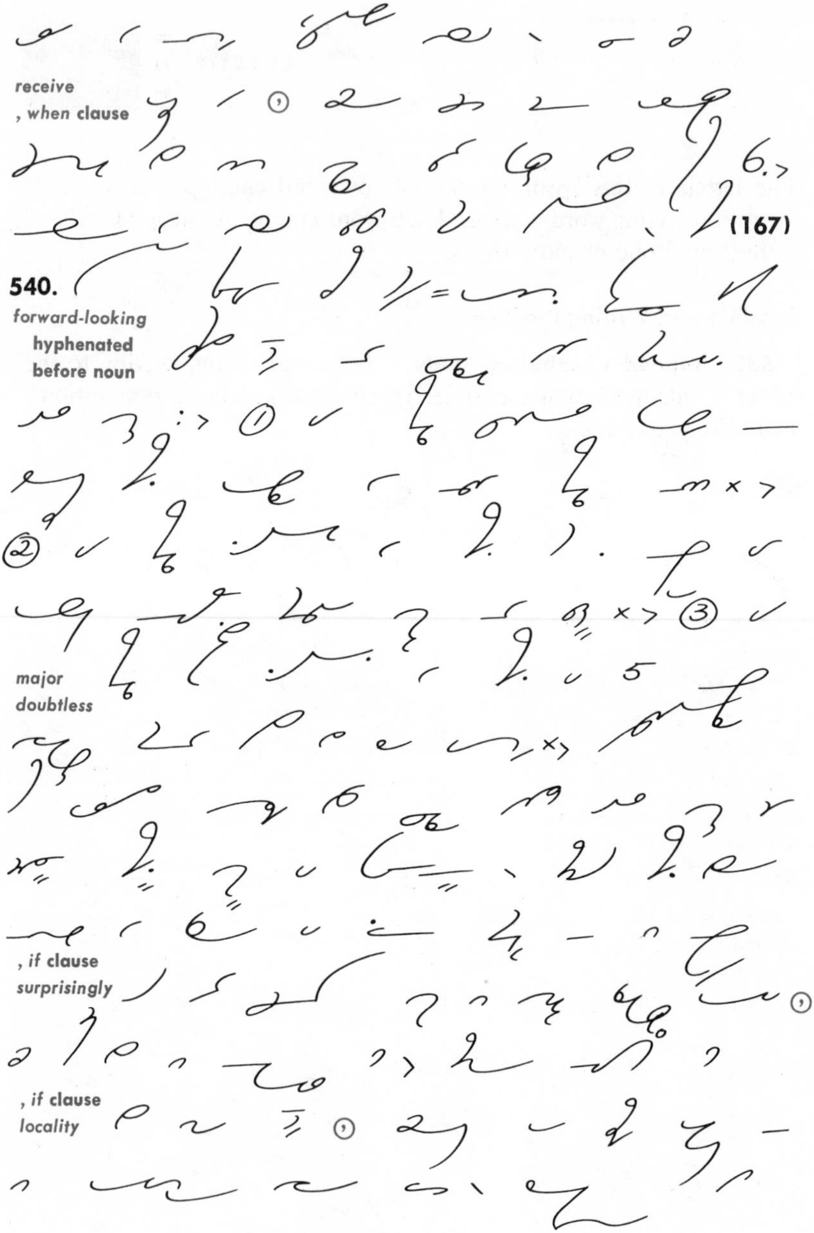

receive

, when clause

(167)

540.

forward-looking

hyphenated

before noun

major

doubtless

, if clause

surprisingly

, if clause

locality

formulate
, *if* clause
compose

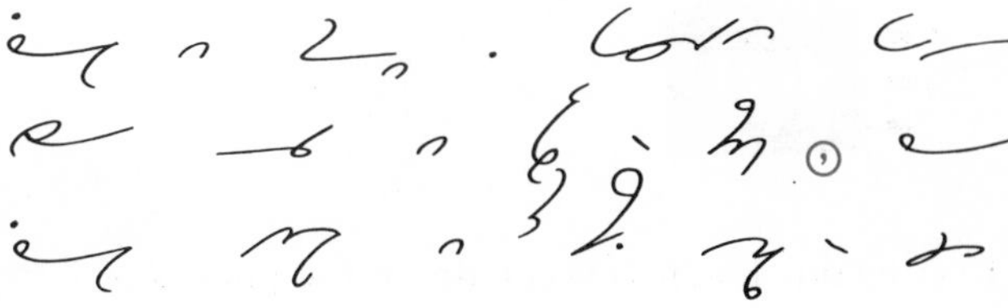

(208)

Pretranscription Quiz. For you to supply: 10 commas – 1 comma as clause, 2 commas series, 3 commas introductory, 3 commas apposition, 1 comma *if* clause; 2 words missing from the shorthand.

541.

(144)

LESSON 68

The letters in this lesson concentrate on the phrases of Gregg Shorthand. The letters contain 112 phrases, with one or more illustrations of every phrasing device.

Reading and Writing Practice

542. Applied Vocabulary Study. *Respond,* answer. *Carried your account,* did not insist on payment. *Successor,* the person who takes another's place.

543.

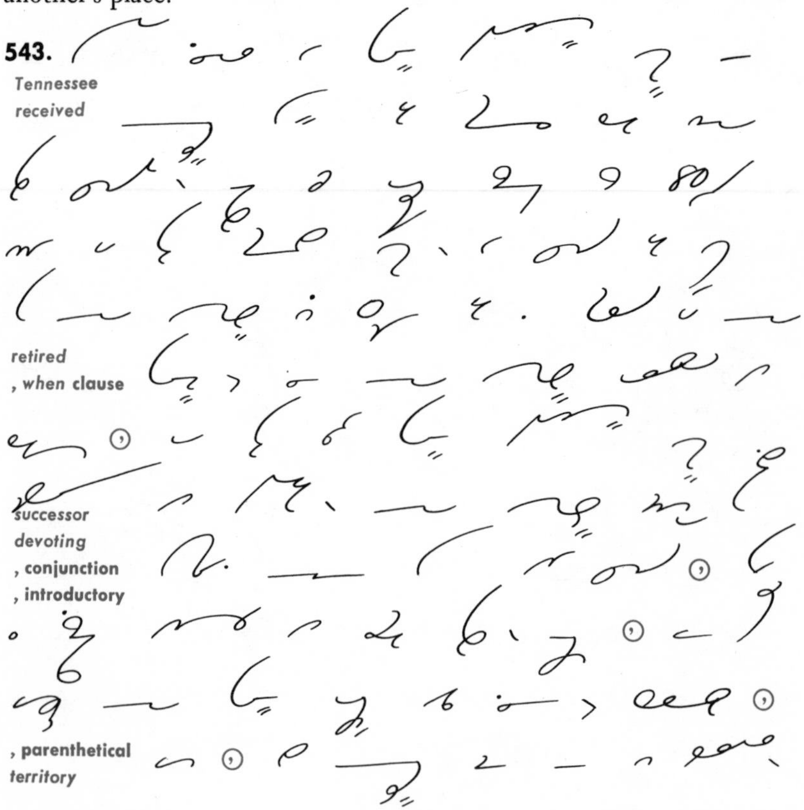

Tennessee
received
retired
, when clause
successor
devoting
, conjunction
, introductory
, parenthetical
territory

, parenthetical
whether

season
, conjunction

, introductory

(183)

544.

owed
, conjunction

, conjunction
repayment

respond

, if clause
, parenthetical
, when clause

, parenthetical
settle

, conjunction

recently

(166)

Pretranscription Quiz. For you to supply: 11 commas – 8 commas parenthetical, 2 commas conjunction, 1 comma *if* clause; 3 words missing from the shorthand.

545.

(145)

LESSON 69

The letters in this lesson concentrate on the phrases of Gregg Shorthand. The letters contain 100 phrases, with one or more illustrations of every phrasing device.

Reading and Writing Practice

546. Applied Vocabulary Study. *Convey,* carry. *Liberal,* generous. *Relationship,* association. *Intimated,* suggested, hinted.

547.

, conjunction
breakfast
everyone
worth while
no noun,
no hyphen
, introductory
, introductory

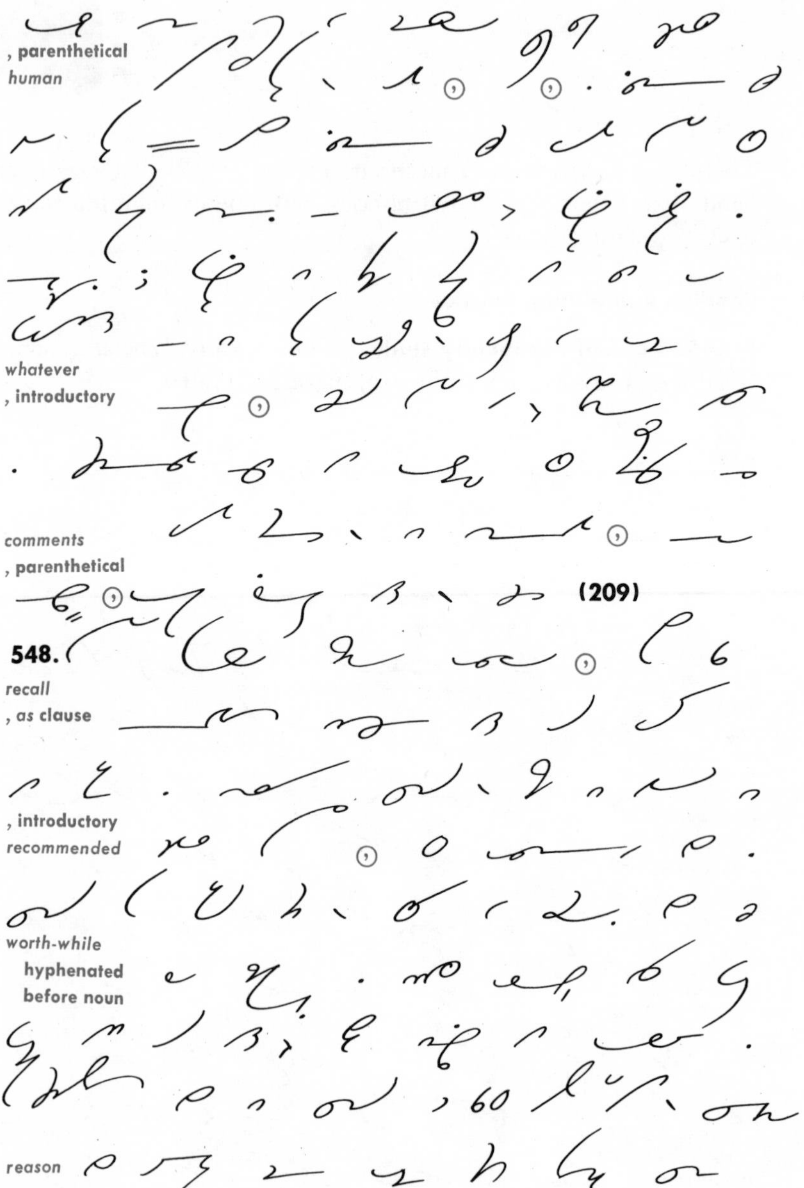

, parenthetical
human

whatever
, introductory

comments
, parenthetical

(209)

548.

recall
, as clause

, introductory
recommended

worth-while
hyphenated
before noun

reason

(122)

Pretranscription Quiz. For you to supply: 5 commas – 2 commas series, 1 comma conjunction, 1 comma apposition, 1 comma *if* clause; 2 words missing from the shorthand.

549.

(144)

LESSON 70

You won't be able to refrain from chuckling as you read the following exchange of letters between a hotel manager and a guest.

Reading and Writing Practice

Reading Scoreboard. Now that you are on the last lesson, you are no doubt very much interested in your final shorthand reading rate. If you have followed the practice suggestions you received early in the course, your shorthand reading rate at this time should be a source of pride to you.

To get a real picture of how much your shorthand reading rate has increased with practice, compare it with your reading rate in Lesson 18, the first time you measured it.

The following table will help you determine your rate on the *first reading*.

Lesson 70 contains 500 words.

If you read Lesson 70 in	your reading rate is
10 MINUTES	50 WORDS A MINUTE
12 MINUTES	42 WORDS A MINUTE
14 MINUTES	36 WORDS A MINUTE
16 MINUTES	31 WORDS A MINUTE
18 MINUTES	28 WORDS A MINUTE
20 MINUTES	25 WORDS A MINUTE

550. Applied Vocabulary Study. *Customary,* usual. *Desolated,* full of gloom. *By the same token,* in the same way. *Conceivably,* possibly.

551.

customary
guest's
, introductory
woolen
occupied
, parenthetical
, parenthetical
luggage
, parenthetical

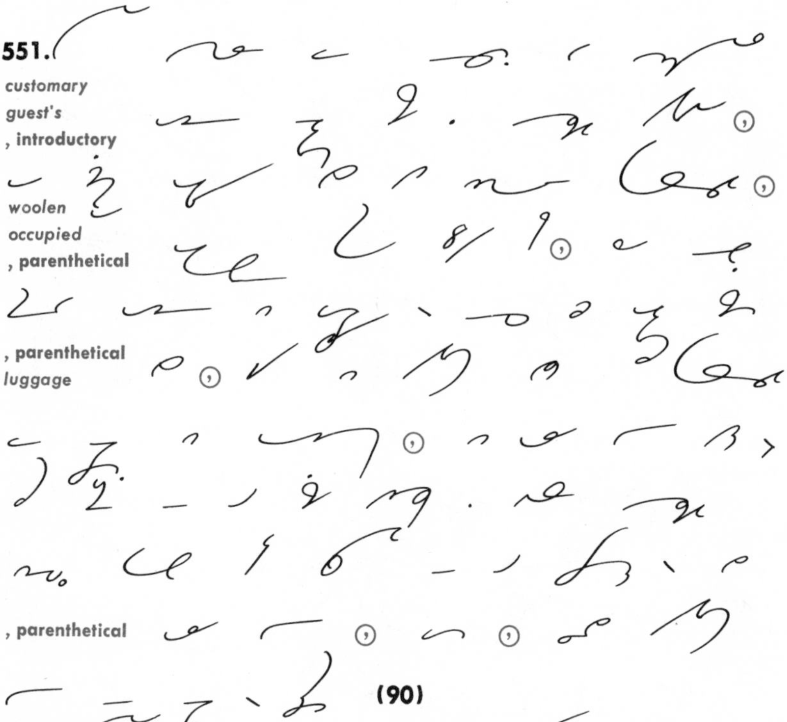

(90)

552.

desolated
, apposition
absent-minded
souvenirs
, introductory

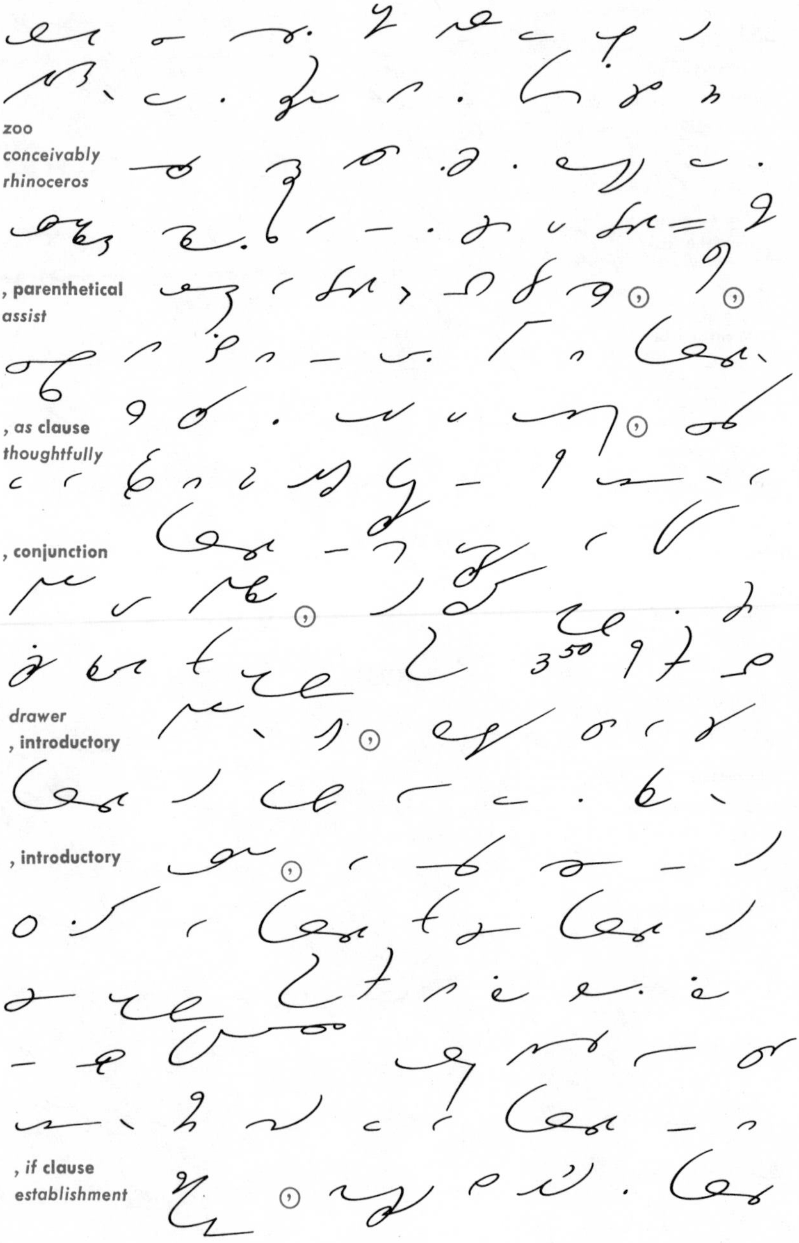

zoo
conceivably
rhinoceros

, parenthetical
assist

, as clause
thoughtfully

, conjunction

drawer
, introductory

, introductory

, if clause
establishment

 (256)

Pretranscription Quiz. For you to supply: 6 commas – 2 commas series, 1 comma introductory, 1 comma conjunction, 2 commas parenthetical; 3 words missing from the shorthand.

553.

 (154)

554. Recall Chart. This chart contains an illustration of every principle of Gregg Shorthand. Can you read the 102 words and phrases in 5 minutes?

Words

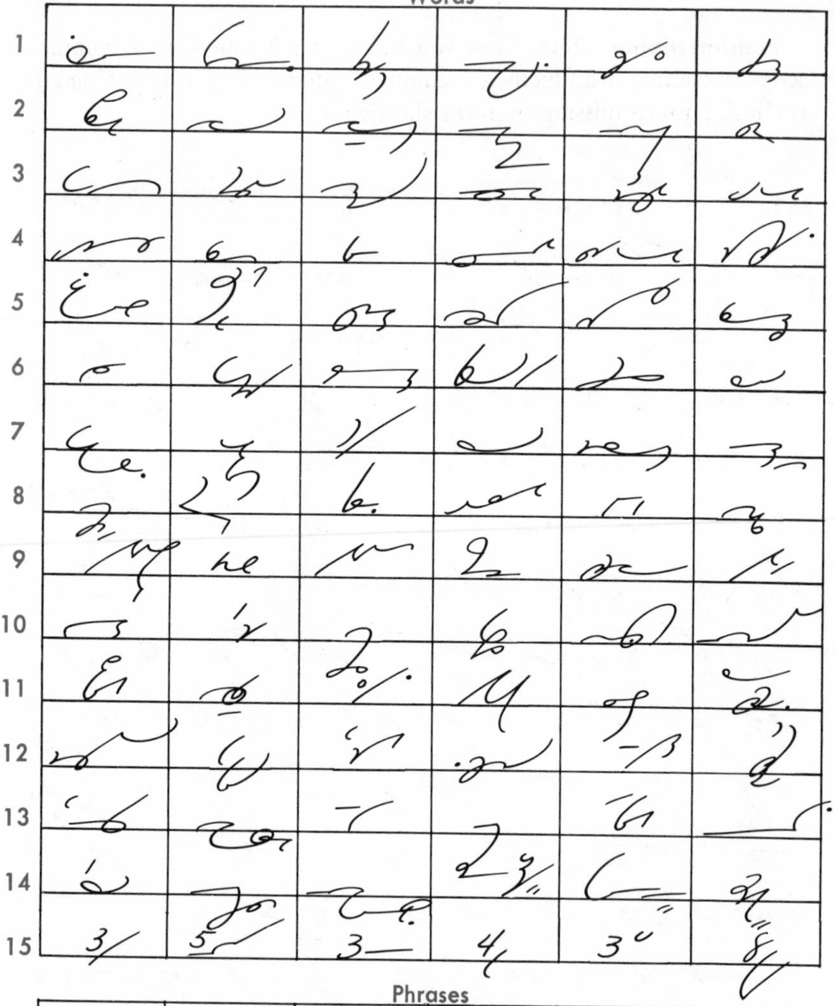
1
2
3
4
5
6
7
8
9
10
11
12
13
14
15

Phrases

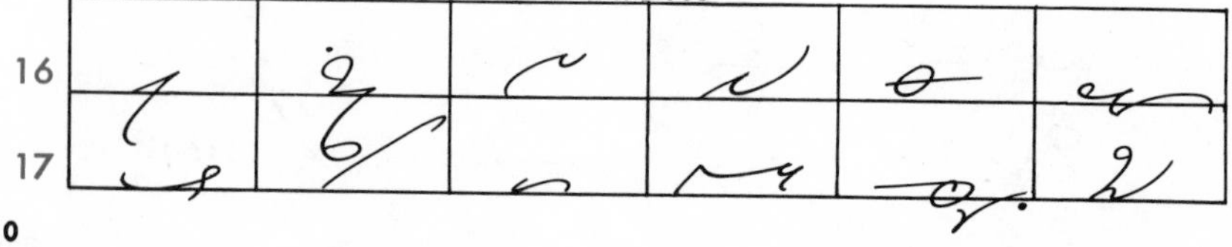
16
17

APPENDIX

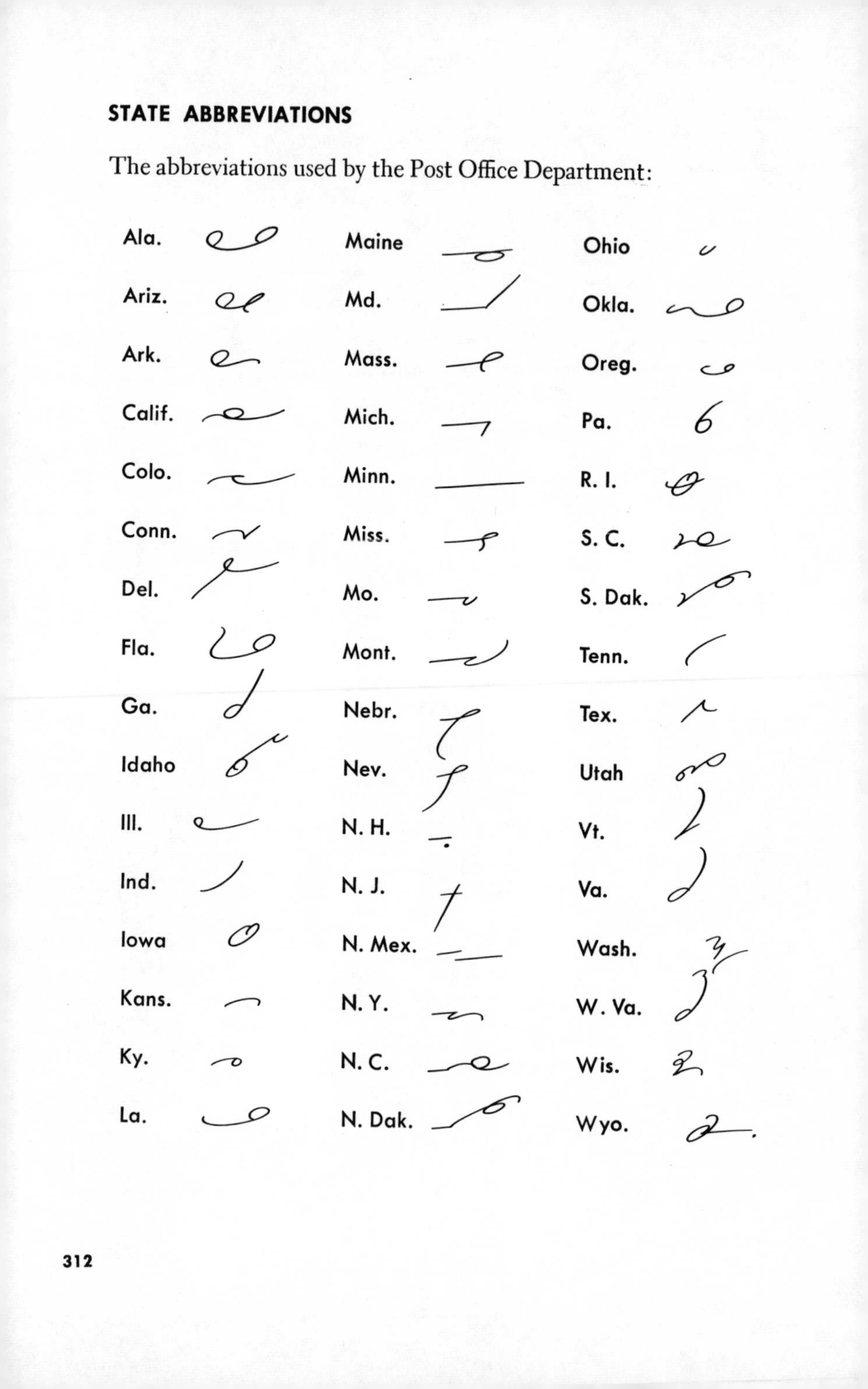

STATE ABBREVIATIONS

The abbreviations used by the Post Office Department:

Ala.	Maine	Ohio
Ariz.	Md.	Okla.
Ark.	Mass.	Oreg.
Calif.	Mich.	Pa.
Colo.	Minn.	R. I.
Conn.	Miss.	S. C.
Del.	Mo.	S. Dak.
Fla.	Mont.	Tenn.
Ga.	Nebr.	Tex.
Idaho	Nev.	Utah
Ill.	N. H.	Vt.
Ind.	N. J.	Va.
Iowa	N. Mex.	Wash.
Kans.	N. Y.	W. Va.
Ky.	N. C.	Wis.
La.	N. Dak.	Wyo.

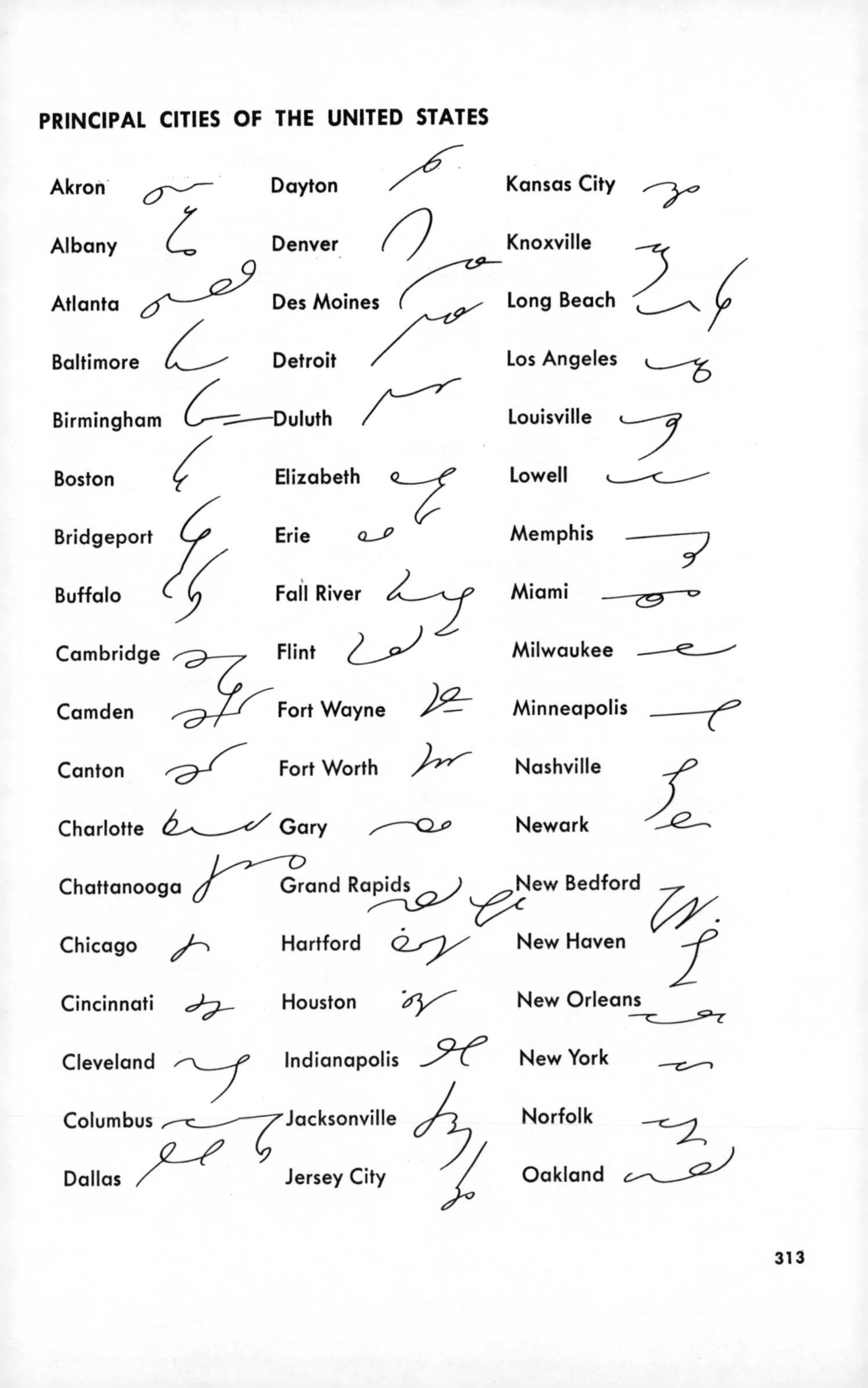

PRINCIPAL CITIES OF THE UNITED STATES

Akron
Albany
Atlanta
Baltimore
Birmingham
Boston
Bridgeport
Buffalo
Cambridge
Camden
Canton
Charlotte
Chattanooga
Chicago
Cincinnati
Cleveland
Columbus
Dallas

Dayton
Denver
Des Moines
Detroit
Duluth
Elizabeth
Erie
Fall River
Flint
Fort Wayne
Fort Worth
Gary
Grand Rapids
Hartford
Houston
Indianapolis
Jacksonville
Jersey City

Kansas City
Knoxville
Long Beach
Los Angeles
Louisville
Lowell
Memphis
Miami
Milwaukee
Minneapolis
Nashville
Newark
New Bedford
New Haven
New Orleans
New York
Norfolk
Oakland

Oklahoma City	St. Louis	Syracuse
Omaha	St. Paul	Tacoma
Paterson	Salt Lake City	Tampa
Peoria	San Antonio	Toledo
Philadelphia	San Diego	Trenton
Pittsburgh	San Francisco	Tulsa
Portland	Scranton	Utica
Providence	Seattle	Washington
Reading	Somerville	Wichita
Richmond	South Bend	Wilmington
Rochester	Spokane	Worcester
Sacramento	Springfield	Yonkers

BRIEF FORMS IN ORDER OF PRESENTATION

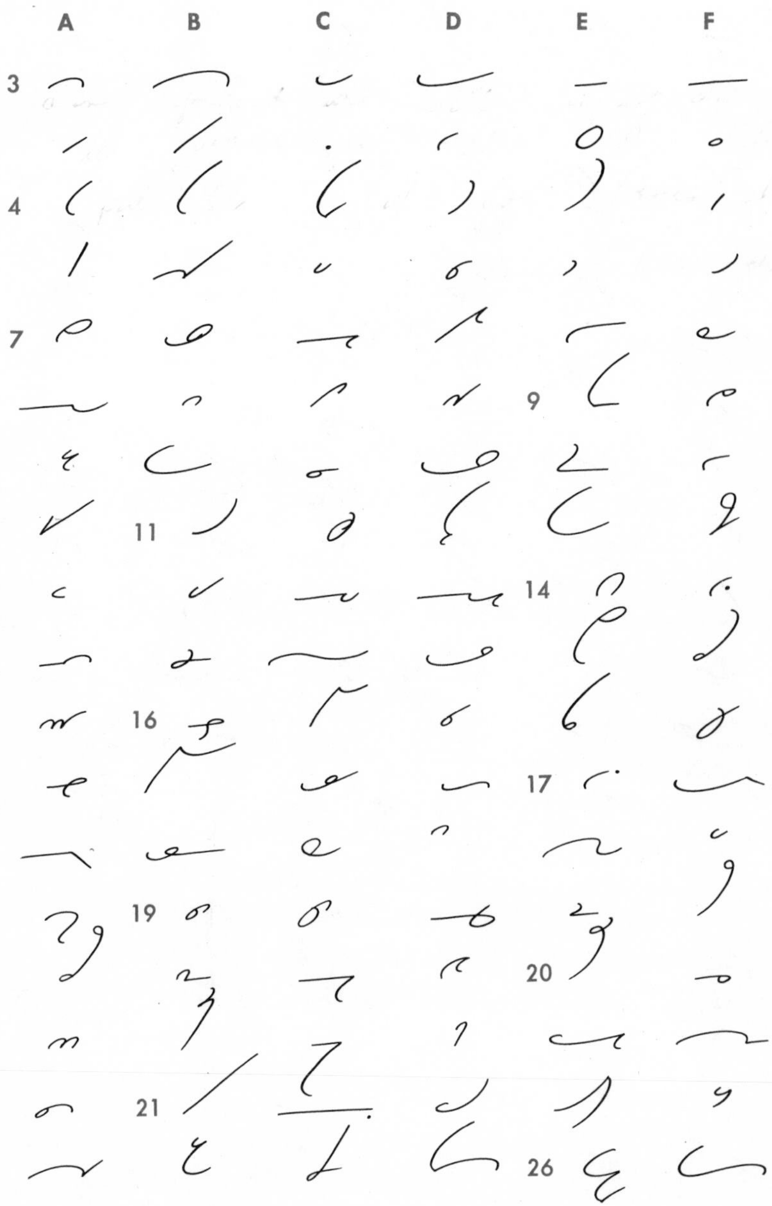
A
B
C
D
E
F
3
4
7
9
11
14
16
17
19
20
21
26

A B C D E F

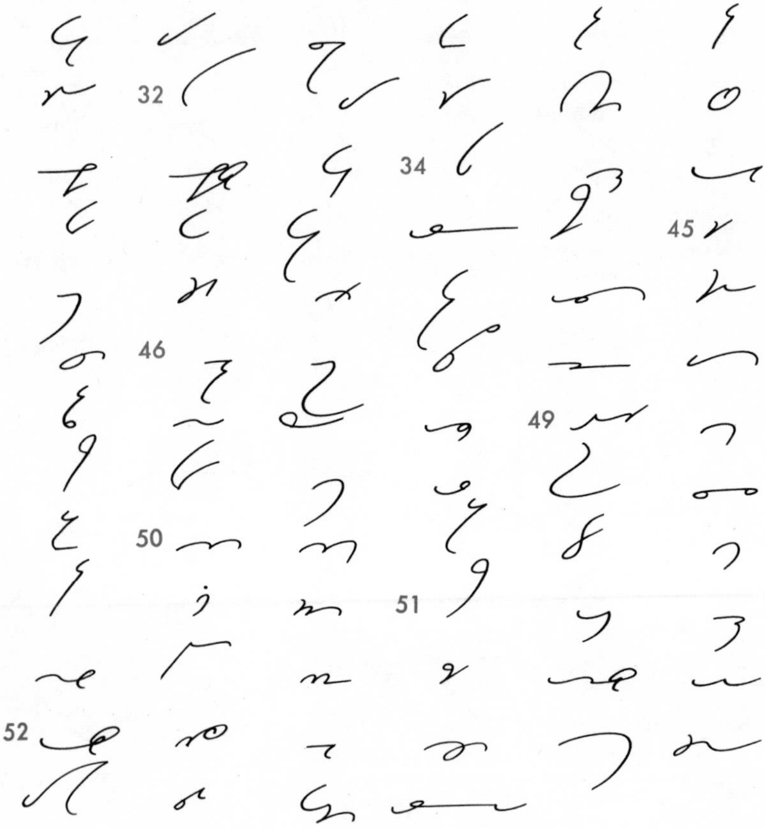
32
34
45
46
49
50
51
52

Index of Manual

In order to facilitate finding, this Index has been divided into six main sections – Alphabetic Characters, Brief Forms, General, Phrasing, Word Beginnings, Word Endings.

The first figure refers to the lesson; the second refers to the paragraph.

INDEX OF BRIEF FORMS

The first figure refers to the lesson, the second figure to the paragraph.